Beyond White Ethnicity

Beyond White Ethnicity

Developing a Sociological Understanding of Native American Identity Reclamation

Kathleen J. Fizgerald

LEXINGTON BOOKS

A division of
ROWMAN & LITTLEFIELD PUBLISHERS, INC.
Lanham • Boulder • New York • Toronto • Plymouth, UK

LEXINGTON BOOKS

A division of Rowman & Littlefield Publishers, Inc.
A wholly owned subsidiary of The Rowman & Littlefield Publishing Group, Inc.
4501 Forbes Boulevard, Suite 200
Lanham, MD 20706

Estover Road
Plymouth PL6 7PY
United Kingdom

British Library Cataloguing in Publication Information Available

Library of Congress Cataloging-in-Publication Data

Fitzgerald, Kathleen J., 1965–
   Beyond white ethnicity : developing a sociological understanding of Native
 American identity reclamation / Kathleen J. Fitzgerald.
      p. cm.
   Includes bibliographical references and index.
   ISBN-13: 978-0-7391-1393-6 (cloth : alk. paper)
   ISBN-10: 0-7391-1393-3 (cloth : alk. paper)
   1. Indians of North America—Ethnic identity. 2. Identity (Psychology)—United
States. 3. Group identity—United States. 4. Whites—United States—Relations with
Indians. 5. Whites—Race identity—United States. 6. United States—Race relations.
I. Title.
   E98.E85F58 2006
   305.897—dc22   2006020802

Printed in the United States of America

⊗™ The paper used in this publication meets the minimum requirements of American
National Standard for Information Sciences—Permanence of Paper
for Printed Library Materials, ANSI/NISO Z39.48-1992

To the memory of my father

Contents

Preface

The seeds of this research project were planted during the introduction of a presenter at a completely unrelated conference, the Drake University Conference on Music and Popular Culture in March 1996. One of the conference organizers introduced an old friend, a former graduate school colleague as I recall, and explained that the woman speaking that day now went by a different name, as she had reconnected with her Latina heritage, a heritage that she was never informed of growing up. This story piqued my interest. I found myself very interested in studying people who were reclaiming a heritage that had been denied them. It began to dawn on me that my embrace of my Irish heritage was an aspect of white privilege, as well as a result of the socio-historical context within which I lived. It occurred to me that for individuals seeking to reclaim a racial heritage, there may be more obstacles to confront than I faced as a white ethnic American embracing her ancestry.

I decided to study Native American reclaimers primarily because demographic data show that the Native American population may be increasing at a rate of four times the national average. A significant portion of this growth is believed to be due to changing patterns of racial/ethnic identification. Understanding the subjective experiences surrounding why individuals would reclaim their Native heritage and what this process entailed became my objectives. As it turns out, sociologists have shown considerable interest in the lingering presence of ethnicity and the ethnic identity of white ethnics, yet have paid fairly little attention to ethnic identity among racial minorities.

My deepest appreciation goes to the individuals who were willing to share their reclaiming stories with me. Their words, while unavoidably presented through my interpretive lens, are what make up the bulk of this work. It is difficult to speak of one's identity search with a stranger, yet so many individuals were generous and trusting enough to do just that. Thank you all. I also wish to thank the two Native organizations that allowed me access to their meetings, members, and even at times their organization's historical documents. Thanks to all of those who may not see themselves directly in this work, but who indeed were significant in my learning process concerning Native reclaimers and Native culture more broadly. I would also like to extend my thanks to the following folks at Lexington Books/Rowman & Littlefield: Joseph Parry and Rebekka Brooks Istrail.

Sincere appreciation needs to be expressed to my dissertation advisor, Dr. Mary Jo Neitz, at the University of Missouri–Columbia for her support throughout this project. She provided valuable feedback on my data analysis and challenged me at every step; and provided structure and certainly intellectual guidance, yet still allowed this project to be mine. For not only her help but her way of helping, I am thankful. The process, of which we sociologists are so very concerned, was easier due to her guidance. Dr. Prahlad Folly introduced me to some useful folklore literature, and Dr. Tola Pearce provided important critiques of the written work. All three challenged various aspects of my analysis, and I believe this book is better due to their input. I would also like to thank Dr. Peter Hall and Dr. Ken Benson for helping to shape my sociological imagination in so many ways. Of course, this work is ultimately my own, errors and insights included. I would like to thank Columbia College for their support in awarding me a summer research grant in 2005, as I began to prepare the manuscript for publication. I extend my sincere appreciation to my favorite sisters and colleagues, Dr. Donna McClure Begley and Dr. Pamela McClure, for their ongoing love, laughter, and support, both personally and professionally. I would like to express my love and gratitude to Kristy for her ongoing support during this project. Finally, I would like to express my thanks to my best friend from high school who first encouraged me to take a sociology class, saying she was sure I would love it. Very intuitive of you, Mari Bridget. I thank all for their input and reiterate that any remaining errors are my own.

Kathleen J. Fitzgerald
Columbia, Missouri
Winter 2006

Contextualizing Native American Racial/Ethnic Identity Reclamation

My ethnic identity is something for which I am rarely, if ever, penalized despite the salience of my Irish-American ancestry. My last name as well as my physiognomy are clues to people that I am of Irish descent. I realize not being penalized is a privilege and is a result of the particular socio-historical circumstances within which I live. I came of age in an era where Irish dancing, music, and even Irish pubs have become internationally embraced and consumed. The same story certainly cannot be told for Irish immigrants or Irish Americans at the turn of the nineteenth century. Indeed, it was not easy for my grandparents, who were Irish immigrants, to find themselves accepted in their new world. Yet, I am able to embrace this ethnicity in ways earlier generations would not have dared. I can eagerly incorporate and celebrate my "Irishness" without it challenging my sense of myself as an "American." My experiences, it turns out, are far from unique for white ethnic Americans.

Most of us probably became familiar with the notion of American society as a "melting pot" in at least middle school. The melting pot ideology implies that each ethnic group blends with the host culture and forms a new and different culture (McLemore and Romo 2005, p. 30). Despite the pervasiveness of this ideology, by now it is clear that cultural and sociological claims of ethnic assimilation and the "melting pot" have not materialized. Beyond my personal experience, even casual observation of North American culture recognizes that ethnicity is alive and well, as evidenced by the success of *Riverdance* and the lingering presence of Irish ethnicity for numerous American. Certainly one can see the influence of Latino cultures in music, food, and other arenas. Numerous sociologists have documented this lingering presence of ethnicity (Alba 1990; Gans 1979; Nagel 1996; Waters 1990; among others). Some refer to the ongoing influence of ethnicity as "symbolic ethnicity," viewing it as a somewhat superficial connection to one's ancestry (Gans 1979). Other sociologists view it as in flux—as part of a larger ethnic transformation, from identification with specific European ethnicities to identification with larger categories such as European American (Alba 1990). It appears that stories of the death of American ethnic identification are indeed premature. Ethnicity is everywhere.

The recognition of my privileged position, in terms of access to my cultural heritage, leads me to speculate on what groups today are denied this privilege. For whom would embracing their heritage contain costs rather than advantages? At a conference in the spring of 1996, I encountered a woman who was reclaiming her Latina heritage after being raised as white. This woman explained to the audience that she found out as an adult that her mother was Latina but had assimilated and raised her children as white, not even informing them of this aspect of their heritage. I find this story fascinating. This woman certainly has to work harder than I do to celebrate her ancestry. It is not difficult to speculate on the reasons why her mother would have denied this heritage to her children. It is clearly easier to be "white" in this country. I am sure she did this to give her children the advantages associated with being white in this country. Peggy McIntosh refers to these advantages as white privilege, that "invisible package of unearned assets that I can count on cashing in each day . . . an invisible weightless knapsack of special provisions, assurances, tools, maps, guides, codebooks, passports, visas, clothes, compass, emergency gear and blank checks" (McIntosh 2001, p. 30). My interest is piqued, especially concerning the woman reclaiming her Latina heritage. I find myself curious as to who else goes through such a reclaiming process and how we can understand, sociologically, their experiences.

Turning to the social scientific literature on ethnicity and ethnic identity, I find that sociologists have plenty to say about white ethnic reclaiming. Some refer to reclaiming one's ethnic heritage as a privilege of the third-generation ethnic (Hansen 1996 [1938]). As historian Marcus Hansen so eloquently puts it, "What the son wishes to forget the grandson wishes to remember" (Hanson 1996 [1938], p. 206). While in some sociological discourse this pattern of white ethnic reclaiming is referred to as an "ethnic revival" (e.g., D'Antonio 1978; Greeley 1978; Novak 1971), sociologist Herbert Gans (1979) refers to it as symbolic ethnicity, where individuals embrace certain aspects of their heritage, yet nothing about this reclamation challenges their middle class, white, American status. It is the lingering presence of ethnicity, specifically among white Americans of European descent, that appears to fascinate sociologists (e.g., Waters 1990).

What is missing in the sociological literature on ethnicity and ethnic identity is an analysis of the salience of reclaiming for groups designated as *racial* minorities. In fact, sociologists often treat racial minorities as if they are devoid of ethnicity. Yet, clearly racially designated groups can be differentiated along ethnic lines (e.g., blacks from Nigeria, Jamaica, and Puerto Rico may share a common racial designation, but their ethnicities are quite varied). However, a racial "otherness" has a very different meaning in this society than a white-ethnic "otherness." As Ringer and Lawless argue, "The theyness imputed to racial minorities by the dominant American society has been qualitatively different from the they-ness imputed to white ethnic minorities" (quoted in Sollors 1996, p. xxxi). Sociologist Mary Waters points out the differential access to ethnicities between whites and blacks:

> Whites enjoy a great deal of freedom in these [ethnic identity] choices; those defined in "racial" terms as non-whites much less. Black Americans, for example, are highly socially constrained to identify as blacks, without other options available to them, even when they believe or know that their forebears included many non-blacks. . . . [T]his shows how some groups may be socially constrained to accept an ethnic identity. (1990, p. 18)

Kibria makes a similar point, arguing that "for racial minorities, the process of defining one's ethnic affiliations is marked by externally imposed constraints more powerful than those that face white Americans" (2000, p. 77).

If a racial/ethnic[1] designation is so different from a white/ethnic designation, then what kinds of differences would individuals who are reclaiming a racial/ethnic heritage and identity face compared to those faced by white ethnics? How much more difficult is it for racially designated individuals and groups to reclaim a heritage? Maintaining, preserving, or reclaiming one's cultural heritage has not been as easy for racial/ethnic minorities as it has been for white ethnics. While many white ethnics initially face severe discrimination due to their ethnic heritage, their eventual designation as white enables them to eventually assimilate, and therefore places their future generations in a privileged position within the racial hierarchy that eventually allows them some freedom to reclaim their heritage.[2] As mentioned, such white ethnics have been the focus of considerable sociological investigation.

There has been some sociological work analyzing the collective reclamation of ethnicity among racial minorities (Nagel 1996; Rhea 1997). Sociologist Joane Nagel (1996) has analyzed what she refers to as American Indian ethnic renewal. She looks at the structural conditions that allow and even encourage Native Americans to reclaim their heritage. According to sociologist Joseph Tilda Rhea (1997), the various assertions of minority cultural identity since the mid-1960s can be thought of collectively as a race pride movement. Rhea analyzes four groups historically designated as "racial" minorities—American Indians, Asian Americans, Latinos, and Black Americans—in terms of how they assert their collective identities and demand representation in terms of what has been deemed "American history" as well as within current American culture. As he argues, "We turn, all of us, to history for a sense of identity" (1997, p. 8). For instance, in terms of Native Americans, he argues, "Red Power was concerned primarily with the recovery and assertion of an affirmative racial identity" (1997, p. 10). This process involves efforts to redefine the past and embrace symbols of Indian resistance to white aggression. "Reaching for a new sense of the past, they developed an active antagonism toward the mainstream representation of their history" (Rhea 1997, p. 15).

While the previous are examples of a small literature concerning collective racial/ethnic renewal, I still find a void in terms of sociological attempts at understanding what it means for individuals to reclaim a racial/ethnic heritage. My goal is to rectify that in this research. Currently there is a resurgence among racial minorities who had previously "walked away from" their cultural heritage in order to accommodate mainstream desires for Anglo-conformity. Some individuals reclaim a heritage that they had consciously distanced themselves from while others are reclaiming a previously unknown heritage that their parents or grandparents had dropped in order to assimilate. According to Karl Eshbach (1993), contemporary census data suggest that the Native American population may be increasing at a rate of four times the national average. A significant portion of this growth is estimated to be due to changing patterns of ethnic identification. It is the subjective experiences of these individuals that I strive to understand in this research. Through qualitative research, I look at what it means for individuals to reclaim a Native American heritage. In what ways is their construction of this ethnic identity similar to or different from what is known about ethnic identity construction among whites? Does the explanatory power of Gans's concept of symbolic ethnicity translate to the experiences of such racial/ethnic minorities? Does reclaiming a Native American identity challenge Gans's notion of the voluntariness of ethnic identity? Does it challenge one's position in the mainstream American culture rather than being non-threatening to that status, as Gans speculates it is for white ethnics?

Clarifying what I mean by *reclaimer* is necessary. I use the term *reclaimer* to signify anyone who has recently learned of their Native American ancestry or is recently identifying with this aspect of their heritage, that is, consciously claiming, embracing, and enacting this aspect of their heritage. One of my interviewees says that she feels the term *reclaimer* is a misnomer because she views herself as in the process of finding her ethnicity rather than reclaiming it. For her, reclaiming implies that she had had it at one time and somehow lost it or walked away from it, which is not the case. Her father was from their tribal reservation and left because there was no way to earn a living there. I took her criticism to heart, but throughout our conversation, I began to feel that my appellative was accurate for this process and, I would say, even accurately describes her situation. She says she feels a "calling" of sorts to pursue this aspect of her heritage. As she describes, "Something inside me makes me pursue this." That is what I mean by reclaiming: that one's cultural heritage is always part of them, whether it is subtle, unconscious, or unrecognized as such. I think there are also important political implications attached to this kind of racial/ethnic reclamation that the term *reclaiming* captures better than *finding*. Native Americans have historically made claims to this land as the indigenous people of this continent. The Native American Rights Fund is actively working to protect their land base and the natural resources of Indian nations from infringement by industrialists, the government, or whomever, and are basing their claims on their aboriginal status (*Native American Rights Fund* 1995, pp. 13–17).

While my focus is on individual reclaiming and what that process means to those involved in it, I think racial/ethnic reclamation has powerful cultural consequences as well. Due to the fact that "race is a system of power" and "racial boundaries reflect the relations of power from which they emerge . . . [and] the dominant group plays a critical role in erecting racial boundaries," racial/ethnic reclamation can destabilize this system of power (Kibria 2000, p. 78). If people consciously reclaim a previously or currently denigrated status, it represents a powerful challenge to the hegemonic racial structure.

I think one can witness such a challenge occurring at a cultural level today, especially in terms of an Afrocentric movement that is influencing Western cultures across the globe as well as the North American embrace of certain aspects of Latino culture. For instance, through even casual observation, one can recognize that more and more African Americans as well as Africans throughout the world are wearing their hair in traditional braids or dreadlocks. Additionally, tattooing and piercing, reclamations of indigenous cultural practices, have become cultural practices embraced by Generation Xers across race, class, and gender lines.[3] I cannot, of course, infer the intentions of all individuals who get tattoos or body piercings or dreadlock their hair. One has to be careful to recognize that when something becomes a cultural trend, original intent may be lost; therefore, not every person participating in such a cultural practice is consciously challenging Anglo hegemony. However, my argument is that the presence of such a return-to-roots movement and the embrace of such indigenous cultural practices can act as just such a challenge at the cultural level. Similarly, as significant numbers of people who formerly considered themselves "white" reclaim an indigenous racial heritage, they will, consciously or not, challenge the racial hierarchy.

Additionally, there is power in the actual reclaiming stories people tell; this power lies in the challenge these stories pose to Anglo cultural hegemony. Sarah Joseph argues, "The critical edge of cultural studies in the United States has come from the project of giving recognition and voice to identities submerged by the dominant culture" (1998, p. 16). I see my work as situated within what is referred to as the "cultural turn" in the social sciences. According to Barrett, this refers to several things, including

> a general shift in disciplines such as sociology away from socio-economic or social structural explanations and towards a recognition of the importance of cultural meaning. Part and parcel of this is the decline of the concept of class as the primary explanatory factor, and the rise of interest in subjectivity and identity. (1999, p. 14)

My research is situated within this cultural turn in that it embraces the turn toward subjectivity and identity rather than emphasizing socio-economic explanations. However, it remains ensconced within sociological tradition in that there is considerable emphasis on structure and its role in constraining or enabling Native reclamation.

My work, then, hopes to fill a void in the sociological literature on race and ethnicity by studying the ethnic identity construction (or reconstruction) of Native American reclaimers. While I intend to focus on the individual reclamation process, I think this research is also useful for generating some understanding of a much larger ongoing cultural transformation—that of the revival, transformation, and adaptation of indigenous cultural traditions, including what gets defined as tradition and who gets to define tradition.

THEORETICAL BACKGROUND

In order to generate an understanding of the process of reclaiming a Native American identity, the sociological literature on race, ethnicity, and ethnic identity provides a starting point. Despite some progressive thought within this body of literature, for the most part, these three concepts are treated as separate and distinct, with the exception of a small literature on racial/ethnic reclaiming to which my research contributes. For instance, while it is currently accepted that the concepts of race and ethnicity are social constructions, in practice, through academic discourse surrounding race and ethnicity, sociologists have almost reified these concepts as not only objective and real but distinct from each other. As previously mentioned, throughout the sociological literature, racial minorities are perceived as being devoid of ethnicity. This is evidenced in the earliest theories of ethnicity and ethnic identity, where theories of ethnicity specifically emerge out of research on white ethnics and become problematic when attempts are made to apply them to racial minorities. This is especially obvious in the dominance of the assimilationist paradigm, the idea that immigrants will merge uniformly into the dominant, Anglo-American culture, as well as the opposing perspective, that of cultural pluralism, where members of every American ethnic group are viewed as free to participate in all of society's major institutions while simultaneously retaining their own ethnic heritage (McLemore and Romo 2005, p. 31). Both treat ethnicity as exclusively the property of white ethnics and as somewhat voluntary; the assimilationists argue that ethnicity is something that could, and should, eventually be dropped, and the cultural pluralists argue for the value of individuals' retaining their ethnic ties, thus still emphasizing the voluntariness of that identity.

During the "ethnic revival" of the 1970s, sociological interest in ethnicity is also rekindled. The recognition that individuals are holding on to and even celebrating their ethnic heritage fascinates sociologists, if for no other reason than the fact that this lingering presence of ethnicity challenges assimilationist expectations and "melting pot" ideologies. This body of research specifically focuses on white, European ethnics and their identity construction while current research focuses on the transformation of ethnicity among white ethnics, from specific ethnic identities such as Irish American or German American to the more generalized notion of a European American identity (Alba 1990; Rubin 1994; Stein and Hill 1977). Beyond simply the fascination with the lingering presence of ethnicity, sociologists of this era also focus on political implications of ethnic identification, from ethnic voting blocs to social movements (Glazer and Moynihan 1963; Novak 1971; Roberts 1978). The transformation of white ethnic identity has resulted in a white ethnic movement according to Stein and Hill (1977) and the formation of European American social clubs according to Rubin (1994). Finally, there is a more current albeit small body of sociological work on Native American resurgence (Cornell 1988; Nagel 1996) and significant work on the current transformation of racial identities (Korgen 1998; Rockquemore and Brunsma 2002).

According to sociologist Werner Sollors (1996), the origin of the term *race* is disputed. However, it is believed to be several centuries older than the term *ethnicity* (1996, p. xxix). He argues that the term *ethnicity*, of relatively modern origin, is "intended to substitute for 'race' at a time that the older word had become deeply compromised by 'racism'" (1996, p. xxix). Yet, *ethnicity* has still not come to replace the term *race*, in popular or sociological discourse. Today distinctions are still emphasized between the two terms. A basic race relations textbook defines race as "a group of people who (1) are generally considered to be physically distinct in some way, such as skin color, hair texture, or facial features, from other groups and (2) are generally considered by themselves and/or others to be a distinct group" (Farley 1995, p. 5). Ethnicity is defined as "a group of people who are generally recognized by themselves and/or by others as a distinct group, with such recognition based on social or cultural characteristics" (Farley 1995, p. 6). Yet, while sociologists differentiate between the concepts of race and ethnicity, and to a certain extent reify them through their use, most acknowledge that both concepts are social constructions of particular political-historical eras (e.g., Farley 1995; Omi and Winant 1994). As Farley points out, "Physical characteristics partially define race, *but only in the context of a decision by society to consider those physical characteristics relevant. . . .* Race is a *socially constructed concept*" (1995, p. 5, italics in the original). Omi and Winant concur: "How one is categorized is far from a merely academic or even personal matter. . . . The determination of racial categories is thus an intensely political process" (1994, p. 3).

Sociologists have long been fascinated with the concept of ethnicity, as a concept distinct from race. Early research in the Chicago school focuses on the experiences of white European ethnic immigrants. Robert Park, W. I. Thomas, and Ernest Burgess, as central figures in the Chicago school, argue that it is necessary for immigrants to retain ties to the old world initially "because a premature severing of his ties to the past left the immigrant in a rootless and demoralized condition" (Persons 1987, pp. 53–54). New immigrants are expected, after this transition phase, to drop their old ways and assimilate into the dominant, Anglo-American culture. The ideology of the "melting pot" took precedence, viewing all immigrant groups as merging into a new identity, that of the "American."

This assimilationist paradigm has been highly influential in the sociological study of ethnicity, although it has not been without its critics. An early criticism was introduced by E. Franklin Frazier, a student of Park's at Chicago, who argues that this model of ethnic assimilation does not adequately capture the experience of racial minorities in this country. It is clear to Frazier that blacks can be extensively amalgamated with whites, acculturated into the Euro-American culture, but not assimilated into American society (Persons 1987, p. 74). In the United States, blacks and whites live essentially separate lives. The ethnicity theory of the Chicago school, then, is not applicable to the experiences of those Americans defined as "racial" minorities: African Americans, Native-Americans, Latinos, and Asian Americans (Omi and Winant 1994, p. 16).

Cultural pluralism is an opposing perspective to the assimilationist paradigm, entertaining the idea that numerous ethnicities can co-exist without threatening the dominant culture. Such a progressive view has never been as widely accepted as the assimilationist perspective, yet there has always been a strain of thought running through American culture that adheres to it. This theory, however, can also be accused of applying only to white ethnics, not extending to those defined as racial minorities because, at least historically, there have been conscious efforts made to eradicate the cultures of racial minorities, for example, weakening the transmission of Native American culture through education of youth at boarding schools; the erasure of African American culture during slavery; and even current attacks on Latino culture, as the "English First" movement exemplifies. Despite the pluralist view that numerous ethnicities can co-exist in American society, there is evidence of less interest in the dominant, mainstream culture for preserving the cultures of racial minorities.

Social scientists refer to the 1970s as an "ethnic revival" era during which white European ethnics—Irish Americans, German Americans, Italian Americans, Polish Americans, etc.—appear to challenge the dominant ideology of assimilation through actively reclaiming and celebrating their ethnicities. Sociologist Herbert Gans argues that this was no revival but merely a new kind of ethnic involvement hinging on ethnic identity, "the feeling of being Jewish or Italian, etc." (1979, p. 193). He refers to this as symbolic ethnicity and argues that it is most often practiced among third-generation ethnics.

For Gans, symbolic ethnicity is more of an achieved or earned status rather than an ascribed status. "In other words, for later-generation white ethnics, ethnicity is not something that influences their lives unless they *want* it to. . . . Ethnicity has become a subjective identity, invoked at will by the individual" (Waters 1990, p. 7). According to this perspective, for white ethnics at least, practicing one's ethnicity is voluntary. Gans does not view their ethnic reclamation as conflicting with patterns of assimilation and acculturation because people are merely trying to find "easy and intermittent ways of expressing their identity, for ways that do not conflict with other ways of life" (Gans 1987, p. 203). Thus, the reclamation and celebration of one's ethnic identity does not affect an individual's status; therefore the "costs" of being ethnic are slight. This reclaimed ethnicity is expressed by nostalgic allegiance to the old country, a sense of pride in one's heritage or cultural traditions, ethnic foods, and ethnic festivals. For Gans, individuals reclaiming an ethnic heritage avoid time-consuming commitments such as learning their native culture's languages.

Sociologist Richard Alba's work *Ethnic Identity* (1990) provides some quantification of the symbolic ethnicity on which Gans speculates. He defines ethnic identity as "the degree to which individuals think of themselves and experiences in terms of ethnic points of origin" (p. 3). Alba retains the sociological tradition of "defining out" racial minorities that could potentially prove problematic to his analysis of ethnic identity construction. As mentioned previously, Alba's concern is with white European ethnics and how there has been a transformation of ethnic identity from specific identities to the broader identity of European American. His work is interesting for my research in that I am curious as to what extent white ethnic identity—or collectively, a white ethnic movement—can act as a catalyst for non-white ethnic identity reclamation. Are the Native American reclaimers I encounter feeling forced out of the dominant Anglo-American culture?

Sociologist Mary Waters's (1990) research provides a further challenge to the sociological notion of assimilation that occurs among later-generation, white, middle-class, Euro-American, Catholic ethnics in the United States. Her objective is to understand the strength and extent of ethnic identification among third-and fourth-generation white ethnics located in suburban communities. As she argues, "Sociologists tend to equate suburbanization and residential integration with assimilation. Yet we know that later-generation suburban residents do continue to answer census or survey questions on ethnicity" (1990, p. 11). She is interested in finding out if this ethnic identity has some meaning in their day-to-day lives. Waters avoids looking at ethnic identity construction among so-called racial minorities because, as she argues, her focus is on "the meaning or lack of meaning of ethnicity to people in the last stages of assimilation—people for whom ethnicity is an option rather than an ascribed characteristic" (1990, p. 12). As Frazier's research points out, assimilation is not the reality for individuals designated as racial minorities.

Gans's concept of symbolic ethnicity also applies specifically to white ethnics. Alba (1990) and Waters's (1990) later work, as with most sociological theories of ethnicity, fails to address the unique circumstances of racial minorities. A small body of research looks at racial minorities efforts to reclaim specific identities. For instance, Rhea's *Race Pride and the American Identity* (1997) explores collective reclamation for Native Americans, Asian Americans, African Americans, and Latinos. In this work he investigates how "in the mid-1960s, a generation of minority activists turned to the task of gaining cultural representation. . . . [T]he net result of their efforts was the cultural transformation of a nation that had already experienced a major legal revolution" (1997, pp. 3–4). Sociologist Kathleen Odell Korgen argues in *From Black to Biracial: Transforming Racial Identity among Americans* (1998) that

> [a] change in the racial identification of mixed-race persons took place during the three decades between the mid-1960s and the mid-1990s. Findings . . . indicate that both young biracial adults and young Americans in general are now more likely to identify someone with both a black and a white parent as biracial

than as black. This is a dramatic difference from the way the previous generation of Americans racially defined children of interracial couples. (p. 25)

While the phenomenon she is analyzing—blacks reclaiming their white heritage—appears to be the opposite of the phenomenon I am studying—whites who are reclaiming their racial/ethnic heritage—the two really are part of a similar process: the destabilization of the existing racial hierarchy. These individuals redefining themselves as biracial represents the disruption of our long-held racial classification system.

Some individuals reclaim a racial/ethnic heritage they had consciously distanced themselves from while others reclaim a heritage that their parents or grandparents had dropped in order to assimilate. The Native American population may be increasing at a rate of four times the national average and a significant portion of this growth is due to changing patterns of ethnic identification (Eshbach 1993). Nagel concurs that there has been "a remarkable recovery of the American Indian population during the second half of the century. The number of Native Americans increased eightfold from 1900 to 1990, with much of the growth occurring in the decades after 1960" (1996, p. 5).

My research hopes to generate an understanding of what this reclaiming process means to the individuals who undertake it. Will the explanatory power of Gans's concept translate to the experiences of such racial minorities? Will reclaiming a Native American identity challenge the notion of the voluntariness of ethnic identity of which Gans spoke? Will it challenge one's position in the mainstream American culture rather than being non-threatening to that status as it was for Gans? I argue that this process differs fundamentally because the individuals who are reclaiming a distinctly racial heritage are, by definition, overtly challenging the hegemony of the Anglo-American culture. We know that groups designated as "racial" minorities have varying and distinct ethnicities and cultural practices. We also have to recognize that the designation "racial" is a social as well as a political construction (e.g., Omi and Winant 1994) and that people don't always fit neatly into such categories. Numerous individuals "pass" and successfully assimilate into the dominant, Anglo-American culture. Some such individuals then attempt to reclaim the cultural heritage they had previously denied or suppressed. What are the political implications of non-white reclamation? Does this challenge and/or threaten the mainstream, Anglo-American culture?

Political implications of ethnicity also receive considerable sociological interest. Nathan Glazer and Daniel Patrick Moynihan in *Beyond the Melting Pot* (1963, 1970) argue that ethnicity is an interest group; in this view, individuals are tied together along racial or ethnic lines by fundamental political interests. For instance, during the late 1950s and early 1960s, blacks were struggling for the removal of discriminatory barriers in order to gain equal access to the "American dream." Once these barriers were removed, however, the responsibility fell on blacks to assimilate into the mainstream, as other ethnic groups had previously done. Again, assimilation into the white mainstream is the unquestioned objective, even among social scientists. As Alba describes, "Ethnic identity should be strongly linked to political attitudes, participation, and behavior" (1990, p. 28). Gans also recognizes the political dimensions of ethnicity, arguing that symbolic ethnicity can take political forms. For instance, as politicians belonging to a particular ethnic group achieve national office, they become symbols of their group, instilling a feeling of pride in their success. He also postulates that this resurgence of ethnicity among white ethnics in the 1970s was a reaction to white perceptions of gains made by blacks due to the civil rights movement.

A more current sociological analysis of the political dimensions of race and ethnicity is found in Omi and Winant's *Racial Formation in the United States: From the 1960s to the 1990s* (1994), which explicitly places race at the center of American political history. They exemplify the significance of new social movements such as the black movement of the 1960s that have challenged "existing patterns of race relations . . . created new political subjects, expanded the terrain of political struggle beyond 'normal' politics" (1994, p. 4).

While Omi and Winant focus on the black movement, Native American activism was also burgeoning during the post-1960s era. In *Return of the Native: American Indian Political Resurgence* (1988), Stephen Cornell documents this resurgence of Native American activism dramatically marked by the 1973 siege at Wounded Knee.[4] As he explains, there have always been politics about Indians, but what is unique about this resurgence of Indian activism is the fact that they "had returned to the political arena with unexpected, often defiant force, and in the process had reversed the four-hundred-year trend of declining Indian influence and power" (Cornell 1988, p. 6). Indians are, once again, demanding a voice in decision-making processes most affecting their communities and lives. Cornell provides a comprehensive account of the history of the political and economic relationships between Native Americans and Euro-Americans, as well as the effects such relationships have had on Indian groups and their opportunities to act (1988, p. 8). One of the primary determinants, according to Cornell, has been the creation of a supratribal consciousness. As culturally diverse as Native Americans are, there is now a self-conscious Indian identity, as distinct from tribal identity. For Cornell, such supratribalism is what has made the resurgence of Indian politics possible (1988, p. 107). For some individuals, a supratribal identity has replaced a tribal identity, especially in cases where tribal culture has been eradicated. However, "it seems evident that for most Indians, supratribalism represents not a replacement but an enlargement of their identity system, a circle beyond the tribe in which, also, they think, move, and act" (Cornell 1988, p. 144). The importance of this new identity lies in its political potential. I am interested in whether reclaimers articulate a tribal consciousness or a distinctly Indian consciousness, and whether such redefinitions manifest themselves politically, for instance, if they see themselves as part of an Indian rights movement. Do reclaimers view this search for a heritage in political terms or cultural terms, or as an individual identity issue?

Joane Nagel's work *American Indian Ethnic Renewal: Red Power and the Resurgence of Identity and Culture* (1996) is a recent look at the resurgence of American Indian ethnicity. Nagel is interested in what she refers to as ethnic renewal, "the process whereby new ethnic identities, communities, and cultures are built or rebuilt out of historical social and symbolic systems. . . . Through common identification, group formation and reformation, and cultural production and reproduction, ethnicity is revitalized and constantly renewed" (1996, p. 10). Nagel is interested in both collective and individual ethnic renewal among Native Americans. She defines collective ethnic renewal as involving "the reconstruction of community: building or rebuilding institutions, culture, traditions, or history, by old or new members" (1996, p. 10). She argues that "individual and collective ethnic renewal are intertwined aspects of general ethnic renewal. Individual ethnic renewal involves mainly matters of personal identity and the groups with whom one identifies and associates" (1996, p. 11).

The strength of Nagel's analysis is her recognition of the role of structure, what she looks to as the explanatory factors for understanding the resurgence of Native American identity. According to Nagel,

> The reason can be found in policies and politics. Demographic, political and cultural currents in American society provided the basis and logic for Indian ethnic renewal. . . . [T]he transformations of identity and culture that mark late-twentieth-century American Indian ethnicity were forged in the crucible of Red Power. Although it was controversial and limited in its constituency, goals, and scope of participation, Red Power activism was the progenitor of an American Indian ethnic rebirth. (1996, p. 113)

She continues, "The cultural renewal under way across Indian country is a second legacy of the activist period of the 1960s and 1970s, and it is at least as important as the resurgence of identity in overall American Indian ethnic renewal" (1996, p. 190). She eloquently argues for the significance of the resurgence of Red Power: "In fact, the argument can be made that there is no more powerful counter-hegemonic statement than one that turns hegemony on its head: the expropriation and redefinition of 'black,' 'brown,' and 'red'

by African American, Latino, and Native American political movements"
(1996, p. 70).

Nagel's structural analysis of the causes of collective ethnic renewal
among Indians is complemented by her look at individual ethnic renewal. Her
analysis of individual renewal comes from interviews with activists in the
Red Power movement and how "the movement had not only led them to a renewed sense of ethnic pride but also permitted them to reconnect with their
tribal and spiritual heritage" (1996, p. 190). While Nagel's primary emphasis
is on structural explanations, my emphasis is on individual identity construction and performance. My work, then, hopes to extend her assumption that individual ethnic renewal, or what I refer to as reclaiming, is a result of changing structural and cultural conditions. My interviewees, however, differ
considerably from hers in that the link between Indian activism and reclaiming their ethnic identity is more indirect: my interviewees were not a part of
the Red Power movement; in fact, many had not even been born at the time.

IDENTITY

Attempting to understand identity, whether ethnic identity or any other di-
mension of identity, can be problematic. As Nagel argues,

> [B]oth identity and culture are ongoing enterprises. Identity changes throughout
> the life course. . . . [I]ndividuals and collectivities adapt, adopt, discard, and
> change continually, according to the needs and vagaries of history and of the
> world around them. However . . . to document the reconstruction, much less the
> construction of an individual's ethnic identity or a community's cultural prac-
> tices or institutions, is often an unwelcome, sometimes vilified enterprise.
> (1996, p. 63)

Douglas Kellner argues that modernist notions of identity are "mobile,
multiple, personal, self-reflexive, and subject to change and innovation. Yet
identity is also social and Other-related . . . as if one's identity depended on
recognition from others combined with self-validation of this recognition"
(1992, p. 141). Nagel adapts this modernist notion of identity to her understanding of ethnic identity: "Ethnic identity lies at the intersection of individual ethnic self-identification (who I am) and collective ethnic attribution (who
they say I am). Ethnic identity is, then, a dialectic between internal identification and external ascription. It is a socially negotiated and socially constructed status" (1996, p. 21). Butler further problematizes identity: "The notion of identity carries several burdens: the meaning of culture . . . the
problem of historical formation and contextualization; the possibility of

agency, social transformation, representability, and recognizability in both linguistic and political terms" (1995, p. 440).

The symbolic interactionist understanding of identity construction fits within this modernist tradition in that it emphasizes the role of significant others and reference groups in our understanding of ourselves as well as the role of individual agency in defining who we are, as Charon says, *"Identity is the name we call ourselves, and usually it is the name we announce to others that tells them who we are as we act in situations"* (2001, p. 86, italics in the original). For symbolic interactionists, "Identity is a process by which individuals understand themselves and others, as well as evaluate their self in relation to others. . . . Analyses that draw on this tradition tend to rely heavily on social interactions as the contextual networks in which identities emerge and are contested" (Rockquemore and Brunsma 2002, p. 23). And Charon adds, "Defining who the self is, as are all other actions the actor takes toward his or her self, is carried out in interaction with others. Others label me, so I come to label myself . . . and these identities become central to us over time as our interactions reconfirm them over and over" (2001, p. 86).

I am curious as to whether reclaimers hold such views of their racial/ethnic identity. Specifically, how much of their newly reclaimed racial/ethnic identity is externally determined? Individuals who are reclaiming a racial/ethnic status that they (or their ancestors) previously walked away from may be less likely to have a recognizable racial physiognomy. Therefore, what dilemmas, if any, will result from not physically resembling Indians, or at least the stereotypical notions of what an Indian looks like? If my interviewees' sense of racial/ethnic identity is reliant on others for recognition and validation, who are the significant others who can influence their sense of ethnic identity? What influence will whites have on their sense of ethnic identity, if any? Or will indigenous peoples, tribal people they meet during their reclamation process, be more influential in their identity development? Or will it be some combination of individuals to whom they turn for identity validation and confirmation?

Kellner points out that postmodernist positions on identity differ from such modernist notions. As he argues, "In a postmodern image culture, the images, scenes, stories, and cultural texts of so-called popular culture offer a wealth of subject positions which in turn help structure individual identity" (1992, p. 173). Instead of identity being "other," related and bound to a certain extent by external ascription, in a postmodern culture, various cultural images influence one's identity choices. Such a situation is seemingly limitless in terms of "new possibilities, styles, models, and forms" (Kellner 1992, p. 174). However, Kellner warns, "The overwhelming variety of subject positions, of possibilities for identity, in an affluent image culture no doubt create highly unstable identities while constantly providing new openings to restructure one's identity" (p. 174).

I view identity as something that is fluid, constantly being negotiated, constructed, and reconstructed. Castells argues, "It is easy to agree on the fact that, from a sociological perspective, all identities are constructed. The real issue is how, from what, by whom and for what. The construction of identities uses building materials from history, from geography, from biology . . . from collective memory and from personal fantasies" (1997, p. 7). To study identity implies a researcher must be aware of the emergent and even the somewhat contingent nature of such. In this respect, I agree with Nagel that studying identity can be an often "unwelcome, sometimes vilified enterprise" (1996, p. 63). Yet, I feel studying racial/ethnic identity construction among Native American reclaimers is an endeavor worth pursuing and something that can generate rich insight primarily because racial/ethnic identity reclamation has the potential to destabilize the racial hierarchy and fixed notions of race operating in our social worlds today. As individuals deny their whiteness and embrace a denigrated racial identity, their process is evidence that race is a social and political construction and, therefore, can be deconstructed. Additionally, it will broaden our sociological understanding of ethnic identity among racial minorities as well as provide us with an understanding of broader cultural change.

METHODOLOGY

In order to generate this understanding of racial/ethnic identity reclamation among Native Americans, I engage in ethnographic research. While qualitative methodologies are capable of providing considerable insight, they are not without their methodological dilemmas in both the research and the writing stages. Ethnographic research concerns over subjectivity, narrative dilemmas, studying outgroups, and researcher reflexivity are problematized in this research. Additionally, as a white researcher studying Native American reclaimers, the possibility of questions surrounding incongruent cultural norms between myself and my research participants and potential misinterpretations due to such incongruencies is an ongoing concern.

According to Waters, "Sociologists interested in white ethnics of European extraction have had to change both their methods and their focus of study. Instead of their studying the 'ethnic group' as a collectivity, attention has shifted to the 'ethnic identity' of the individual" (1990, p. 8). This is also a shift I want to make in studying non-white, non-European ethnics. As mentioned previously, while the collective ethnic resurgence of Native Americans is well documented by Nagel (1996), her work is limiting for understanding what this ethnic identity means to the individuals who embrace it. In this way, I see my work as situated between Waters's look at third- and fourth-generation white, European, suburban Catholic ethnics and Nagel's look at Native American resurgence.

Waters, for instance, intentionally chose suburban community residents for her sample because she wants to "discover what kind of ethnicity exists when the structural forces that maintain it are not evident" (1990, p. 11). My sample is intentionally drawn from mid-Missouri. I believe that for someone to reclaim a Native American heritage in this location is a very different process than if that person lived even a mere two hours west of here, where there is a much more visible Native American presence. The extreme "whiteness" of this location is something pointed out to me by an individual who had been raised on an Indian reservation in Oklahoma. In fact, she told me her four-year-old son asked her if the president of the United States lived here, because there sure were a lot of white people! And, I presume, it seemed reasonable enough to him that with all these white people, the most powerful white person of all could be here as well. The importance of geographic location lies in the fact that the structural forces traditionally viewed as necessary for maintaining culture are necessary for someone reclaiming a particular heritage. Those structural forces are less likely to exist in mid-Missouri, similar to Waters's non-ethnically defined suburban communities. Alba similarly justifies his research setting with this statement: "There is value in studying ethnic identity in a specific setting because ethnicity is, in important aspects, a localized phenomena, dependent on context" (1990, p. 31).

Despite claims to the importance of location, I want to problematize the significance of geographic location for racial/ethnic reclamation. Many reclaimers I spoke to, for instance, are not from this area. So, their entire lives may not have been lived in such a white location. And surprisingly to me, one reclaimer, who grew up in Oklahoma, feels that, for her, despite the fact that Oklahoma is "officially" Indian country, this area has been more conducive to Cherokee reclamation, simply due to the fact that she has been able to connect with other Natives and Native reclaimers. Despite her Indian country origins, throughout her school years, she was one of only a few students of Native descent. So, the presumed influence or significance of location must be treated with caution, particularly due to the fact that Native Americans suffer from low visibility throughout this country, and certainly so in the Midwest and the eastern United States. According to Farley, Native Americans constitute less than 2 percent of the overall population of the United States, and their geographic breakdown can be summarized as follows:

In 2000, 48 percent of the American Indian population lived in the West, 29 percent in the South, 16 percent in the Midwest, and 7 percent on the Northeast.

However, just three states, Oklahoma, California, and Arizona, account for nearly one-third of the Indian population . . . [with] a little over half a million Native Americans living in reservations. (Farley 2005, p. 239)

Additionally, it is important to distinguish between personal and collective racial/ethnic identity. Stein, in writing about the construction of lesbian identity, differentiates between personal identity and collective identity: "One might say that in addition to collective identity, there is *personal identity*, which may be defined as 'a sense of continuity, integration, identification, and differentiation constructed by the person not in relation to a community and its culture but in relation to the self and its projects'" (Stein 1997, p. 19). She argues that we need to begin to "theorize the interweaving of personal life and social worlds without falling into voluntarism or overdeterminism, on one side, or biological or psychological reductionism, on the other" (1997, p. 19). Korgen, operating from a symbolic interactionist perspective on identity, stresses that personal identity is enmeshed with group identity and that "the transformation of identity takes place on both the individual and the societal level" (1998, p. 83). Again, Nagel's focus is more on collective reclamation while my work focuses primarily on the individual racial/ethnic identity of reclaimers. I think it is important to recognize the "interweaving of personal life and social worlds" in terms of Native American reclaimers, however. For instance, in what ways do they deviate from ethnic identity construction for non-reclaimers? From white European ethnics? In what ways is their process similar?

In this research, I generate this sense of personal racial/ethnic identity construction (or reconstruction) through ethnographic research. According to Creswell (1998), "An ethnography is a description and interpretation of a cultural or social group or system. The researcher examines the group's observable and learned patterns of behavior, customs, and ways of life" (1998, p. 58). Put another way, "Ethnography means describing a culture and understanding another way of life from the native point of view" (Neumann 1997, p. 346). However, as Hall and Neitz (1993) point out, "How to do this has changed markedly in recent years as scholars have become more reflexive about their own processes in creating the meanings they ascribe to those they study, and as scholars have attempted more fully to give voice to the subjects of their studies" (p. 265). As an ethnographer, I am committed to research as an arena where participants' voices are integral to the research. My hope for this research is that it provides a space for the voices of individuals who are reclaiming an indigenous heritage. According to Creswell, "The final product of this effort is a holistic cultural portrait of the social group that incorporates both the views of the actors in the group (emic) and the researcher's interpretation of views about human social life in a social science perspective (etic)" (1998, p. 60).

Yet, I want to take this ethnographic understanding even further. In the spirit of Dorothy Smith (1987), my goal is to practice institutional ethnography. Babbie (2004) describes institutional ethnography as

> A research technique in which the personal experiences of individuals are used to reveal power relationships and other characteristics of the institutions in which they operate. . . . This approach links the "microlevel" of everyday personal experiences with the "macrolevel" of institutions. . . . Institutional ethnography departs from other ethnographic approaches by treating those data not as the topic or object of interest, but as 'entry' into the social relations of the setting. . . . The institutional ethnographer starts with the personal experiences of individuals but proceeds to uncover the institutional power relations that structure and govern those experiences. (p. 295)

As significant as reclaimers' stories are, I contend that it is important to recognize them as challenging white hegemony, the "power relations" behind our racial hierarchy. Smith is concerned with what she refers to as the "relations of ruling," by which she means "that total complex of activities, differentiated into many spheres, by which our society is ruled, managed, and administered. . . . These are the institutions through which we are ruled and through which we . . . participate in ruling" (1990, p. 14). Smith elaborates on the value of this approach:

> Thus taking the everyday world as problematic does not confine us to particular descriptions of local settings without possibility of generalization. This has been seen to be the problem with sociological ethnographies, which, however fascinating as accounts of people's lived worlds, cannot stand as general or typical statements about society and social relations. (1987, p. 157)

While this work is ethnographic, I think the stories reclaimers tell here help to bring into focus the generally invisible relations of ruling, thereby providing counter-hegemonic accounts of race.

True to the claims of qualitative research, my intent is not to find a representative sample in the hopes of generalizing the research findings. My objective is to generate an understanding of the subjective experiences of individuals engaged in racial/ethnic identity reclamation and the reclaiming process they go through. It is important to recognize that reclaiming is a process—identity construction is always a process—and therefore my objective is not to present any reclaimer as finished. As Cornell and Hartmann state, "Construction refers not to a one-time event but to an ongoing project. Ethnic identities are constructed, but they are never finished" (1998, p. 80). I then extrapolate the effects racial/ethnic reclaiming can have on race, interpreted as a system of power.

Beyond individual interviews, and for a more complete perspective on this reclaiming process, I turned toward two bounded groups: a Native American student organization and a local Cherokee culture organization. Although the process of reclaiming isn't unique to a particular setting, I feel some field observation is necessary for several reasons. First, individuals do not construct identities in isolation. Identity construction, according to symbolic interactionists, is the product of social interaction, it is an ongoing negotiation with others. By going beyond the individual to a group, I seek to understand the role of larger social processes in one's racial/ethnic reclamation process. Does the support of a group or organization, for instance, trigger individual reclaiming? A second reason for conducting some field observation is that it can help me to understand how Native American reclaimers define themselves on a collective level. I want to find out if reclaimers articulate a tribal consciousness, or a distinctly Indian consciousness, and whether such redefinitions manifest themselves politically; for instance, do these individuals see themselves as part of an Indian rights movement? Do reclaimers view this search for their Native heritage in political terms or cultural terms, or as an individual identity issue?

Additionally, observing these two Native organizations allows me to immerse myself in Native culture on a semi-regular basis. It allows me, as a white woman, to generate an understanding of interactional styles of Native people (some members of the organizations were reclaimers, but not all) and their concerns. I struggled with researcher reflexivity throughout the research process, attempting to fully acknowledge my social location and how that influences my interpretation of what I see and hear.

In terms of research subjects, I engaged seventeen individuals in formal, in-depth interviews. I conducted formal interviews between 2000 and 2002. I also spoke to at least five others for informal interviews at pow-wows. I attended numerous pow-wows between 1996 and 2002, and talked informally to reclaimers at all of them. Interviewing allows access to the individuals' understanding of their racial/ethnic identity; how they practice, enact, or perform it in their daily lives; and the potential political ramifications of such an identity. My formal interviews lasted from one and one-half hours to two hours, with follow-up interviews necessary for two subjects. These interviews were tape-recorded, transcribed, and coded for themes and patterns. The informal interviews varied in length and I took notes on them afterward. I use pseudonyms for the three interviewees I highlight in the narrative chapter (chapter one), and other than that, I use descriptors rather than names throughout the text to protect the identity of the interviewees. I have also changed some biographical data, other than gender and tribal affiliation, to conceal identities even more.

NARRATIVE: NOT JUST TELLING STORIES

Ethnographies simultaneously capture as well as produce stories. Yet, to paraphrase Marx, the stories that both the participants relate and the ethnographers generate aren't always produced under conditions of our own choosing. Anthropologist Edward Bruner (1997) argues that "ethnographies are guided by an implicit narrative structure, by a story we tell about the peoples we study" (1997, p. 264). He uses ethnological studies of Native American cultural change to explicate his point. He argues that in previous eras, the stories produced portrayed Native Americans as facing a future of certain assimilation into the white, dominant, mainstream American culture. "Now, however, we have a new narrative: the present is viewed as a resistance movement, the past as exploitation, and the future as ethnic resurgence. . . . The ethnographic problematic is now one of documenting resistance and telling how tradition and ethnicity are maintained" (1997, pp. 264–65). He is careful to point out that while he refers to these differing stories as dominant during different eras, they are dominant in anthropological discourse, "not necessarily in Indian experience. Our anthropological stories about Indians are representations, not to be confused with concrete existence or 'real' facts. In other words, life experience is richer than discourse" (1997, p. 267).

Yet, while these stories may be simply representations, they are also to be recognized as "structures of power as well . . . [and] carry policy and political implications" (1997, p. 269). Bruner continues by arguing that ethnographies are inherently co-authored because "ethnographer and informant come to share the same narratives" and views "both anthropologist and Indian as being caught in the same web, influenced by the same historical forces, and shaped by the dominant narrative structures of our times" (1997, pp. 272, 274). While, as Bruner claims, "stories make meaning," they do not do so under conditions of the teller's choosing. Bruner argues that new narratives emerge when there is a new reality to be explained: "When social arrangements are so different that the old narrative no longer seems adequate. . . . After World War II the world changed, with the overthrow of colonialism, the emergence of new states, the civil rights movement, and a new conception of equality. Narrative structures changed accordingly" (1997, pp. 275–76). What this implies for my research is that, beyond the larger political forces that Nagel views as contributing to a climate where individuals can more easily reclaim a Native American heritage, one must acknowledge the role of academic discourse in the research process as well as in the reclaiming process individuals go through.

Through ethnographic research, I generate reclaiming stories. "Personal identity, the answer to the riddle of 'who' people are, takes shape in the stories we tell about ourselves" (Hinchman and Hinchman 1997, p. xvii). Gloria Ladson-Billings's critical race theory in education emphasizes the importance of stories of non-dominant group members. Critical race theory (CRT) in education is an outgrowth of critical legal studies and emerges out of the work of Derrick Bell and Alan Freeman. CRT begins with the notion that "racism is 'normal, not aberrant in American society' . . . and because it is so enmeshed in the fabric of our social order, it appears both normal and natural to people in this culture" (Ladson-Billings 1999, pp. 212–13). This theoretical perspective informs the methodology as well as is evident by CRT theorists' commitment to an understanding of the racial experiences related by the stories of people of color. As Ladson-Billings articulates, "One of the major principles of CRT is that people's narratives and stories are important in truly understanding their experiences and how those experiences may represent confirmation of counterknowledge of the way the society works. . . . [N]arrative is a way of knowing that can provide valuable insights into our social world" (1999, p. 219). Stories by non-dominant group members are powerful antiracism tools as well. According to Delgado and Stefancic (2001), "Stories have a powerful psychic function for minority communities. . . . Stories can give them voice and reveal that others have similar experiences. Stories can name a type of discrimination; once named, it can be combated. If race is not real or objective, racism and prejudice should be capable of deconstruction" (p. 43). And according to Ladson-Billings and Tate,

> Naming one's own reality with stories can affect the oppressor. Most oppression does not seem like oppression to the perpetrator. . . . Delgado argues that the dominant group justifies its power with stories—stock explanations—that construct reality in ways to maintain their privilege. . . . Thus, oppression is rationalized, causing little self-examination by the oppressor. Stories by people of color can catalyze the necessary cognitive conflict to jar dysconscious racism. (1995, p. 51)

Therefore, I argue that while ethnographies are indeed stories, I am not "just telling stories" here. There is power in reclaiming stories; these stories will challenge the dominant narrative as well as the dominant methodology in sociology. "If people experience their lives as stories, then why shouldn't historians, or anyone who hopes to memorialize human affairs, adapt their methods to the kind of object they are studying?" (Hinchman and Hinchman 1997, p. xxii). It also, by definition, allows for individual agency. As Hinchman and Hinchman argue, stories "put the individual in the position of being author of his or her own story, an active shaper of outcomes, rather than a passive object acted upon by external or internal forces" (1997, p. xix). Additionally, relying on individuals' stories to understand their sense of ethnic identity is pos-

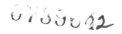

sible because, as Reissman argues, "When we tell stories about our lives, we perform identities" (Couch-Stone Symposium, Jan. 2000). While I am committed to the value of reclaimers' stories, and this work relies on the stories reclaimers tell, ultimately it remains my account—my interpretation of Native reclaiming.

REFLEXIVITY

As a white researcher, I must constantly reflect on the obstacles to understanding that exist between Indians and whites and how this affects research, both the process of and the product of. The dilemmas posed by studying outgroups are well documented in the social science literature, and numerous anthropologists have pointed out specific difficulties encountered while studying Native Americans (e.g., John 1990; Maynard 1974; Mohawk 1985; Trimble 1977; Wax 1991). It is important for me to recognize how my position and status as a social science researcher, as well as a white woman, affects the interactional dynamic between participants and researcher. At the same time, I want to be careful not to overestimate the differences between myself and my interviewees. Will they see me as "white" and themselves as racially "non-white"? Most of these individuals spent a considerable part of their lives in mainstream, American culture, the "white world," as have I. We may actually have more similarities than differences. How enmeshed they are in Native American culture when we met may have determined whether cultural differences between myself and my interviewees became potential methodological dilemmas.

At the first campus organization meeting I attend as a researcher a film titled *Native American Rights: Plundered or Preserved?* was shown. This documentary dealt with the history of the repatriation issue, from burial ground desecration in which thieves make thousands of dollars off the items plundered from burial ground sites to the "institutional immorality" of government sponsored desecration such as scientific analysis and museum exhibits of ancestral remains. At some point in the film, my observation notes indicate, I found myself quite uncomfortable. There is obviously quite a bit of distrust among Native Americans and scientists and it was well exemplified in this documentary. The repatriation battle is often between archeologists/anthropologists and Native peoples. I cannot help but wonder if these people view me as someone out to "take" what is rightfully theirs. Am I a "culture vulture," as the movie described? I recognize that I may not have anything as tangible as their ancestor's bones, but prying into their identities can certainly have some negative ramifications.

There has been an overall trend toward more self-reflexive ethnographic work, a focus that emphasizes the relational character of ethnographic interactions and attempts to avoid false portrayals of objectivity (e.g., Clifford and Marcus 1986; Lewin and Leap 1996; Adler, Adler, and Johnson 1992). Reflexivity emphasizes the relational character of ethnographic interactions. Researchers who view themselves as distant and objective, as accurately representing reality in their written report, are more likely to be criticized than embraced today. Reflexivity demands that the researcher ask difficult questions concerning "how sociological knowledge is created, how the relationship between analysts and their subjects affects the story/account that is told, and the consequences to individuals and society of producing one kind of story versus another" (Adler, Adler, and Johnson 1992, p. 6). Ethnographers influence those they are studying and are influenced by them. Ethnographies, therefore, must acknowledge such. As Clifford and Marcus point out, "Ethnography is actively situated *between* powerful systems of meaning. . . . It describes processes of innovation and structuration, and is itself part of these processes" (1986, pp. 2–3). As Nussbaum only half-flippantly remarks, "Pity the poor ethnographer. No longer can a curious researcher gather data without at least acknowledging the Postcolonialist Uncertainty Principle: your very presence distorts the data you collect" (1998, p. 53).

While reflexive ethnographic work is often viewed as a recent trend within the social sciences, it actually emerges out of a significant methodological tradition within sociology and anthropology, that of participant observation. Such an approach allows researchers to get inside the subjects' world, to understand the world from the point of view of those who are living and experiencing it. Weber describes this as *verstehen*, or empathetic understanding. As valuable as this methodological approach has been in the social sciences, however, fieldwork accounts often inadequately portray the research process, depicting it as much more linear and sanitized than it really is. While emphasizing the importance of studying social life in context, social scientists have less often emphasized the embeddedness of science in social life. Scientific accounts of ethnographic work rarely expose the messiness of life, the idea that "fieldwork is a deeply human as well as scientific experience and a detailed knowledge of both aspects is an important source of data in itself" is rarely articulated (Powdermaker 1966, p. 9).

If one considers research to be a social process, explicit self-reflexive accounts are an essential part of the written report. Yet, despite a long tradition of such self-reflexivity associated with Weber's methodological technique, it is still unwonted (though increasingly less so) in ethnographic work. Despite the dearth of self-reflexive research, there is a clear need for it in ethnographic accounts. For instance, feminist researchers such as Reissman acknowledge dilemmas posed by incongruent cultural norms between interviewer and interviewee. Her work focuses on the different ways a white interviewee and a Hispanic interviewee construct accounts of the same event, a marital separation, and how problematic this is for the Anglo interviewer. The Anglo interviewer had difficulty understanding the Hispanic woman's account because it was organized episodically rather than temporally, but fully understood the white, middle-class interviewee's linear, temporal account (Reissman 1987, p. 173). Such work seriously challenges the early feminist notion that the commonality of experience among women is enough; race, ethnicity, and social class, among other variables, all influence researcher and subject interactions (Edwards 1990; Reissman 1987). Traditional, unreflexive ethnographic accounts cloud such difference instead of explicating it and treating it as part of the data. Reflexivity encourages acknowledging "embedded assumptions about authority, power, gender, voice, relations with subjects, and the appropriate location of the researcher's self" (Adler, Adler, and Johnson 1992, p. 4). Clifford and Marcus argue that the subgenre of ethnographic writing emphasizing self-reflexive accounts "provide[s] an important forum for discussion of a wide range of issues, epistemological, existential, and political. The discourse of the cultural observer can no longer be simply that of the 'experienced' observer, describing and interpreting custom" (1986, p. 14).

It is also important to recognize how intertwined modern-day social scientists may be with the people they study. No longer is there a safe, objective distance between the researcher and the subject. For instance, urban Indians who had been forced off reservations and into urban areas during the 1950s and early 1960s due to the federal government's termination policy (1953) found themselves exposed to scientific exploitation of their ancestors in the form of museum and other public displays of burials. This became the organizing issue for the formation of AIM, the American Indian Movement, as they fought for repatriation, the traditional reburial of Native American ancestral remains. One can't help but wonder if Native peoples had still been overwhelmingly isolated on reservations, would the awareness of this form of exploitation have arisen?

When one turns to research specifically focusing on Native Americans, there is a paucity of such reflexive research, yet, as Vine Deloria Jr. has critically pointed out, there is no shortage of researchers: "Every summer when school is out a veritable stream of immigrants heads into Indian country. Indeed the Oregon trail was never so heavily populated as are route 66 and Highway 18 in the summer time. From every rock and cranny *they* emerge. . . . 'They' are the anthropologists" (1988, p. 78). The most prominent of such self-reflexive works are those of anthropologists Murray L. Wax (1972; 1991) and Rosalie H. Wax (1961; 1971; 1972). Numerous field experiences on Indian reservations have enabled them to reflexively expound on Native Americans and white relations and the study of such. Rosalie Wax argues that a primary difficulty between white researchers and Native Americans is miscommunication. The groups have very different styles that result in interaction patterns that alienate, puzzle, and sometimes anger the other (1961, p. 306). An important issue for anthropologists is how Indians and whites are problems to each other, rather than the traditional approach of simply referring to the "Indian problem" as if it were unidirectional (Wax, "The Enemies of the People," 1972, p. 178; 1961, p. 305). Such an approach focuses on the generally unarticulated relational character of anthropological research.

As a white researcher studying racial/ethnic reclaimers, awareness of this body of research alerted me to the potential dilemmas of studying outgroups. However, the reclaimers I spoke to are members of the white, mainstream society despite their racial/ethnic identity claims. Thus, we had enough similarities for understanding one another. However, the social distance between the reclaimers I interviewed and myself became most obvious during some interviews, when references were made to Native culture or particular terminology was used that I was unfamiliar with. Despite my observations at Native organizations and despite my interest in Native cultures, it became clear that there is a lot I do not know about Nativeness and Native cultures and that I am an outsider.

CONCLUSION

As a qualitative researcher, I embrace the emergent character of research. Despite that commitment, there is no doubt that I enter the research with some preconceived notions as to what I think might be significant themes among reclaimers. My overall objective is to generate an understanding of the subjective meaning of this newly embraced ethnicity for reclaimers I speak to and how they practice, enact, and perform it in their lives, the significance of this newly reclaimed ethnicity for them, what triggers their search for this new identity, what the process of reclaiming entails, and how significantly they see it as changing them and altering their perceptions of the world, if at all. Additionally, I wonder to what extent physical appearance plays a role. Will there be differences between reclaimers who "look" Indian and those who do not hold the stereotypical physical characteristics associated with Native peoples? A final theme I view as potentially important is that of activism. Will reclaiming a Native American heritage trigger political activism? Will the people I speak to alter their political views in any way due to their transformation of their racial/ethnic identity? Will they view reclaiming in individualistic terms or will they see themselves as part of a larger Indian rights movement? If they become Indian rights activists, will they make demands for inclusion into the existing political/economic system or will they embrace calls for sovereignty? As mentioned previously, much of the literature on ethnicity emphasizes the political importance of ethnic groups, and I am interested in whether the reclamation of a racial/ethnic heritage plays itself out politically the way it has for white ethnics.

While I enter this research with the previously mentioned guiding questions and a commitment to researcher reflexivity, I try to remain open to shifts in the direction of the interview. Chapter one provides detailed stories of three reclaimers. A number of objectives are behind this chapter. First, is to allow readers a more complete understanding of the Native reclaimers I interviewed. Providing a relatively lengthy narrative of each allows for a more holistic understanding of these individuals and allows for more of their subjective understandings to be recognized. This chapter provides the best overview of what reclaiming means, why someone would pursue their Native heritage, how they pursue it, and some of the dilemmas this reclaiming process entails. Additionally, this chapter provides an opportunity to explore the role of structure and agency in reclaiming. Throughout my interviews, the constraining and enabling aspects of structure are exposed. Reclaimers speak of the structural constraints that their ancestors faced to embracing their Nativeness as well as the current enabling aspects of structure that provide an opportunity for them to reclaim this heritage. The three individuals I choose to highlight in this section are exceptionally articulate about the constraining and enabling aspects of structure; therefore I chose to emphasize their stories here, but it is a consistent theme throughout my interviews.

Chapter two analyzes the various ways Native reclaimers engage in struggles of cultural representation, from the misrepresentation of Native peoples to misinformation, invisibility, and stereotypical portrayals in popular culture and educational institutions. Without defining it as such, reclaimers engage in a poststructuralist endeavor, actively challenging historical metanarratives. This theme, as it turns out, contradicts what I initially theorized. I assumed that increased multiculturalism and Native images in academic curriculum and popular culture would contribute to the ability of people of Native descent to reclaim that heritage. What I found instead is that despite the presence of diversity, multiculturalism, the development of the new social history, poststructuralism, and all the various ways scientific and historical metanarratives have been challenged, the story of the elimination/assimilation of Native peoples still perseveres and is being perpetuated throughout educational institutions. Reclaimers fight such images and narratives, most often in educational institutions, whether colleges or universities that they attend or their children's elementary schools. It is through these challenges that reclaimers are also making political challenges on the dominant culture. While most reclaimers I speak to do not define themselves as political in the traditional sense, meaning in terms of active participation in the government, their actions discussed in this chapter are political and powerful. They are actively challenging the racial hierarchy, actively challenging white hegemony.

In order to understand the particular ways Native reclaimers enact, practice, or perform this newly reclaimed identity, chapter three directly addresses reclaimer practices. Enacting cultural practices are a way of performing one's identity, and certainly among individuals who are reclaiming a racial/ethnic identity, there is an intentionality behind this enactment. In this way, as Meyerhoff argues, "Self and society are known—to the subjects themselves and to the audience" (1978, p. 32). Generating an understanding of the enactment of culture is not entirely unproblematic, however. Often, there is a tension in this arena. Reclaimers are individuals who have spent their entire lives in the white, mainstream society and, while still ensconced in that world, are reconnecting with their Native heritage. They actively try to differentiate their current, reclaiming selves from their previous white, mainstream selves, yet this distinction is not always clear-cut. In many ways their embrace of Nativeness is similar to that identified among white ethnics. However, there is something distinct about Native racial/ethnic reclamation as well. This tension is best exemplified with a sociological understanding of reclaimer practices. They are involved in a struggle to differentiate themselves from the mainstream, yet it is difficult to achieve.

One question I had as I began this research was, what role does physical appearance play in one's reclaiming process? In other words, will someone who has stereotypical Native features, such as dark hair, eyes, and skin, and high cheekbones, have an easier time reclaiming this heritage? In chapter four, I explore the role of racial physiognomy for reclaiming a Native American heritage. This exploration necessarily addresses the notion of race versus ethnicity and the idea of both as social constructions. One way to understand the role race plays in the day-to-day lives of Native reclaimers is to look at the role of appearance in racial/ethnic identity construction. Do people rely on physical appearance as a marker of their "Indianness?" Past sociological research exposes a connection between appearance, race, and identity. This chapter seeks to understand whether there is such a link for the reclaimers I spoke to.

Chapter five addresses the policing of identity among reclaimers. I find that, among the Native reclaimers I spoke to, authenticity challenges or claims to authentic Indianness are pervasive, including and going beyond issues of appearance. Authenticity questions surround debates over blood quantum requirements and the reliability of "official" measures for generating one's Indian ancestry; they inform challenges to new-age co-optng of perceived Native practices and beliefs, and the presumed presence of "wannabes," individuals who claim to have Native ties that do not exist. Additionally, there are questions of authenticity at the collective level, with state-recognized tribes struggling to gain federal recognition and the dilemmas surrounding attaining such recognition.

I do not intend to make generalizable claims with this research, in the traditional, positivist, quantitative research sense of the term. In order to understand Native reclaiming, I employ qualitative research methodologies, which implies that I am seeking reclaimers' subjective understandings and experiences. I do not intend to generalize the experiences of these reclaimers to all who engage in a racial/ethnic reclamation project, nor am I seeking to uncover universal laws concerning reclaiming in order to help explain this social phenomena. My objective, instead, is to generate an understanding of the subjective experiences of the reclaiming process these individuals go through and to understand it within its particular social context.

Despite that, I do feel this research can go beyond understanding individual racial/ethnic identity reclamation. Again, in the spirit of institutional ethnography, I start with the personal experiences of individuals, but through this process it is possible "to uncover the institutional power relations that govern and structure those experiences" (Babbie 2004, p. 295). An understanding of Native reclamation exposes the regime of truth (Foucault 1980, p. 131) surrounding race in American society, and it exposes race as a social and political construction. Individual reclaimer narratives exemplify the ways race is policed in our culture; they expose the efforts extended to keep racial distinctions alive and functioning.

Such knowledge is important for understanding larger cultural transformations. The demographic changes taking place in American society are no surprise to sociologists. As Rumbaut explains, "Today's new and rapidly accelerating immigration to the United States is extraordinary in its diversity of color, class, and national origins. . . . [M]ost new immigrants reported themselves to be nonwhite in the census" (1996, p. 121). Increasing immigration of non-whites combined with increasing numbers of individuals reclaiming a non-white heritage they had not previously embraced is clearly going to present a challenge to the racial hierarchy in the United States. They become a political force against dominant group control as well as a cultural challenge against the dominant ideologies.

NOTES

1. I intentionally use the term *racial/ethnic* throughout this work as a way to remind us that the two concepts are not mutually exclusive, as they have all too often been treated in the sociological literature as well as in mainstream discourse. I use this in the spirit of Evelyn Nakano Glenn's work, "From Servitude to Service Work: Historical Continuities in the Racial Division of Paid Reproductive Labor," in *Feminist Frontiers IV*, edited by Richardson, Taylor, and Whittier. In this work, she explains her use of the term *racial-ethnic* "to refer collectively to groups that have been socially constructed and constituted as racially as well as culturally distinct from European Americans and placed in separate legal statuses from 'free whites.' . . . Historically, African Americans, Latinos, Asian Americans and Native Americans were so constructed" (2001, p. 77).

2. There is a growing body of scholarly literature exploring this notion of the changing definition of whiteness in American society. See Ignatiev, *How the Irish Became White* (1995); Roediger, *The Wages of Whiteness* (1991); and Rothenberg, *White Privilege: Essential Readings on the Other Side of Racism* (2004).

3. As Wojcik argues in *Punk and Neo-Tribal Body Art* (1995), dreadlocks are "a symbol of defiance that proclaimed [one's] dissatisfaction with the dominant society. . . . The disheveled, 'unclean' appearance of dreadlocks [are] (an explicit transgression of dominant ideas about hygiene)" (p. 30). Adornment such as body piercings and tattoos "create a tension between the 'primitive' and 'barbaric' and that which is believed to be 'civilized' and 'cultured'" (1995, p. 33). Additionally, such "body alternations [can be seen] as being rites of passage and expressions of estrangement from mainstream society" (1995, p. 35).

4. Wounded Knee refers to the most notorious massacre of Indians by the white American government in history, perpetrated on the Pine Ridge Reservation in the winter of 1890–1891. In 1973, at this same location, there was an American Indian Movement (AIM) protest, which resulted in a two-month standoff between the FBI and Indians. Two Indians were killed in this standoff and an FBI agent was paralyzed, yet the situation ended in a peaceful mass arrest. Rhea explains, "Although Indians won no concessions from the government, their act of defiance was an important step in the reformation of Indian identity in America" (1997, p. 14).

Chapter One

Reclaimer Narratives: Exposing the Duality of Structure in Identity Formation

This work is informed methodologically and theoretically by critical race theory (CRT), and therefore I consider reclaimers' stories to be of great significance to understanding racial/ethnic reclamation. The narratives reclaimers share are powerful in that they challenge the societal narrative concerning race. In the process of relaying such counter-hegemonic stories, reclaimers' sociological imagination is exposed as well. Sociologist C. Wright Mills's concept of the sociological imagination is a useful tool for thinking about how individual reclaimers' lives intersect with history and social structure. Steven P. Dandaneau (2001) emphasizes encouraging the development of one's sociological imagination as "a form of self-consciousness that grasps the interrelations between history, biography, and society" (p. xi). The fact that Native reclaiming is a phenomenon at this particular historical juncture is evidence, I argue, that there must be some cultural and/or structural changes that have opened up the possibility for individuals to reconnect with their Native heritage. In other words, I argue that in order to understand racial/ethnic reclamation, it is essential to understand how the intersection of history, biography, and social structure interacts and contributes to reclaiming one's Native identity. Joane Nagel (1996) describes the characteristics of Native renewal and resurgence of Native cultures:

> Indian country abounds with instances of political reorganizations, linguistic revitalization, membership growth, and cultural revival. . . . [T]here has been a steady and growing effort on the part of many, perhaps most, Native American communities to preserve, protect, recover and revitalize cultural traditions, religious and ceremonial practices, sacred or traditional roles, kinship structures, languages, and the normative bases of community cohesion. (p. 6)

31

Her work *American Indian Ethnic Renewal* (1996) explores the reasons for the resurgence of Native cultures. She argues, for instance, that the Red Power movement inspired Indians to be proud of their heritage and to reaffirm Native cultural traditions: "the Red Power movement was not only a political mobilization; it was also a wellspring of transformation and renewal. . . . American Indian ethnicity became a more valued social status in the 1970s and a more attractive ethnic option" (p. 140). Reclaiming one's indigenous heritage is not only a North American phenomena; there is evidence of global indigenous reclamation as well (e.g., O'Toole 1997).

There are a number of objectives behind this chapter, the first of which is to relate in detail several reclaimer narratives in order to provide a more in-depth understanding of reclaimers as individuals and the reclaiming process they are engaged in. The narratives also provide readers with an understanding of structure and agency; embedded within the personal narratives are the reclaimers' perceptions of the structural constraints faced by their ancestors to maintaining the reclaimers' cultural heritage and the opportunities contributing to their current ability to reclaim this heritage that their ancestors had distanced themselves from. This chapter also provides an opportunity for understanding the process of racial/ethnic identity formation. While I focus on three narratives in particular, I also use this chapter as an opportunity to explicate the constraints and opportunities faced by other reclaimers, whose partial stories are interwoven with the three primary narratives.

I chose these three particular narratives for several reasons. First, all three were extraordinarily reflexive about their reclaiming process. It was my assumption going into the research that people would be able to articulate what reclaiming meant to them and describe the process they engage in and the challenges they face since their reclaiming is consciously chosen and their embrace of Native culture is overt rather than the more subtle ways culture is generally transmitted. While this is certainly true for many, others are clearly less articulate about the process. That is not to deny its significance for them; while they are actively engaged in their Native reclamation, they more than likely have not been allowed the necessary space to reflexively understand the process and what it means to them. Thus, reclaiming their Native heritage is not quite at a discursive level. Giddens refers to this as practical consciousness, "what agents know about what they do, and why they do it . . . without being able to give them direct discursive expression" (1984, p. xxiii). He describes discursive consciousness as "the ability to comment rationally on our activities—to describe and discuss the reasons for our behaviour" (p. 135). Second, all three of these reclaimers recognize and articulate the structural constraints and opportunities between their parents' and/or grandparents' efforts to distance themselves from this heritage and their ability to reconnect to it. Their cognizance of this is useful for understanding the ways structure both constrains and enables reclamation. While the constraints and opportunities of structures for reclaiming are not unique to these individuals, they are able to articulate such issues more clearly than most. Therefore, not only is their reclamation process at a discursive level but the role of structure is explicitly recognized by these three individuals. And finally, all three stories are poignant and unique in some ways, whether in terms of obstacles faced trying to reclaim, or the dilemmas surrounding their racial/ethnic identity construction, thus justifying in-depth description and analysis. At some level, of course, the decision concerning which reclaimers to emphasize in this chapter is a rather arbitrary and subjective one, bound to be influenced by the interview dynamic itself.

Using a structure/agency approach to understand generational differences in one's embrace of one's Native heritage is valuable because it allows us to understand to what extent reclaiming is an individual choice and to what extent it is reliant upon particular socio-historical circumstances. According to Giddens, "[a]gency refers not to the intentions people have in doing things, but to their capability of doing those things in the first place" (1984, p. 9). Such an understanding of agency implies the power of social structures; to what extent are individuals active agents in their own lives, actively constructing their own identities? And to what extent is their agency constrained by social structures over which they have little control?

Functionalist interpretations of structure refer to "some kind of 'patterning' of social relations or social phenomena . . . as a source of constraint on the free initiative of the independently constituted subject . . . an intersection of presence and absence" (Giddens 1984, p. 16). Yet Giddens challenges us to go beyond what such a functionalist interpretation allows, to understand structure as not only a constraint but also enabling (1984, p. 25). "Structure has no existence independent of the knowledge that agents have about what they do in their day-to-day activity. . . . Human history is created by intentional activities but is not an intended project; it persistently eludes efforts to bring it under conscious direction" (pp. 26–27).

Giddens proposes what he refers to as the theory of structuration in order to attempt to address this duality of structure. "The basic domain of study of the social sciences, according to the theory of structuration, is neither the experience of the individual actor nor the existence of any form of societal totality but social practices ordered across space and time" (p. 2). In other words, for Giddens, structure and agency need to be thought of as two sides of the same coin. He does not see structure as having an independent existence apart from being enacted by people; he instead sees structure in the actions of people. Therefore, according to Giddens, social analysis should focus on social practices. Analyzing reclaimer narratives does just that—exposes the constraining and enabling aspects of structure through practices.

RECLAIMER NARRATIVE #1: STACEY

Stacey's story provides a good starting point for understanding the constraining and enabling aspects of structure for an individual's racial/ethnic reclamation process. Stacey is a forty-nine-year-old, married mother of two, a recent college graduate, earning both a bachelor's and a master's degree as an adult, non-traditional-aged student, and is now working as a social worker. I met Stacey at her home, an old farmhouse in a rural community. As I pulled in the gravel driveway for our first meeting, I was immediately greeted by dozens of curious cats. A woman with long brown hair with gray streaks as the only betrayal of her age emerges from the back door to greet me and offer an explanation of sorts: "My husband calls it 'Stacey's Home for Handicapped Animals.'" Later she explains what she refers to as "the animal thing . . . [there are] all kinds of strange critters out here. We try to treat things right. They come our way—and they deserve an existence and respect too." That attitude, I soon discover, appears to be a core philosophy for this reclaimer, as her narrative exposes respect toward the earth, her family, her Native community, humanity in general, and, particularly, the mentally ill.

We meet on a warm afternoon in June and sit in her living room for the interview. Her home, warm and inviting, is a very lived-in combination of antique furniture and children's toys, with walls full of old framed photos of family members and what appear to be Native peoples. I find her to be intelligent and forthcoming not only about her reclamation process but also about life in general. Her two children, an eight-year-old boy and an eleven-year-old girl, are home and inside with us as well that afternoon. They are both shy but polite, and only rarely show their summer boredom and impatience with this stranger occupying their mother's time. Her interactions with the children display a patience, kindness, and placidness that I, perhaps misguidedly, attribute to her maturity level and age. She is an easygoing person and displays this in her interactions with me as well as her with children.

In the very beginning of our interview, she provides me with her basic demographic information, adding abruptly, "My dad is Native American and my mother has a little Hopi in her background. My dad is Cherokee. All my life I was told to tell people I was Italian, that being Indian will just get you in trouble. . . . And so, don't tell. Just pass for white." She later adds, when asked how she answers questions concerning her ethnicity, "as a child I would be punished if I answered that way [saying she was Native American]." I respond, "Literally? So they [her parents] were explicitly hiding it?" To which she replies,

> Yeah, oh yeah. When we were kids, you'd get crosses burned in your yard. . . . Yeah. It was against the law for us to practice our religion so people watched you to see if you did it. Until 1978, it was against the law for me to practice my religion. I had to keep that private. . . . No freedom of religion for Indians. Carter passed the Native American Religious Freedoms Act in 1978. . . . No one ever thought about that.

As a child, she explains that while her family moved around a lot, much of her childhood was spent in the Midwest. She says her appearance has always been a "problem" for her in that "I've been told all my life, you know, as a little kid even, people would say, 'You're Indian, aren't ya?' And my parents and my grandparents would always say, 'Tell 'em you're Italian.' And that was always my answer, 'I'm Italian.'" I ask her if answering that way feels strange to her. She confirms that it does. "Yeah. You lied your whole life. But they said . . . there was such fear, you know, you could *feel* fear in adults, you know, that if you said anything you could be harmed and it was a dangerous thing to say, so you did what you had to do."

I ask her to talk about some of the discrimination she remembers experiencing as a child. As she relays her first story in response to this query, I am struck by the poignancy of it, specifically that it is such a sweet childhood memory that is forever tarnished by racism and the accompanying fear it instilled in her as a child:

> I remember one incident when I was little and I was with my grandmother and we went to, it was a little farming community in Iowa, and we went to a restaurant and we were going to get ice cream and on the door was a sign that said, "No dogs, no Indians." And she squeezed my hand and she said, "Remember, you're Italian." And I remember being really scared, thinking somebody's going to catch us, you know? Because I was afraid they were going to catch us and find me out. I wondered what would have happened to her. She's white, very white, Lutheran lady, you know?

Despite experiencing such fear and feeling the fear adults felt over being identified as an Indian in this community when she was young, Stacey still reclaims her Native heritage as an adult. I ask her what triggered the reclamation of her Native heritage. She responds,

> I've always known that it was there . . . but, I guess . . . [long pause] . . . probably about ten or fifteen years that I can actually, I've been able to say it—that

> I was [Native American] . . . my dad was very against me doing that. And all of a sudden it seems to be becoming cool to be Indian and he stopped feeling so paranoid about it, so I just started claiming it and he seemed to roll with it a little bit. He's okay with it now.

Her answer exposes an interesting dilemma. Since it was her parents who distanced themselves from this aspect of their heritage, their attitudes, even into her adulthood, act as a potential constraint on her reclamation process. In order for her to be able to fully embrace who she is, it is at least somewhat necessary for her father to stop "feeling so paranoid about it." She explains to me that he has come a long way in his feelings toward his Native heritage, adding "this spring he called me up and asked me it I'd take him to a pow-wow. . . . It was huge for him because he didn't want to claim any of it. He wanted to pretend he wasn't an Indian all these years."

She goes on to explain that her father distanced himself from his Native heritage, but that this distancing was not an "ethnic" option in the way sociologists like Gans, Waters, and Alba speak, because his parents were forced to hide their Indian heritage, which inevitably influences the amount of voluntariness associated with his "ethnic options." As she explains,

> His grandmother walked the Trail of Tears as a child and was one of those who kind of escaped up the river into Iowa and didn't complete the walk. And she was in a community where it became illegal for Indians to own land and there was an Irish community [that] neighbored and so she married an Irish man in order to keep her land. . . . [T]hat happened with a lot of Indians—a lot of them were married, intermarried in order to keep their landholdings. There were a lot of white men who married Indian women to get their land and then killed them. . . . Yeah, it worked out real well [sarcastically]. The Osage in Oklahoma and Missouri and that area—a lot of them had oil rights and a lot of white men married Indians to get the oil rights and then killed them. . . . It's still on the books in Missouri that I [as a Native American woman] can't own land.

Her final comment that, as a Cherokee woman, she cannot own land in Missouri warrants interrogation. She and her husband own their home; clearly she can own land because such laws, if still "on the books," are not being enforced. But, her point can be understood more symbolically. It is significant that such a law still exists and, potentially at least, can be acted upon. One cannot help but recognize that the mere existence of such a law is evidence of white hegemony in law.

As I look around Stacey's home, she catches me looking at an old photograph on her living room wall of a woman. She explains without my asking, "That's Donna Murphy. She's the daughter of the Irish and Indian marriage . . . . Donna Blake Murphy. The Blake is a changed name. I think it was . . .

something in Cherokee, [but] it's changed by white people to 'Blake.'" I ask her who changed the name, and she replies, "When the census takers reported names they tried to, you know, English-ize them or Anglo-cize them. . . . A lot of missionaries Anglicized the names . . . making white-sounding names." This is interesting to me since I have heard of this happening to immigrants at Ellis Island, but up until this point am relatively unaware of it occurring among Native Americans.

I am particularly interested in what triggers someone to reclaim their Native American heritage. For Stacey her response exposes a confluence of influential factors:

> Actually, I had bought into Christian principles most of my life and was pretty adamant about that and . . . in some Western Civ. class [at college] I started doing a lot of reading about Christian history and about Native history and doing the comparisons and most of what I learned about Christianity is, it's a bunch of bullshit. That it was created by a rich aristocracy to keep peasants under control. And reading what their missionaries did to Native families and how they were treated and the children, how they were tortured and abused at boarding schools . . . all in the name of Christianity, and I basically discarded Christianity. . . . And I started researching what my natural history would have been had there not been that Christian influence.

I ask her what she thinks has changed in our culture that has made reconnecting with a Native heritage easier. She speculates,

> there are a lot of white people who, [with] this New Age thing going on, that want to be Indians. We call them wanna-bes. You know, and they go to reservations and they get into ceremony and they build sweat lodges and they think they're being Indians, you know, and they think that's very cool. And I guess where it used to be being an Indian was a horrible thing to be, now everybody says, "Wow! I really want to get to know you, I want to know more about you!" You know, it's tokenism, it's really kind of disconcerting. They don't want to get to know you because they think you're an interesting person, it's because, 'Oh, you're Indian! I want to collect you like they collect beanie babies. [laughs] You know . . . which is kind of a bizarre feeling.

Her problem with "wanna-bes" is that a lot of these people, she explains, set themselves up to be experts on being Indian and they do not have "one drop of Indian" in them. "You know, until somebody's spit on you and told you, 'no dogs and Indians allowed,' you don't get to say you're an Indian." What I find sociologically interesting about this point is how it directly reflects her socio-historical locatedness. I doubt a twenty-one-year-old reclaimer has ever encountered this kind of racism where they see signs that say, "No dogs or Indians allowed." This statement indicates the socio-historical locatedness of her experience, as a woman of Native heritage, a woman with Native features, who is of a particular generation.

Later she adds her frustration with the trendiness of Nativeness: "At this point in history, white people seem to think I'm just the coolest damn thing they ever saw, you know? It just blows me away. You grow up your whole life trying to pretend you're not something and now all of a sudden it's the cool thing to be." I respond to this comment with a request for clarification: "You don't sound like you appreciate that very much." To this she replies, "Well, I guess when you've been punished for who you are as a child, you know, it leaves a kind of bitterness." Again, what this narrative exposes is the intersection of history, biography, and social structure. How one's lived experience is informed by one's socio-historical locatedness.

While almost all of my interviewees recognize that there is something about the current era that provides them with some safety to reclaim, Stacey is one of the most articulate concerning the matter and is able to recognize the baggage that comes with it as well. "You know, I don't know . . . sometimes I think that we're all just going to disappear and pass for white and nobody will ever notice. . . . Yeah and then there are other times when I get a real uneasy feeling that there's a revolution brewing, you know, and what will happen with that? Will we be demolished again?" After this comment, I ask her, "You don't seem very comfortable with the fact that the culture will be open to Natives much longer . . . and I even put 'open' in quotes." She responds,

> Well, Native culture is very different from the dominant culture. The Western culture is a competitive culture, the capitalist, everything is bottom line, everything is, "What can I get?" Individualistic and profit-oriented. And the Native culture is very community minded, what's good for the community . . . how do we get consensus, you know? . . . It's just a very different way of thinking.

By this, Stacey is implying that Native culture and the dominant, white, mainstream culture are so discordant, that even an "openness" toward Native cultures by the mainstream culture is not enough. One could read more into her statement, in the context of her previous concerns over whether Native people would simply disappear and "pass for white" or whether there will be a "revolution" of sorts, that as more and more people of Native heritage reclaim that cultural heritage, it poses a threat to the dominant culture, which, as her concern explicates, could result in the subordinate groups being "demolished again." Yet, without actually articulating it, her embrace of her Nativeness may also be evidence of the potential for success in this endeavor, that collective reclaiming has the potential to seriously disrupt the racial hierarchy.

Stacey's education level and academic inclinations are often expressed during the interview. For instance, she makes numerous academic references as support for various points she makes, and it does not appear to me that she does this for my sake, to authenticate her points to an academic. Instead, it comes across as simply her style, her way of thinking and being. As a social worker, she describes a counseling method called the "Red Road Approach," created by two Dakota men. This counseling method, she explains, emphasizes a phenomenon known as cultural schizophrenia, "where Indians live in two different cultures. In order to survive, you have to understand the dominant culture and the competitive model if you want an education. But if you live in the traditional Indian system, it's a cooperative model, so you have to be able to walk in both worlds in order to survive and most can't." This idea has a long history in the sociological literature on minority groups, despite the fact that we do not use the psychological jargon "cultural schizophrenia" to explain it. DuBois describes it explicitly in *The Souls of Black Folk* (1989 [1903]) as "born with a veil, and gifted with second-sight in this American world, a world which yields him no true self-consciousness . . . it is a peculiar sensation, this double-consciousness. . . . One ever feels his two-ness" (p. 5). I ask her if she experiences cultural schizophrenia, since she was raised in the white, mainstream society and now is embracing her Native heritage. She replies,

> Sure, yeah, it's difficult because it—especially in academia because if you want to adopt the cooperative principle of living—academics are very competitive and very cut throat. . . . A lot of Native Americans, the majority, don't survive a bachelor's program, let alone a graduate program. . . . I found it a hostile environment; graduate school was very difficult. . . . I don't feel it was really supportive at all.

She sees herself as an activist, proudly exclaiming, "Most of our legislators recognize me when they see me. . . . They know my name." She says her Nativeness informs her activism in terms of her environmentalism as well as her respect for the mentally ill. In this way, her Native "self" informs her social worker "self." She provides an intriguing example:

> I've done a lot of advocating for mental health. . . . White people don't have any respect for people with mental illness. They blame them like it's their fault. Somehow it's somebody's fault. Um, in Native culture the mentally ill are just another unique creation and they have a purpose. They have value. I find that really enlightened. And when you work with the mentally ill, you see how unique they are and they have a value, they have their own—they're a different

creature, you know? Just like we're all unique and they have lots to offer. And a lot of them just need help having a peaceful existence. And we all deserve that. Anyway, schizophrenics are amazing people—very creative, very imaginative if people help them with being peaceful. So, if you can take the torment out of it, which you can do with medication, you'll find a lot of interesting people. Some of my favorite clients are schizophrenic. Mental illness doesn't have to be a curse, just like disability isn't a curse. It's just another feature of an individual. You know, I guess . . . we [Native Americans] have bizarre ways of looking at things, I know.

Stacey's environmentalist ethos is something that is nurtured through her Native reclamation rather than being something difficult to reconcile. She explains,

I'm what they call a tree hugger. Consolidated Electric hates me 'cause they always want to trim my trees and I won't let them touch my trees [laughs]. They think I'm a pain in the neck. "You're going to lose electricity when that line comes down." Not necessarily, I've got propane and stuff, I've got oil lamps—we'll live. [We'll] take our chances.

When asked how important her Cherokee identity is to her, she responds, "Very important. It's my identity. It affects about everything I do." When asked what she thinks it does to people to distance themselves from their cultural heritage, to not embrace it, celebrate it, and practice it, she replies,

I know what it did to my dad. He's very unbonded from anybody. He's very unable to get close in any relationship. I don't know if you're familiar with . . . attachment disorder research . . . there's a cultural attachment disorder . . . it comes with being so disconnected with who you actually are. And I guess I see my dad as a classic example of that because he grew up not telling anybody and denying his heritage and asking his children to deny it. Um, and he's just the guy, he can't cope with any kind of connection with anybody. And the family thing is just too much for him . . . he's just totally disconnected from the family thing.

She continues, "He's retired like three times and he can't stand to spend time with his family so he goes back to work. . . . The day I graduated with my master's, a *big* day in my life, it took like thirty years to get there, you know, a long road, man [laughs] . . . he had a committee meeting he couldn't miss [shrugs]." She then adds, "I accepted my parents a long time ago for what they are."

Interestingly, she says that when she began her reclamation journey, she expected everything to be wonderful but has been shocked to find out it has not necessarily always been:

I guess the one thing that when I started down this path I saw it as, you know, this is going to be really cool, I'm going to reclaim this, "I'm an Indian and I can say it now." And I found that it's been very difficult . . . it's one of those where for a while I would wake up in the morning and go, "God, I'm still Indian," wishing I could shirk it off, it was just very uncomfortable for a very long time. . . . I thought it was going to be this really fun, cool skin to wear and it didn't turn out to be that way. I'm finding now, as I've gotten into it a lot further and time has gone on, that I'm embracing those things that, um, are meaningful to me and not taking in other people's criticisms and rules about what it means to be an Indian. . . . I'm getting more comfortable with "this is the skin I've got" and what I do with what's inside me.

I find her language interesting in this quote, specifically that she speaks of "skin." As she says, she initially thought, "it was going to be this really fun, cool, skin to wear" and that "this is the skin I've got." First, the use of the term *skin* to refer to Natives is something I find in Native literature. Crow Dog (1990), for instance, says that she cannot wait for the summer sun to "make me into a real skin [Indian]." It is also a direct reference to race. Race is a social construction that is literally embodied in our skins. Native Americans have historically been defined by Euro-Americans as a racial "other." Stacey is someone who sees being Native as being non-white. "It's not something you can choose to be or not to be. . . . You know, you got the skin, you're wearing the skin, it doesn't matter what your religious practices are. It's a race."

Later she elaborates on her point about how surprisingly difficult reclaiming her Cherokee heritage has been for her, "I guess the point I was making is it wasn't the easy thing that I thought it would be—the transition to being the cool Indian wasn't easy." I ask her for clarification, stating, "I can see how it wasn't easy, but earlier you said how it wasn't necessarily comfortable. Why?" She responds by citing the struggles she faces passing her heritage on to her children:

No, because of things like, my children having their own Pledge of Allegiance or my children coming home with a poster about Columbus being a hero. . . . And what do I do with that, you know, how much conflict do I create for my children? How many lies do I let them believe so they can get by? It is an uncomfortable place to be.

She continues, "I want them to know the truth and I want them to grow up knowing their heritage and being proud of it. But, how much risk is there in that? You ask yourself those questions all the time. It's not a comfortable place to be." I respond, "For some people, they talk about it being comfortable because it's who they are and so it fits . . ."

To this she adds,

> I feel like it's, in that way, I feel like it's what I have to be, you know, I can't pretend I'm something I'm not. I'm not going to go through this life denying what I am and pretending I'm something else because it's safe. That's not a valuable life. I feel like I have something to offer. I'm a very intelligent woman and hopefully I will contribute something that will make things better for my kids and other little half-breed Indians to come, so they can be proud of who they are. You know, hopefully pass on some understanding that it is okay to be who you are no matter how unique you are.

As she describes the dilemma of reclaiming, expressing that on the one hand, it's not a comfortable place to be, yet clearly *not* embracing this heritage is also uncomfortable, the duality of structure becomes obvious. While individuals are active agents in their own lives, and to a certain extent racial and/or ethnic reclamation is evidence of human agency, at the same time Stacey's story forces us to recognize the power of structure as well. Structural opportunities may enable one to reclaim a previously denigrated heritage. Yet, while one can reclaim, there are still structural constraints faced by reclaimers as well as non-reclaiming Indians. The dominant group can still influence whether this reclamation process will be conflictual or problematic for those engaged in it.

Stacey is someone who recognizes the difficulties as well as the benefits of Native reclamation, as well as the constraining and enabling aspects of structure. She describes her social activism as informed by her newly reclaimed Nativeness while, at the same time, her racial/ethnic identity reclamation informs her activism. While this narrative explicitly exposes the duality of structure, it is important to recognize that there is more to her story than I am able to capture here. The following chapters provide more information on Stacey and her reclamation process, particularly how this new identity informs her parenting, her religious practices, and her educational experiences.

RECLAIMER NARRATIVE #2: JAMES

I meet James at a local coffeehouse. I get there early, anxiously awaiting the arrival of one of my earliest project interviewees. I scan the crowd to see if he is already there. We have yet to meet, but I have been given a description: long, dark hair, in a pony-tail; a goatee; wearing a flannel shirt and jeans. Finding no one who fits that description, I order a coffee and find a table near the door. Within minutes, he unassumingly enters the room, figuring out who I am before I even have time to register his arrival. He is easy to talk to, telling his story without much prompting. Unlike some of the other reclaimers I meet, the only clue to his Native heritage in terms of his appearance is his long hair, which, while not entirely uncommon, is rare for a professional man of his age. I find him to be extremely reflexive and articulate concerning his reclaiming process.

James is a forty-year-old single father of three children and a college professor. His narrative also exposes the constraining and enabling aspects of structure. James refers to his Native ancestry as a "dirty little secret," at least that is how he perceived it in his family when he was growing up. He explains, "I was born in Tampa, Florida, with Indian blood on both sides of my family. My mom's family was from Georgia, entirely from Georgia." He describes an interesting clue to his Native heritage, which he was unable to define as such until his adult, reclaiming years:

> There was always something I attributed to be rural and southern in their [his parents' and grandparents'] teachings that I found out later on wasn't necessarily southern, it was Indian. The thing is, from the time of relocation from the Trail of Tears to about 1978 or 1979, it was illegal to be a Creek Indian inside the borders of the state of Georgia. Yes, that's how long the law stayed on the books. Yes. My grandmother was born in 1918, grandfather 1912.

He goes on to provide an example of those rural/southern cultural practices that he later identifies as Native. Additionally, this quote explicitly exemplifies the constraining aspects of structure. The heritage that James later reclaims was denied him as a child due to such structural constraints as legal proscriptions and even the threat of forced relocation. Other reclaimers speak of similar constraints.

James proceeds with an explanation of the conflation of "rural ways" with "Indian ways": "Granddaddy never said too much but he would teach you a lot. You would learn, [but] you didn't realize you were learning it." He provides an example of this subtle transmission of culture:

> I don't think they were intentionally giving me my heritage. . . . I think it came natural to them. But the part about not telling me was intentional, yeah. That was dangerous. . . . When I was like three, my grandfather would take me all over the place with him. When he was working in the tobacco fields or cotton fields, for instance, I would ride on back of the mule or on the tractor with him. I was just a little guy and it was incredible to see this older fella, fiftyish, dragging me all through the swamps and stuff. Why would you take a three-year-old into the swamps? Well, he was taking me there to teach me. He never said this, he never said, "This is the way you approach nature . . . this is the respect you have for it." But it was things like, you always knew where to hunt and fish. And he was always very respectful of whatever he was hunting. If he was

hunting deer, for instance . . . he would cross over into the ditch and he would stop there and just bow his head like this. I always thought he was listening, but what he was doing was praying for the deer. He was actually talking to the deer. We [Native peoples] have this idea that hunting is a good thing, and when a deer wakes up in the morning, he knows and he makes a decision that today is the day that he's going to leave this earth. To have some effect on the ongoing health of the earth, he's going to put himself in a position to be consumed by another being . . . a brother or a sister, whether it be a bobcat or a human being. In doing so, there would be a continuation. . . . He [his grandfather] was praying, thanking the deer. So, he would hunt the deer, shoot the deer. And he would take what I thought was tobacco out and sprinkle it on the deer. He was sprinkling sage on the deer. I just thought [later in life], how quaint, a cool, southern, rural thing, everybody here does it. And you later learn that those aren't things that everybody does and they're not things that everybody talks about, either. That would have immediately identified him as an Indian. You didn't do that then.

This narrative exposes his understanding of the constraining aspects of structure, describing an environment where people live a certain way but are forced to deny the cultural legacy they enact. He explains that due to this discriminatory climate, he was not explicitly told of his Native heritage until he was a grown man. While never being explicitly told, he says he knew of this heritage, but it is significant that he was never told outright. He continues with an explicit acknowledgment of how the constraining and enabling aspects of structure play themselves out in his and his family's life:

I was a grown man before my granny, and I already knew this, but she told me one time, when she was getting up in years, she said, "You know, my grandma is full-blood Creek." And I said, "Yes, ma'am, I know that." She says, "She was Ellen Thomas and her husband was half Creek and she was full-blooded Creek. I just thought I'd tell you that." So this woman who had lived under the threats, either real or only perceived, of the threats of racism toward Indians, to live that long, to be that old and to finally open her mouth and tell me that, even though I already knew it, everybody in the family knew it, you just didn't say it, was amazing to me. It became a little game after that. Every time she saw me, when I would go home six months later, she'd say, "You know, my grandma was a full-blood Creek." I'd say, "Yes, ma'am, you told me that." "Yep, I told you that."

I ask him why he thinks she chose to broach this subject at this point in time: does he think she had gotten to a more comfortable place to be able to say this, or had the world come to a more comfortable place, or was it simply because she was getting old and felt that this needed to be said? In his response, there is an explicit recognition of the constraining aspects of structure:

It's definitely part of that [the latter]. . . . She knew she only had a few years left on this earth; she just died a couple months ago, and she didn't want that to die. 'Cause granddaddy couldn't ever talk about it. . . . He died in '71 and that was still not the time to talk about it. And I think part of it was the fact that she was getting old and wanted to make sure that I knew what was going on, and the other part of it was the fact that I think she kind of judged me, in a way, to see if I was responsible, if I would protect the family. . . . I think she kind of judged me as being someone who would be responsible with that information and that I wouldn't let anything bad happen to my family. . . . As many wonderful, bonding experiences that I had with her, I think that's one of the foremost.

A few years after this, he approached his grandmother to tell her he wanted to get the family tribally enrolled. "Granny, I'm going to get us enrolled at the reservation. Do you mind?" She said she did not mind, but when he asked her if she wanted a card, she declined. "'No . . . you have to enroll me or else you can't get enrolled, but don't get me a card . . . not right now. Let's wait a while.'" He explains, "She was still hesitant to have something as simple as a reservation card." He had to explain to her "It's cool. Nobody's going to mess with you anymore." To which she replied that he should use his judgment; if he thinks it is right to enroll the family, then he should enroll them. He recognized that it was hard to convince her that there is not a threat anymore, a perspective that did not surprise him at all: "There's a great deal of paranoia and distrust, especially toward the government, among Native Americans. I don't hold a BIA card, although I could. But I don't. [And] I'm not as paranoid as many are . . . I am tribally enrolled, not federally enrolled."

I ask him about the comment that his Native heritage is a "dirty little secret" and if he knows of any specific stories of things that happened to family members because they were Indian. He says, "I don't know this for a fact, but I suspect that my great-granddaddy was ruined financially by the Klan. Why he was allowed to live I have no idea." He provides more detail:

Granddaddy . . . he was just a poor, half-breed dirt farmer, had nothing. . . . [Yet] this man owned a chunk of land by 1908 . . . now, he's around fifty years old by that time. He worked and got all that land. . . . Legally, Creeks could stay there [in Georgia] according to federal law, but according to state law, it was illegal for them to be there. So, they stayed. Anyway, great-granddaddy became an affluent farmer. He had all kinds of land. He had a big, pretty house, things like that. Before the Depression, there was a blight of cotton down there. Weevil came and just trashed the place. So, he started losing some land there. Another way he lost land was when his farmhands would get in fights, he would go down and post land [bail] for them, and somebody would convince them [the farmhands] to leave town; therefore his land was lost. According to court records, the same guy was buying up the land from the county. . . . In my mind, it is connected to Klan activity in that county because the guy who was buying that land was a Klan activist in that county. . . .They had a problem with grand-daddy because he was an Indian. They had a problem with granddaddy because his momma wasn't married. And they had a problem with him because he would pay a black man in the fields the same thing he would pay a white man in the fields. They didn't like an Indian holding the reigns of control over a white man, and certainly not if he was going to pay a black man the same thing as far as wages. So they were pissed at him. Somebody told me that they came to his house one night and burned a big oak tree in the front of his yard . . . that is when this land scam started. They were trying to force him out financially.

One of the ways he knows of his Native heritage even though no one ever spoke explicitly about it in the past is because it was often spoken of in code. As a child, he explains, he used to linger and listen to "the old men talking. And everyone accepted me as part of the furniture. And I would just listen and I would remember things."

There used to be cane grindings, when they made syrup out of cane. And we'd stay up all night, sitting around fires all night and talking. I would just kick back and listen. . . . They talked about the "old people." . . . I think a lot of the people in the community were Indian and that was the code word from far back in the tribal days was "old people." . . . I think that was the code word when they were talking about before relocation and the time when there was a strong cultural identity, before they had to go underground. I think that's what they were talking about, that period.

James explains that his reclamation process is triggered as he sees "the old people passing [away]":

I'd always been interested [in genealogy] from hearing it, the stories about the old people, and it laid dormant for a long time. Unfortunately, most of the old people had by then died before I figured out that this was something that I needed to know about.

His Native reclamation, however, is triggered not only by his life events and/or interests. Instead, it is something that was imposed upon him by a family member, an "old maiden aunt," as he describes her. He explains, "When I graduated from college, she called me to the house. So I went around, and she said, 'Son, I'm proud of you . . . you're educated.' Hugging on me and stuff, 'And I want to give you something.'" He says at this time she told him,

that I'd been listening to the old people for so long, that she was going to give me something for it. She gave me everything she knew about our family history. She gave me two big boxes full of news clippings, scraps of paper with dates on it . . . nothing constructed about it. Just all these archives. She said, "This is your job, now. I can't do it anymore."

He adds, "I was essentially issued a mission at the age of twenty-three or whatever. I was always interested . . . genealogy is a hobby of old people normally . . . at least everybody I've met in the practice of it has been. . . . So, there was this innate interest, hearing all the old stories prompted further interest. And this mission from my aunt made it formal: now I have to do it. I can't back out."

He later explains, "Family is of the utmost importance to Indians." I find from his narrative that this is true for him; family appears to be of the utmost importance to James. He attributes this to his Nativeness; however, as a single father, one could argue that he is forced to be family centered in a way mainstream, non-Native men in this culture are not because all too often our definition of fatherhood is based exclusively on the breadwinner role. As Hamer describes mainstream American fathers, "Men measured their success as men in terms of their breadwinning role and the standard of living they were able to provide for themselves and their families" (2001, p. 17). Yet, his concern for his ancestral family certainly extends beyond his single-father status; in other words, genealogy is not something he has to pursue, except for the fact that his aunt charged him with the search. He says that his grandmother told him about their Creek heritage because "she kind of judged me as being someone who would be responsible with that information, and that I wouldn't let anything bad happen to my family."

His Nativeness also seems to inform how he treats elders, a perspective not unique to this reclaimer and one I will expand on in later chapters. He tells of an interaction he had with an Indian elder who lives near him:

> There's this elder up in . . . [town] . . . that I just met the other day and . . . it was kind of funny. Whenever we meet an elder, we take a little piece of red cloth and put tobacco in it . . . it's nothing, but it's to show respect. So, I went up there to meet him the other day for the first time and when he reached out to shake my hand, I reached out with this medicine bundle in it . . . he said, "This is how I know you're a real Indian." And I said, "Okay, cool!" We were off to a great start. Whenever we meet someone who is an authority, an elder, someone who is older and wiser than us, we pay tribute. It's not a matter of subjugating ourselves; it's a matter of complimenting them.

He later relates a story that exemplifies how important elders and family are to him. Speaking of his great-grandfather, he recounts,

> He lived to ninety-two years of age and toward the end of his life, as was traditional in my family, he was getting old and infirm and the children would pass

him around. He would live with this one for a week, that one for two weeks, etc.
They all lived within twenty miles of one another. He was always taken care of.
That was a man that always inspired me, the little that I know about him, he al-
ways inspired me a great deal.

Since his parents had to deny their Creek heritage, and so far he has only
spoken of his grandmother's acknowledgment of it, I ask how his parents feel
about his reclaiming, to which he replies they are not nervous about it. "Because my mom had left Georgia, met my dad in Tampa. The environment was
different. So, she felt a little bit more freedom." I think his answer is interesting and similar to Stacey's in that there is an expectation that this will not
be something their parents' generation would embrace, simply due to their
historical experiences. Yet, he makes a comment that implies geographic location also plays a role. Once his mother left Georgia, a much more restrictive place for Creeks, she "felt a little bit more freedom."

James' Native identity influences all aspects of his life, including his sense
of family and parenting. Beyond that, he explains why this aspect of his heritage is so much more influential to him than his other heritages:

> I have some Irish and a great deal of Scottish blood in addition to Native Amer-
> ican blood. I'm very proud of my Scot and Irish heritage, just as proud as I am
> of my Native American heritage. You can be Irish American or you can be Scot
> American, but neither one of those people are thoroughly and totally disenfran-
> chised as a people. That is why it's impossible to be a Native American in one
> segment of your life and a white, middle-class individual, with a white mental-
> ity, in another segment of your life. And that's not saying this is better or that is
> better . . .

He continues,

> I don't celebrate my Scottish ancestry, although I am proud of it. I am involved
> in genealogy and obsessed with knowing who these people were, and they are
> as important to me as ancestors as my Native American ancestors are. I think the
> similarities between tribal structure in Scotland and tribal structure here is what
> led those Scots to affiliate with the Native Americans. . . . But what I am trying
> to say is that my understanding of being Native American is that it is all perva-
> sive.

This quote seems rather contradictory. On the one hand, he does not want to
deny the non-Native parts of himself. But, he finds that they are, for the most
part, incompatible identities. He then works to ameliorate some of the incom-
patibilities by emphasizing the similarities in tribal culture between the Scottish
and Native Americans. His efforts exemplify the negotiation that necessarily

goes into understanding ourselves in terms of race and ethnicity, particularly among biracial and/or bicultural people.

James further notes that the further along he has come in his reclaiming process, the more empathetic he feels he has become. "For instance, some of the events make me extremely sad. The fact that my grandparents and their parents and their parents had to deny who they were is very sad to me . . . that is some of what motivates me." In regard to his children, he admits:

> I'm biased. Every parent wishes for their child to maintain the same set of values. I try to consciously allow freedom there. . . . I try to teach them the same way my grandfather and my grandmother taught me, which is through quiet emulation. . . . You teach through lessons, you don't teach by answering questions. . . . So, as far as teaching culture? No, I don't teach them culture. I have language tapes laying around the house. . . . I never say, "You need to learn this." I never do that. I have the books, I have a bookshelf full of various accounts of Creek culture, I have old manuscripts written by educated, old Creeks. I have a whole computer full of lineage. Any question they ask, I'll direct them to it. But, I'm not going to say, you're a Creek kid, you're going to learn this, because they're going to resent that.

Additionally, he talks about his brother who does not embrace his Native heritage. He explains, "My brother, who is six years younger than me, he knows about being Creek, but his hair is short and he lives in the white world and he's happy there. And I love him and I respect him. . . . But, I think in his dreams people talk to him in another language. I really believe that." I ask him, do you think he will ever reclaim? To which he replies, "Probably, when we're both old men. He'll want me to tell him stories."

Another arena where one can see the Native influence on James is in his profession as a college professor. He explains that as a generalist teaching at a small college, his approach to whatever subject he is teaching tends to be holistic: "I'm much more comfortable teaching that way, and I think it makes more sense to them that way." He adds, "I have a lot of fun in American history classes! I just start talking about treaties and I see their eyes roll back into their heads and they're thinking, 'Come on! Let's talk about white folk history for a while!' My response to that is, 'You've been talking about that your whole life. Let's talk about something else.'" While his students may not entirely appreciate his approach, he argues that "there's the assumption that when you empower a disenfranchised segment of the population, they immediately disenfranchise someone else . . . and I don't believe that." He also explains that he views himself as a role model for Native students on campus, "I have Indian students following me around all the time." He says this is partially attributed to the fact that he has long hair and that is a marker of his Indianness.

"I have longer hair than probably 90 percent of the female faculty . . . and certainly than most of the male faculty. . . . But a lot of people think I'm weird, a lot of people are trying to figure out what my niche is, if I'm a dead head or what I am."

He says that a characteristic of his personality that can also be attributed to his Nativeness is

> you don't go through life drawing attention to yourself. . . . If you ever run into an Indian who is boastful, then they have forgotten the way they were raised, or they weren't raised properly. Just like if you ever run into an Indian who is disrespectful to elders, whether they're white, black, or Indian, doesn't matter, they're still elders, then that person has either forgotten how they were raised or they weren't raised properly. You go through life not drawing attention to yourself, as seeing yourself as part of a collective, as opposed to an individual. Which is why flash doesn't mean a great deal. When an Indian walks into the room, you don't want to draw a lot of attention to yourself.

At least in terms of my interactions with him, he certainly seems to live up to this assessment of Nativeness. He extends this point to include

> the way people talk. There seems to be a tendency in the dominant society that the less one has to say in an argument, the louder they talk. People are moved to increase volume, for, to me, what are irrational reasons. The way to talk to people is in a soft voice. Because the softer you talk, the more you can listen. . . . That's not the way we're taught. We're taught to be collective, not to make people see us as being an integral part . . . the most humble people that you can meet on a reservation or in a community are the chiefs.

When asked how his new racial/ethnic identity has altered his life or sense of self, he replies,

> it's made me . . . the more I learn, the more introspective I get. But, I think that may be true had I been born and raised on the reservation because as you go through life, you become more introspective. And doing that, you feel other emotions. You feel the empathy of other people. For instance, some of the events make me extremely sad. The fact that my grandparents and their parents had to deny who they were is very sad to me.

Similarly to the previous narrative, James's story explicitly recognizes the constraining and enabling aspects of structure. He moves from feeling that his Creek heritage is the "dirty little secret" of his childhood to, as an adult, reclaiming and embracing that heritage and being in a position to pass it on to his children. His interest in genealogy and explicit acknowledgment of the importance of family are also attributed to his Nativeness, a point I will discuss in more detail in the chapter on reclaimer practices.

RECLAIMER NARRATIVE #3: SARAH

I initially meet Sarah at the campus Native American student organization meetings, and she turns out to be a rather high visibility student on her college campus—an activist on Native and women's issues and someone I see everywhere on campus. While she has always been very polite to me, for some reason I do not manage to interview her until several years into my project. I can not help but wonder how similar or different it would have been had I been able to interview her in the early stages of my project. Since Native reclamation is a journey, a process, I assume there would be some fundamental differences had I spoken to the twenty-six-year-old undergraduate activist instead of the almost thirty-year-old, soon to be graduate student. I meet Sarah at the campus food court after she gets off work. It is summer and she is working full-time before she begins graduate school in the fall. The interview goes very well. I find her to be forthcoming, intelligent, reflexive, and patient. We have to schedule a second interview in order to get through the questions, so her patience is certainly tested.

This final narrative exposes the identity struggles of someone of a racial/ethnic bicultural heritage. Sarah is a twenty-nine-year-old reclaimer currently pursuing her Ph.D. in psychology. To me, Sarah "looks" Native American, in that she has long, black hair, dark eyes, and a dark complexion. Despite my assessment of her appearance, she explains that she gets "everything but" Native when people try to guess her ethnicity. She, probably rightly so, attributes this to an overall invisibility of Native Americans in this society. She grew up in an urban area, but recognizes that she is raised with "Indian ways." Her father, who died when she was twelve, was Lakota. She still has family on the reservation, and she says she is "beginning to learn that life."

She is one of the only people I speak to who, when asked about her ethnicity, the inevitable "What are you?" question, responds, "I am bicultural. I mean, because I have, my mother is of German and French and, oh, a whole bunch of European ancestry, but there is also Delaware in her background . . . but her family didn't claim that. . . . My father's side, he's . . . Lakota." While she is my only interviewee to use the term *bicultural*, she has not always been comfortable with the concept. She describes one incident where the inevitable "What are you?" question emerged and she laughingly replied, "I'm my own worst enemy! I'm like, [laughter] you know—I'm just like, I'm

the Native person and I'm also the people that came over. What's going on?
. . . But, I mean really . . . I don't feel that in myself." And she adds,

> I think sometimes, too, when I was—when I was still trying to form my identity
> and trying to figure out who and what I was, um, by being bicultural, uh, or mul-
> ticultural I should say 'cause it's—it's more than two 'cause my mother's mixed
> with more than one culture, um, by being multicultural, it was very hard to, to
> feel legitimate enough, you know? To say legitimately, now, "I'm Native Amer-
> ican" without "and blah, blah, blah." You know? But being able to say, "You
> know what? I'm just Native American." And that's what I feel like I—that's
> what I feel like I am. . . . That's what makes sense to me. I mean, the teachings,
> the family structure, the—everything makes sense to me.

Later she explains, "If people ask me, I am Native American because that
is what I connect with. That's what I know. I don't know anything about my
German or French ancestry." So, despite the fact that she is not from the reservation, she feels that is the heritage that was most salient in her home growing up. As she says,

> even if you're removed from the reservation, even if you, if your family is no
> longer on the reservation, you still have a parent or parents that have Indian ways
> and that's the way you're raised . . . that's how you learn how to associate with
> people. That's how you learn how to be with people. . . . You learn familial pat-
> terns from that. And so all of that was Native and so, yeah, by all means, yeah,
> when I claim my ethnicity, it's Native American, but if I get the chance, then I
> put . . . Lakota. Because that's me.

Her answer makes me wonder what influence, if any, I, as a white researcher, have on her answer. Why does she go through the trouble of explaining that she is bicultural, and then work toward the conclusion that she
is Native, specifically Lakota, because that "is what she knows?" Certainly
her explanation might refer to her changing perceptions of herself and her
process of coming to terms with her Nativeness. But, as a researcher, I cannot overlook the influence I may potentially have on the interview interaction. Her response may be a standard response she provides to whites, dominant group members who are quick to question one's authenticity,
particularly if one's physical appearance is not a distinct marker of one's
racial/ethnic identity. An additional point of importance about her identity
claim is that she defines herself in terms of her tribal affiliation, over and
above being Native American (Cornell 1988). Most, but not all, the reclaimers I speak to emphasize their tribal affiliation. For those who did not
emphasize their tribal identity, it is usually due to the fact that they are unsure of their specific heritage.

To clarify a previous point, I ask her, "So, growing up, you, you haven't changed over time in terms of your self-identification?" She responds, "Oh, no, I have . . . yes, by all means." And she goes on to explain in detail:

> Let me give you background on my father because that kinda helps . . . [understand] what I am and then kinda where I came in to. But, my father, uh, was born in 1925. He was quite a bit older than my mom. . . . He was actually seventeen years older than my mom. . . . He was this . . . good-lookin' guy and so that's . . . how he got her . . . but anyhow. . . . He passed away from cancer when I was twelve. So . . . he was born on the . . . reservation, one of the poorest in the country. And one of the only ways to get out was to go into the military or something like that. And actually World War II was going on when he was able to go in . . . see he, uh, did his service over there and, and, for a lot of Native people, as well as African Americans who went into the service, as well as Hispanic people . . . for a brief period of time, they were treated like human beings. They were treated like citizens . . . they were honored, they were revered for being a soldier. And I, I think that that, that happened with my father as well. So, they come back to civilization or come back to America and then they come back to their towns and all of a sudden they're just another dirty Indian. Even if they have the skills, they're not treated like they have the skills. They're treated like they're incompetent . . . substandard . . . those kinds of things.

She continues,

> I think my father really hated going back to that. . . . He talked to my mom about this. Of course, I didn't hear the stories from him because I was twelve when he died, but . . . he made the decision when he came back, um, to leave the reservation. There's no way to make money [on the reservation]. I mean, it's, it's just very poor. There's, there's no industry. There's no way to make money. . . . It's like people collapse in on themselves because they wanna stay on the reservation to maintain their cultural pride, but yet, at the same time, if you can't feed your family . . . it really comes down to eating . . . It's not even like, "Oh, we can't buy a new car." You know? . . . And that was certainly the case in the forties . . . and he made the decision to move off of [the reservation] and look for work out in the world.

She adds, "So, my dad brings us into [the] city, raises us in an urban area because he wanted things for us that he didn't have as a child . . . the opportunity for education, the opportunity for medical care. . . . We grew up urban, but we were raised the Indian way."

So far Sarah may not appear to be someone who fits my description of a reclaimer, since she describes herself as having been raised "the Indian way." However, I think she does fit as a reclaimer because she has not always recognized that she has been raised in "the Indian way" due to some particular life circumstances. Although she has always been aware of her Native heritage, due to the death of her father when she was twelve she was "removed from the family, 'cause most of the family was back on the reservation.. . . . After he died it was, um, it was a struggle, uh, as a teenager trying to figure out my identity." This is one of the primary reasons I chose her story to be represented in this chapter, because she explicitly recognizes and discusses the identity struggles surrounding her Nativeness and, through doing so, exposes the processual nature of identity construction and the role of significant others in identity construction. Symbolic interactionist Joel Charon points out, "One of the most important qualities that we all develop over time is some idea of who in the world we are—our identity. Identity is really a process; who we are is an ongoing development" (2001, p. 160). To continue with her story in her own words:

> Not having my father there as a central figure, um, not having relatives around me, um, all the time. Not having those people as mentors/role models. It became very confusing what it meant to be bicultural for me. Um, it also became very confusing what it meant to be Indian for me, you know? Anyway, so I went through a lot of identity faltering. . . . I went through tons of different phases of people who I collected as friends and masks I would wear . . . just really trying to figure out who I was, but never fitting, ever. Never feeling like I was in the right community, like I was clicking into the right place. And, um, it was a very hard time for me . . . a lot of days being very sad. And, and not understanding, I don't know, why my ways of being and doing were so incongruent with [mainstream] American ways of doing and being, you know? . . . It was also trying to find people who connected with me and understood what was going on. It was very hard to find that in the group of friends I was making that were not Native, um, or at least with an understanding of Native ways. Um, and it was, um, not until about two years before I came to college here that I decided to start going back to these roots. Kind of going back to understanding who I am as a person, as a relation to my father. Um, I think I carried a lot of anger for many years against my father for dying so there was—there was a part of me that pushed that part away, um, that didn't acknowledge that that was part of me. Um, because if he was gone, really what was I then? And it was hard. . . . There were a lot of times that I felt very lonely and very isolated . . . a lot of depression coupled with that.

She later adds that, for her, being Lakota "ties so closely to my father and for—and for me to remember him and honor him . . . that's kind of the integral part of being. . . . Lakota to me . . . is, is being part of my father." She acknowledges that there had been a lot of adolescent angst accompanying this ethnic identity crisis, but that "certainly that was a huge pressure, uh, was the identity . . . the lack of identity. The lack of knowing who I was and—and I didn't feel like I had, um, the right to claim my Native heritage." I think this last point is particularly interesting and ask her to elaborate on it. She adds,

Um, because I mean, I wasn't hooked into the community anymore because they were back on the reservation and they were, you know in [another state] and here I was. . . . I didn't look a certain way, I didn't act a certain way, I didn't speak the tongue, you know, so really what was I?

Sarah's narrative exposes a symbolic interactionist understanding of identity construction. She repeatedly emphasizes that to be Native and especially to understand herself as a Native person, requires others, particularly family and a Native community, particularly in addition to not looking "a certain way." "At the heart of identity is social interaction because it is through social interaction that identities are formed, maintained and changed. It is important to understand identity formation as a negotiation process that unfolds as we interact" (Charon 2001, p. 160). For this reclaimer, it is significant that her Nativeness is rarely reflected back to her in her daily interactions, thus her racial/ethnic identity is contested. Identity is not something one can construct in isolation; meaning is, in fact, negotiated through interaction. As O'Brien and Kollock emphasize, "The self, like other objects, is viewed as a social construction that takes on meaning through interaction . . . we learn about who we are through observing the responses of others to us" (2001, p. 202). And as Charon articulates, "The work of Goffman reminds us that creating identity is an active negotiation process between who others tell us we are and our continuous attempts to present who we think we are to others" (2001, p. 165).

Due to the death of her father and the distance from the rest of his family, Sarah finds it difficult to understand what it means for her to be Lakota. She remembers her father being very proud to be Lakota. As she explains, "I remember always feeling very proud about who I was and—and, um, and that was really important, um, because my dad would, uh, my dad would be very direct with people when they would ask about me or him or whatever, you know, he was always just like 'No. I'm Indian.' You know, I mean, it was always in your face." Later she adds that being Lakota "is very important to me and it's something that, um, I'm also very proud of." Therefore, despite the fact that she has been raised with "Indian ways" and her father not only did not deny his Nativeness but was proud of it, coming to terms with her Nativeness still involves a reclamation process.

There are additional aspects of identity construction that necessitate interaction with a collective. For instance, symbolic interactionists make the following argument concerning the development of a person's self-concept through the reactions of significant others:

Studies indicate that whether one identifies with a group in which she can claim membership depends on how easily one can be identified as a member of that group, for example, by name or skin color. . . . It also depends on the general

salience or visibility of that group in society. The adoption of a role identity involves a process that occurs over time. First, the individual recognizes that the
identity is available. Through contact with others, he or she learns the behavioral
expectations and the social evaluation associated with the role. (Michener and
DeLamater 1999, p. 82)

For this reclaimer, the absence of her Native father and his family in her
life makes the acquisition of her Native identity problematic, despite the fact
that her mother, a woman of primarily European descent, does her best to
keep their Native heritage alive. She describes her mother's approach to her
Native ethnicity as follows:

She tells me all the time that I'm basically a carbon copy of my dad and it's—
it's really, I mean, it's this huge compliment . . . so she refers to her side of the
family as her family and she refers to my father's side of the family as my family. . . . I think in some way she's trying to help me with my ethnicity . . . and
she says all the time that we—we were raised in the way that my father wanted
us to be raised, so. . . . So, again, it kinda goes into the ethnicity question again
where she, um, acknowledged and respected, um, the ways of Lakota . . . and
she continued [after her father's death] to raise us in a lot of the same ways, you
know?

Several of her comments allude to the fact that physical appearance plays a
role in her struggle for her racial/ethnic identity, particularly in the white world.
Sarah feels that she has constantly faced ethnic identity challenges due to the
fact that she does not "look Native." She explains, "I get the 'What are you?'
question a lot . . . that's a constant reminder . . . and it doesn't bother me anymore, but when I was trying to kinda hook into my identity . . . and others
would say, 'Well, you don't look it.' 'So, what do I look like? Do I look like a
potato?'" She continues,

It's so difficult in this society to be something when you don't take on an appearance that says you're this thing. . . . And it's so difficult because then if you're a
person who's still trying to find your identity and you have people telling you
"Well, you don't look . . ." I mean I got everything but Native and so then with
that, being kind of split from the family and it's just like, "Wow, what am I?" . . .
And eventually I just kinda said, you know what? I am. It's not what am I anymore, it's just what I am. And it took me doing a lot of searching to come to that
and realizing that it was up to me to decide what I am. . . . And I am Native. And
I am . . . Lakota.

Sarah says that once she came to this decision, her "life kinda started to go
in the right direction." She has a group of friends on her college campus,
members of the Native American student organization, that she says she fi-

nally "clicked" with. She relates the following: "There's a lot of folks in the student group that had very similar, uh, feelings. Um, backgrounds. Um, situations similar to what I went through, uh, which was really empowering." Later she adds, "It's been an incredible journey but at this point, um, I feel more solid in my identity than I ever have in my entire life. Except for maybe when I was six, I mean, like you know, back then . . . you know who and what you are." Again, within this narrative we find evidence of the necessity of others for the development of identity. "Finally clicking" with fellow Natives helps validate her Nativeness.

While her looks have not provided her with an easy road to her Nativeness, she explains that her surname does. Her reclamation journey has brought her to her family's reservation numerous times and she feels she receives a warm reception there, primarily because "my last name gives me a ticket already . . . . I mean, there's like, over five hundred . . . on the . . . reservation and we're all from one guy! . . . We're all family. And, like, that's a big name at the [reservation]. . . . There's not a question of authenticity at all. Um, there's not a question of whether or not I belong."

Sarah recognizes that still having family on the reservation, and a last name which provides her with a "ticket," places her in a relatively advantaged position in terms of reclaiming her Native heritage. She explains, "I think it would be very hard for people who don't have, um, the direct connection like I do, um . . . I mean, with my father coming directly from the reservation, my family still being on the reservation, you know . . . that kinda gives me an in where someone else . . . it makes it a lot harder for them to make a connection, which is, I'm sure very, very difficult."

She also recognizes the role of structure in limiting her opportunities to meet other Natives. She explains,

on the soil of Missouri, you could be killed, period. For just being here, you were trespassing on the land of Missouri. . . . And that wasn't actually repealed until the 1960s. . . . And so that's . . . actually the history of Missouri—I don't know if you're aware of this, but the history of Missouri, um, there was a law that was passed, um, in the nineteenth century and I always get the date wrong but it was like—I wanna say it was like early 1890s, '92, something like that. There was a law that was passed in Missouri that said if you're Native American—of course, they didn't call us Native Americans back then—but if you were Indian and you were on the soil of Missouri, you could be killed, period. For just being here. You were trespassing on the land of Missouri and Missouri made the law . . . the law that Indians were not allowed on this land and you could be killed . . . and that's why there's not many Native people in Missouri. . . . People scattered out of Missouri after this law was passed and so if you'll notice a lot of Native people are on the peripheral edges of Missouri. Why is that? Because they didn't wanna leave what they knew but they couldn't live . . . in Missouri. . . . So, yeah, actually the infusion of Native blood back into Missouri has been pretty recent as so that's why the numbers are so small in Missouri.

Sarah has been politically active throughout her undergraduate college years, actively involved in the campus Native American student organization, which maintains a pretty heavy activist agenda, particularly during her years as an undergraduate. She is also a women's rights activist, working with the campus women's center. Currently, as she begins graduate school, she describes herself as "on sabbatical" from such types of activism. She plans on looking into a national organization for Native graduate students, "if they exist. I don't know if they do . . . [and] I know that there's a professional, um, Native women's organization that I wanna get involved in as well." She is not involved with Native political organizations such as AIM (American Indian Movement), explaining that there are various ways to be an activist on behalf of Native America: "We need people in all different areas but—but for me it's—it's not the in-your-face kind of thing anymore. It's more about education and—and talking with people. Um, and, um, hopefully doing research and publishing. And teaching. And talking . . . I wanna teach in counseling psych and I wanna teach from a . . . Native perspective." She continues, "I also wanna . . . make sure that when we're teaching multicultural issues, uh, in psychology, that we include Native people." She feels that her Nativeness influences every aspect of her life,

> from what I'm gonna do with my life . . . what I'm doing is, I'm giving to the next seven generations, I mean, because there was a lot of struggle that got me to be where I'm at and there was a struggle that kept me alive. . . . I see that as— as the driving—really, a driving force in my life, um, in the respect of, uh, giving back. Um, it's very important that I'm doing something purposeful. Um, and, uh, hopefully it's involving Native people . . . and hopefully it'll also involve women and hopefully it'll also involve, um, racial/ethnic minorities in this country altogether because the voices have been silenced for too long.

Sarah wants to correct the distorted version of Natives that has been presented throughout her educational history. For instance, she says, "When I go to classes and they're talking about race/ethnicity, Native people aren't in there! That makes me very aware of who I am and very aware of my heritage and very aware of wanting to get that information out there." At the same time, she appears to contradicts herself by arguing, "I'm also asked, um, quite a bit, um, at this university to talk. . . . Sometimes you get a little tired. . . . And I'm glad to do it sometimes. But sometimes you get a little tired of being the instructor. . . . The frustrating thing . . . is that people want you to be the voice for all . . . and you can't be." She also fears that, when she speaks to white audiences from her Native perspective, white people then mistakenly assume they are knowledgeable about the subject, "'I know all about Indians, now.'" This may appear to contradict her stated desire to teach, to educate about Nativeness, to address the invisibility associated with being Native in the mainstream culture, but later she addresses this by stating, "My ancestors have put me here . . . and I don't have a choice in this matter . . . you know? . . . I mean, I really don't because, I mean, because I've made it to the point where . . . I'm still alive at thirty, and that's pretty exciting. . . . So, actually, making it to where I'm at, I know that I had a lot of help. . . . I think it's very important to confront racism when it happens." This apparent contradiction seems instead to be a tension she constantly faces within herself—feeling that she has been put in an opportune position to educate others on Nativeness and, more broadly, racism, versus feeling resentment at always being called on to speak *for* Natives to people (predominantly mainstream white people) who make little to no sincere effort to learn about Native cultures on their own.

While Sarah is well educated, she is somewhat surprising with her answer to my question, "How do you go about learning about your Native heritage?" Her first response is expected, as she explains, "I just talk to my family . . . my Native friends in Missouri, uh, have . . . taught me a lot of things. Um, as far as Indian country culture, I learn that from other folks from all over the country, you know. . . . Also from people who are not Native. . . . You can pick it up from just about anywhere." The surprising part is her follow-up comment, "I don't trust books. Um, unless they're written by somebody who— who's been vouched to me . . . I do not trust books." From someone working on a Ph.D., literally ensconced in the educational system for most of her life, I find this comment somewhat surprising. Sarah continues,

> There's, um, I'm not putting down this man at all, but there's a writer . . . his name is William Least Heat Moon . . . and he, uh, he kinda sold himself for a long time as being Native and he's not at all. See, that's actually his Boy Scout name. . . . I mean, so that . . . I'm not saying that he's . . . he writes fiction, so it's not a really big deal. It's not like he's trying to write books on, like, how to be Indian or something . . . but if you kinda go into this idea that—that, you know, that something's gonna be legitimate because it's in—because it's on paper it's, um, that's not necessarily true. So I'm kind of apprehensive of books unless they're referred to me by somebody who I do respect.

I think having a healthy skepticism of what is in print is essential, and certainly in higher education encouraging critical thinking and critical interrogation of written texts is integral, but I still find it intriguing that someone pursuing a

Ph.D. is this skeptical and even further, tends to rely on the opinion of others as her reference for quality.

Many of my interviewees express similar feelings. And certainly, many rely on the Internet for information and community connections. There are numerous websites to help individuals find their Native roots, many on Native cultures, tribal histories, and so on. While these are valuable sources of information to many, particularly to those disconnected from their tribal culture, there is also a significant amount of distrust of the Internet as a source. Sarah continues with her skepticism:

> Um, the Internet, you know, people can put whatever they want out on the Internet, so that's really—that's really a dangerous area . . . [but] it's kinda neat to find out what's going on, though, politically in Indian country by getting on the Internet, so I do that. . . . News from Indian country is actually online, so you can go out there and find out what's going on.

The important thing for Sarah in terms of learning her Native heritage is that it is accomplished through social interaction. I ask her if she has a mentor, and she replies,

> [My] Aunt Mary . . . in that arena. But, I mean, I have academic mentors as well . . . and I have personal mentors. And I have friends that I will hold up to the status and the level of mentor, um, so, but as far as like, Indian ways, my Aunt Mary . . . and then also, the—the memory of my father. . . . He's still mentoring me even now, um, even though he's passed on . . . and my niece and nephew sometimes. . . . Because children are just so—just so much more aware. I mean, they're just so much more cognizant of how to treat people. . . . They just— there's just this wonderful connection to people that—that kids have, um, with people. Or with animals. Or with the earth or whatever, um, that we can continue to learn from . . .

She describes what she perceives to be the benefits of being of Native heritage. Her description emphasizes a richness of culture, involving rituals, tradition, and identity. In her words:

> I mean, here's these customs and here's these traditions and this, that, and the other [associated with Nativeness]. And—and being a European American there's— unless you have a family that is very strong back to its mother country or whatever, there's—there's kind of a loss of culture, a loss of identity . . . kinda just being one of the many. And, uh, and I think that that can be very hard if you're trying to kind of figure out who and what you are. And I think that anybody, uh, any American, will eventually realize that being an American itself is part of a culture and an identity as well . . . that [having this richness in terms of Native cultural heritage] has been a privilege.

When asked to describe any discrimination she had experienced as a result of being Native, she says poignantly, "I think a big discrimination for me was losing my father, you know, so young. If he had not come from where he had come from, perhaps — perhaps — I would still have a father who was active in my life." She continues,

> I mean, I, I — I'm the product of — of — of poverty and oppression, and my father would not have died of cancer had he not come from the reservation I am quite sure . . . I think . . . well, there's a couple very strong physical reasons. Um, one, was because he didn't have any dental care as a child, uh, being on the reservation . . . and he died actually because of an abscessed tooth that turned cancerous. . . . But I think also, too, because of, um, because of all the oppression and because of all the racism and all of the things that happened to him from being from the reservation, um, he — he was also a drinker, um, which then I think made him not pay attention to the abscessed tooth early enough. And so then that's kind of a more philosophical reason why.

Another arena where she feels discriminated against due to her Native heritage is in academia. Even though she earned her undergraduate degree with a very respectable grade point average and worked on seven research teams that led to publications, she finds that her acceptance in graduate programs is often questioned, as if she is not qualified and they are simply accepting her to meet a racial/ethnic quota, to satisfy affirmative action requirements. As she says, "But still, somebody is always gonna think, 'She's here because she's Native American.' General . . . anti-affirmative action statements said around my presence, which I know were directed at me." She feels that there is a lot of anti-Native American ideas embedded in our overall, mainstream, culture that "you [as a Native person] become more sensitive, so you get hurt more . . . and people try to be funny and it's not, you know?"

Similarly, she feels that the stereotypes surrounding who is Native and what it means to be Native, including the association of Native people with a propensity toward alcoholism, are damaging and therefore a form of discrimination she experiences. "At one time they [stereotypes] were very harmful and very hurtful, um, and they really made me question who and what I was . . . because I didn't fit the stereotypes. But then after confronting the stereotypes and fighting the stereotypes, I find that I become even stronger being what I am." In terms of the association between alcoholism and Native people she explains her frustration in this way: "It doesn't happen all the time, but like, when I talk about my father's death, people automatically assume it's because he was an alcoholic . . . and he died of cancer. He died of cancer because of an abscessed tooth. I mean, he was an alcoholic. He was, but it was bad dental care, not the alcoholism, that killed him." And in true feminist fashion, she recognizes that this situation, while indeed very personal, is also political. She adds,

> I'd say that there's probably lots of stories like that for Native people or for people who are immigrants or whatever. Just lack of—lack of health care—of good health care . . . and I think it probably even happens to a lot of folks that have to use, like um, public health services in general, through Medicaid or Medicare . . . . I'm sure that they miss a lot and they do not get good care and it's very hard for them to see doctors. And, um, and it's a real problem in this country . . . it's a real problem in this country.

She also discusses discrimination toward herself and her father from her maternal grandmother. As she describes, "They hated that my mom was married to him. Yeah, and he never came to visit with us. It was always mom and me and my sister going and he never came. . . . They were very discriminatory against my father. *Very* discriminatory." As far as racism directed at her by her grandmother, she relays a poignant childhood story as an illustration:

> I did get some racism from my grandmother, my mother's mother who is not a Native person, um, who disliked me because I was too Indian. . . . She told me . . . pretty straightforward, too. . . . There was one time that we were at their house and it was the summer and um, I was taking a bath and she came in and . . . she takes this washcloth and she starts scrubbing my arm really hard and she says, "You see that?" and I'm like, "What?" You know, I'm kinda freaked out 'cause she's scrubbing my arm. She's like, "That's your dirty Indian blood. It won't wash out."

This story, while certainly tragic in itself, has an element of sociological interest beyond the explicit racism. That is, this person can't seem to "win" in terms of appearance. To those, such as her grandmother, who are prejudiced against Native people, she has the look they despise and there is some essentialism embedded in the way she describes it: "It won't wash out." On the other hand, this reclaimer is constantly being challenged in terms of her racial/ethnic identity, as discussed earlier, getting every guess but the right one—Indian. (For more on the significance of physical appearance to reclaimers, see chapter four.)

I ask all of my interviewees what they think assimilation does to a person, specifically what happens to people who reject their Native ancestry and assimilate into the dominant culture. Sarah is empathetic toward those who feel the need to assimilate. She explains her position on this topic as follows:

> I think it's very normal to do that. Um, you know, I mean, uh, unless you're—
> unless you're surrounded by people who really kind of celebrate your heritage,

I mean, what does this country teach you? . . . To follow the American dream. So, you buy the house in the suburbs and you have the 2.5 children and you get a good-paying job and you buy things. . . . I mean, my dad, in some ways did that. . . . He left the reservation and didn't want to go back and he wanted to make a way for us, you know, so that we would have enough money to be able to buy food, you know? . . . Um, I don't think he ever assimilated, though. I don't think he ever gave up his Nativeness. . . . I think we see a lot of people giving up their heritage because of this—this grass is always greener on the, uh, American side, or in the . . . dominant . . . mainstream culture. . . . I mean . . . it's hard, I mean, to fight that. . . . I'm not saying people who pursue that are— are in the wrong. It's just wrong for me.

Throughout this narrative it is clear that she recognizes the role of structure, the influence the dominant, mainstream culture has on people of Native heritage (and any non-dominant heritage, for that matter). She continues with her reasoning in this way:

I think that the visibility of Native Americans in this country is still very low and so for people who do wanna come back to their culture—let's say that they've assimilated or their parents have assimilated so they're trying to come back. Um, it's hard sometimes to find those resources and it's even harder sometimes to feel like you're accepted into those resources, too, 'cause, um. . . . And it's very sad. But, I think the Internet has really helped a lot because . . . the information is out there so that they can actually go and look at websites by Native people, you know what I mean? And they can kinda make those connections online that maybe you can't make if you're in a small town in Missouri . . . and you have no other Native people around you . . . the only thing is . . . sometimes you can get a lot of really, um, uh, faulty information, um, out there.

She feels that how assimilation affects people depends on the situation, but that especially for those who actually leave the reservation with intentions to assimilate, "I think that there would be something with their identity that would be askew. . . . Because there would be a piece of themselves that they just decided to give up altogether and never go back to and I think there would be some kind of pain. . . . I mean, I didn't grow up that way, so I don't know . . . it's just very individualistic." She further elaborates,

I mean, it would just depend on the person and—and why they decided to do that. I mean, did they decide to do that because they were discriminated so greatly against and they're—they're frightened? You know? I mean, a lot of people's grandparents were like that . . . [saying], "No, no, no. You don't say that you're Native. . . . I've heard so many stories like this of—of people's grandparents going like, "Oh no, no, no. You tell 'em you're anything else but Native American." Or just, you know, try to pass because if you do that then people won't hate you and try to burn your house down or whatever. Um, so there was a lot of fear so at that time I think that's very different than somebody who decides to leave right now.

Overall, she says that being raised in the mainstream Anglo culture has affected her in that she never feels she fit in and it took her until adulthood to embrace that she is slightly different than everybody else. She continues,

It's very hard sometimes being the only Indian in, you know, a classroom . . . it was difficult . . . sometimes, sometimes it made you special so you kinda liked it, you know . . . especially when you were a kid . . . but, you know, sometimes it also was the thing that, you know, you kinda wanted to hide, you know, because it—it was the thing that people were gonna ask you horrible questions about, you know, and when you're not really capable of articulating your answers. It was—it was difficult 'cause they sometimes made you feel bad.

She explains that doing interviews like this helps her understand herself better; in Giddens's language, it brings her racial/ethnic identity reclamation to a level of discursive consciousness, "the ability to comment rationally on our activities" (1984, p. 135). As she says, "You know, I'm just like *oh yeah, I've kinda got a grasp on this now, finally.* And I feel really good about myself and really good about my background and my heritage. Um, and I couldn't have said that, you know, maybe in some of those years that I was really wandering around trying to figure out who and what I was."

And similarly to Stacey, at the end of our interview, Sarah adds that reclaiming "is really difficult. Sometimes it's really painful. . . . Sometimes you kinda—you feel overwhelmed with the plate that's in front of you—of all the things that you have to do . . . 'cause there's so much to be done and so much to be . . . gosh. There's so much to undo that has been done as well." She says at those points, when it feels overwhelming, is especially when it is important to remember "there's only so much that you as an individual can do but no matter what you're doing, you need to be doing something. . . . Sometimes I wanna be able to fade into the background, but I realize that I can't do that anymore and that's okay because, again, I mean, I was given a big gift to make it to where I'm at."

Like the previous two narratives, Sarah's story provides us with some evidence of the constraining and enabling aspects of structure, particularly in terms of her father, his reasons for leaving the reservation, and her reclamation of his cultural heritage. However, her narrative is somewhat unique in that there is an overwhelming focus on identity construction, particularly emphasizing the role of others in identity construction and how one develops a sense of self through social interaction, a classic symbolic interactionist understanding of identity construction. In this narrative, Sarah leads us through her identity development, from knowing she is Lakota, to losing her father and that connection to the culture, to questioning what it means to be Native, to describing herself as bicultural, and finally to being able to say, "I am Native . . . I am Lakota" and not feeling forced to add the other heritages, which carry less salience for her.

CONCLUSION

There are several major themes embedded in the previous three narratives that are not exclusive to these reclaimers and warrant more in-depth sociological analysis. One significant theme that several reclaimers I spoke to mention is a familial story of land loss through questionable means. Another theme pertains to the significance of naming. Stacey, for instance, speaks of the missionaries Anglicizing her relatives' names as part of their forced assimilation. Other reclaimers speak of the importance of naming, although not all tell stories of the dominant group's forced assimilation through name change. Some speak of taking names as a way to embrace their Nativeness, for instance. And, of course, most narratives of the reclaimers I speak to provide evidence of the constraining and enabling aspects of culture.

Embedded in Stacey's narrative is a recurring theme that I hear throughout my interviews with Native reclaimers—the theme of Native land loss at the hands of whites. At one level, of course, there is nothing new to thinking about Indian-white relations in terms of land loss. It is something even the most neutral history textbooks emphasize—that whites of European ancestry came to the so-called New World and, along with various other exploitative practices, proceeded to take the land from indigenous peoples. While this historical fact is not lost on most of us, and we have some understanding of the collective land loss Natives faced, I think we tend not to recognize the significance of it on an individual level.

Land is, among other things, equivalent to wealth. Oliver and Shapiro (1995) discuss racial disparities in wealth accumulation between whites and blacks in their book *Black Wealth/White Wealth: A New Perspective on Racial Inequality* in a way that I find useful for this discussion as well. They discuss, for instance, the racialization of the state, emphasizing "the context of one's opportunity to acquire land, build community, and generate wealth has been structured by state policy itself. . . . Slaves were by law not able to own property or accumulate assets" (1995, p. 37). While their focus is on state policies that historically and currently inhibit black accumulation of wealth, one could clearly make similar arguments for the accumulation of white wealth and the disadvantage of Native wealth accumulation based upon land swindles. And instead of thinking only of the giant land swindles that are perceived to have been engaged in by the American government against Native tribal governments, one can focus on the smaller, everyday, localized swindles that took place all across the country. As one woman explains, "In the state of Missouri it wasn't until . . . the 1950s or something like that until they could actually say they were Cherokee [because] if they did they took a chance of losing everything. You weren't allowed to own land in the state of Missouri until 1950-something." We tend not to think about the difference it would make in one's life today if their parent, grandparent, or great-grandparent had the wealth associated with land that they had once owned and lost through questionable means. Oliver and Shapiro emphasize that such historical circumstances have significant effects on current lived realities. As they argue—and again, a similar statement could be made in terms of white wealth and Native disadvantage—"Just as blacks have had 'cumulative disadvantages,' many whites have had 'cumulative advantages.' Since wealth builds over a lifetime and is then passed along to kin, it is, from our perspective, an essential indicator of black economic well being" (1995, pp. 5–6). They continue, "Assets expand choices, horizons, and opportunities for children while lack of assets limit opportunities" (1995, p. 7).

The exploitation of Native's land by whites historically occurred when whites were in a position to benefit (Farley 2005, p. 124) and they established a structure that enabled such exploitation. They did this through the establishment of laws that did not permit Native people to own land, through turning a blind eye to land swindles instead of taking legal action against swindlers, and, as pressures for land increased, through forced relocation of Native peoples to reservations. Native Americans faced considerable constraints to obtaining, or holding onto, their land during the eighteenth and early nineteenth centuries. Reclaimers are embracing their Indianness during a time when such actions by the dominant group are less likely to occur. And even beyond the enabling aspects of the current structure, one can look to minority group agency for precedents surrounding reparations. In the 1980s, for instance, Japanese Americans interned during World War II and their children established the "Campaign for Redress" to press the United States government for an official apology and a cash payment to each living internee (Rhea 1997). According to Rhea, "President Reagan signed the Act, which promised a formal apology, and authorized payment of $20,000 for each survivor" (1997, p. 58).

In order to avoid an abstract understanding of this issue of land loss, a discussion of disadvantaged access to wealth needs to be understood at the tangible level at which it is experienced. According to Farley, "African Americans, Latinos, and Native Americans all have far greater percentages of their population living below the poverty level than do white Americans" (2005, pp 251–52). The extreme poverty Native Americans face, particularly those living on reservations, is not an abstract statistic lost on the reclaimers I speak to. Many comment on the desperate poverty disproportionately experienced by Native Americans. One woman describes the following:

> You have all this poverty on reservations and, uh, I'll talk about that every chance I get with people 'cause a lot of people just don't understand beyond their own community what poverty there is on these Native American reservations . . . far worse than any inner-city poverty and anything we have in the United States. . . . People do not understand that there are still reservations out there that don't have running water. And, you know, don't have adequate electricity. I mean, you're talking about what we as the American people would call the Dark Ages, and it still exists.

Therefore, I see the recognition of familial land loss at the hands of whites, or state policies that inhibit the accumulation of wealth, such as the comment made by Stacey that as a Native woman, it is still illegal for her to own land in Missouri, as powerful in terms of claims reclaimers may make on the state. There is now a precedent for such. As noted earlier, the United States government paid reparations, for instance, to Japanese Americans who had been interned during World War II. Robinson outlines such a precedent and makes an argument for reparations to be made to Black Americans for slavery:

> For twelve years Nazi Germany inflicted horrors upon European Jews. And Germany paid. It paid Jews individually. It paid the state of Israel. For two and a half centuries, Europe and American inflicted unimaginable horrors upon Africa and its people. Europe not only paid nothing to Africa in compensation but followed the slave trade with the remapping of Africa for further European economic exploitation. . . . While President Lincoln supported a plan during the Civil War to compensate slave owners for their loss of "property," his successor, Andrew Johnson, vetoed legislation that would have provided compensation to ex-slaves. . . . Black people worked long, hard, killing days, years, centuries — and they were never paid. The value of their labor went into others' pockets — plantation owners, northern entrepreneurs, state treasuries, the United States Government. (2000, p. 207)

Will reparations be in order for Native American land loss? Do Native reclaimers perceive the government as owing them anything in return for land loss, cultural genocide, and exploitation? One interviewee is explicit about this very fact when discussing the money federally recognized tribes get from the government, commenting, "I don't call it a hand-out or welfare. It's the stuff that's due to the Indian after they gave up the whole darn country." If such attitudes are widespread among Native reclaimers, they are quite possibly the result of the current era, where a historical precedent has been established for reparations, and reclaimers can use this opportunity to make demands for reparations to Native peoples.

In terms of the significance of naming, Strauss (1997) emphasizes the importance of names to one's identity, arguing "the person wants to have the kind of name he thinks represents him as a person . . . [t]he phenomena of 'passing' is often marked by name-changing: you disguise who you were or are in order to appear what you wish to be" (p. 18). While his discussion recognizes voluntary name change, forced name changes share some of the same qualities, yet differ on significant others. For instance, Strauss argues that "new names also mark passage to new self-images. Conversion, religious or otherwise, is often marked by a complete change of name . . . some names . . . [tell oneself] that this is what he is and that other people think so too" (p. 19). In the case of dominant group members "Anglicizing" Native names, as in Stacey's story, we see clear evidence of attempts at forced assimilation into the white mainstream and away from Native cultures, evidence that Natives were encouraged to "pass" as white. But, when such name changes are involuntary, Strauss is inaccurate in describing them as part of a subject's attempt "to appear what [they] wish to be." There is power in the act of naming: "To name, then, is not only to indicate; it is to identify an object as some kind of object. An act of identification requires that the thing referred to be placed within a category" (Strauss 1997, p. 21). This quote powerfully points out the objectification process whites engage in their interactions with non-whites. Name-changing is one way the dominant group objectifies subordinate group members.

However, as my interviewees point out, not all name changes are part of the dominant group's objectification of the subordinate group. Many Natives, for instance, undergo a name-changing ceremony where they take on new names. One reclaimer goes by the name Eagle. He explains the origins of his name in this way:

> I've had it for about five or six years, I guess. It was given to me by my clan mother, adopted mother. In the process of proving my lineage, I was going to be adopted into her clan. Anyway, she called me one day and asked if I was ready to take a name. . . . I said, sure. She told me about a dream she had where I was running and ran over the edge of a cliff and just like you see in cartoons, I'm still pumping, doing running motions in the air, and an eagle swooped down and grabbed me by the back of my shirt and brought me to safety. She had had this dream several nights during the past week and decided it was significant. The astonishing thing was, is that I had had almost the exact dream, recurring, as a child. The only difference is that in her dream it was raining and in my dream it wasn't. But essentially, it was the same dream. So Eagle is my given name.

This last point is particularly interesting to me. (I discuss the significance of dreams and mystical experiences to reclaimers in chapter three.) Many reclaimers from this study emphasize the significance of dreams and how they believe dreams influence their life. The validation of such mystical experiences is found in Native cultures and tends to be less validated in the mainstream, white culture. In many cases this is explicitly recognized by reclaimers I speak to. For instance, Sandy, a forty-one-year-old reclaimer, explains, "When I was growing up, to find out you were Native American was a pretty cool thing . . . a lot of kids were, 'That's neat.'" But, she adds, that while at a surface level her Nativeness is validated by others, she feels she could not really emphasize what being Native means to her. "To explain to the kids . . . what I can do as far as my abilities goes, would've been considered crazy . . . dreams and spirits and [talking to] trees. It would have been considered something very crazy. I'm not a shaman. I'm not a medicine woman. Um, I've just been given gifts that I've tuned into that everybody has." This woman recognizes that her connection to the mystical and the significance and value of dreams, talking to spirits and the idea that trees can speak, are all culturally validated or invalidated. So, there are limits to what mainstream cultural members understand or even tolerate in terms of her Nativeness. This exposes the constraining and enabling aspects of structure—that while there is a current "openness" to Nativeness, at the same time what that means, what is considered appropriate, is still defined by the dominant group.

The importance of voluntary name-changing is expressed by another reclaimer I spoke with. She explains the difficulty in proving one's Cherokee heritage through a reliance on federal rolls because Cherokees have a practice of changing their name at different points in their life:

> Depending on what phase of life they're in . . . [and] they have a Native name, they have a very private name they don't give to the public. And they have a white name, or the Christian name, or whatever. So, finding them is sometimes a needle in a haystack kind of thing. . . . Frequently when the Indians encountered missionaries and they heard the Bible stories they would pick a name from a part they liked. . . . So, the . . . rolls will have the Indian names but the census usually doesn't have the Indian names.

This statement exemplifies hegemony of white culture in terms of setting the "rules" for who is considered Native American. As the discussion in chapter five emphasizes, getting officially "counted" or recognized as Native depends on whether one can find and prove the presence of an ancestor on one of several government rolls from the 1800s.

Finally, throughout reclaimer narratives the duality of structure is exposed. By this concept, Giddens refers to the fact that "structure is not 'external' to individuals . . . structure is not to be equated with constraint but is always both constraining and enabling" (1984, p. 25). He continues,

> The flow of action continually produces consequences which are unintended by actors, and these unintended consequences also may form unacknowledged conditions of action in a feedback fashion. Human history is created by intentional activities but it is not an intended project; it persistently eludes efforts to bring it under conscious direction. (p. 27)

In Stacey's narrative, for instance, the duality of structure is explicitly recognized as she ponders the dilemmas of her current socio-historical location regarding her racial/ethnic identity choices and how that manifests itself in the transmission of her Native heritage to her children. She does not simply recognize a current "openness" where it is "cool" to be Indian. She recognizes as well that there are structural constraints wedded to reclaiming this racial/ethnic heritage. I think this is important to recognize because it exposes both the power of reclaimers' agency and the hegemonic racial structure that still exists in the United States. To use Giddens's language, we see the unintended consequences of numerous actors in the U.S. racial drama as an explicitly *raced* human history is being created, maintained, recreated, and reformed. Her narrative repeatedly exposes the continued presence of a hegemonic racial structure. Giddens's statement, "it [history] persistently eludes efforts to bring it under conscious direction," also exposes the power of the duality of structure when thinking about racial/ethnic reclamation: there is nothing inevitable about the current white hegemonic structure.

Evidence of such structural constraints takes many forms. For another reclaimer, the denial of her Nativeness takes the form of actually denying her grandfather, a person she lived with for many years as a child. As so many reclaimers profess, she says that as a young person she knew of her Native ancestry but was not allowed to talk about it. In her case, she was also forbidden to speak of her grandfather. Due to this prohibition, she says, "I thought he was a criminal, I grew up thinking he was a bad guy. . . . I was kinda afraid of him. . . . I just thought there was something wrong with him and that's why we weren't supposed to talk about him." She explains, "Even though I lived with him, I wasn't allowed to talk about him. I was supposed to pretend like I didn't know him when I was out in public. . . . I wasn't supposed to talk about him when I was at school." Much later in her life, while in a college American history class as a non-traditional, adult student, she discovers "it was against the law in Missouri to be Native in the state of Missouri until 1935 . . . and it blew me away when I discovered that I had been afraid of and did not build a relationship with my grandfather . . . because he was full-blood Cherokee."

Another reclaimer tells a similar story of how the legal system works against Natives and therefore is a major obstacle to embracing one's Native heritage. She explains,

> I have an uncle in South Missouri that had property and land and his neighbors plotted against him, I guess. It was a law in Missouri that if you were Indian you couldn't testify in court against a white person, so a white person, as it turns out . . . his neighbor takes a mule on my Uncle's property and accused him of stealing a mule. So it went to court and my uncle couldn't testify and lost all of his property . . . over a mule. And his kids were put in boarding school . . . they had to go to the Carlisle Boarding School because Uncle George lost everything in court because he was Indian. . . . I think that maybe that's why my family was so adamant about not letting anybody know because they'd seen what had happened to Uncle George and they didn't want the rest of us being shipped off.

In this quote we see the theme of individual Native land loss through questionable means at the hands of whites. The individuals I speak to are often speculating, piecing together their history from stories told, aspects left untold, and documentation (such as land titles). To me, it is of less significance whether they can prove such claims. We know there is a long history of land loss by Natives to whites, as Wahrhaftig and Thomas (1972) point out, "Incredible land swindles were commonplace. At the turn of the century, every square inch of eastern Oklahoma was allotted to Cherokees; by the 1930s, little acreage remained in Indian possession" (p. 82). I think it is essential to recognize that for many reclaimers, the recognition and acknowledgment of such discrimination is a potentially mobilizing force. No longer are stories of white exploitation of Natives, specifically in relation to land loss, simply abstract stories of our nation's past. Instead, with such stories, reclaimers are linking specific examples of their ancestor's exploitation to the larger cultural stories surrounding the "founding" of this nation. This may provide them impetus to make redistributive claims on the federal government, again, similarly to the demands for reparations Japanese Americans made over their internment during World War II.

It is not surprising that in the face of such overt discrimination that many people deny their Native ancestry. Another reclaimer expresses her understanding of such denial in this way:

> Because of the 1910 census, there was so much discrimination going on that a lot of Natives checked white if they could pass for white. . . . You know, they disowned their heritage. But, you know, at the time, with so much discrimination if they could pass for white, and that would save them from persecution, you know, that was a choice they made. Um . . . and I wasn't in those circumstances

so I don't know. . . . You know, I don't really blame them. Who's to say I wouldn't have done the same thing?

She is cognizant of the fact that this era of denial is when *her* family lost their cultural connection, lost a lot of their Cherokee heritage, but she does not blame the individuals, her ancestors and others like them, for denying their heritage. She instead looks to cultural constraints, such as the discrimination against Natives and the fact that the legal system exacerbates the problem rather than protecting individuals of Native heritage. This is an especially blatant violation of the civil rights of Natives because the U.S. legal system has long been accused of protecting property with more vehemence than it protects people, yet clearly, not all people's property has been defined as warranting protection. Without using Mills's language, this individual uses her sociological imagination to interpret her ancestor's rejection of their heritage, and later to her ability to embrace hers. She adds,

> It is a personal choice, I guess, on whether or not you claim your heritage. I kind of wonder anymore today what makes people not claim it. Because a lot of the Native American culture is about community and belonging. But, I mean, I guess there is still some racism and discrimination that just puts people to that edge where they identify as white; they don't want to deal with it, I guess.

Her final point here is that while there may be a current openness in the mainstream culture to Nativeness, there are still cultural constraints to reclaiming a Native identity.

Chapter Two

Challenging White Hegemony: Reclaimers and the Culture Wars

Reclaiming a denigrated racial heritage is a challenging process on many levels, from struggles surrounding identity formation to the lack of access to one's heritage due to a history of genocide and forced assimilation into the dominant culture. In addition to those challenges, the reclaimers I speak to all engage in struggles of cultural representation in some way, constantly challenging the dominant culture in terms of Native representation, from Native invisibility to misinformation and stereotypical portrayals. In this way, I see them as recognizing that "representation is guided by power. . . . [C]hanges in representation must be described as changes in the relative power of groups with competing visions of the past and the present" (Rhea 1997, p. 18). Indigenous peoples no longer sit passively by as dominant groups control their representation. This represents more than the perception of potential for change on the part of indigenous peoples but, I argue, an actual shift in power relations.

One of the primary ways reclaimers challenge the dominant group's cultural representation of Native peoples is through their challenge to Anglocentric American history lessons and educational systems. They challenge historical metanarratives, what Lookingbill describes as "continuously recycle[d] localized stories [presented] as . . . grand and unified" (2001, p. 8) that have previously gone unquestioned. Dean describes this as a problematizing practice,

an analysis of the trajectory of the historical forms of truth and knowledge without origin or end. This form of practice has the effect of the disturbance of narratives of both progress and reconciliation, finding questions where others had located answers. . . . [S]uch a discourse remains critical as it is unwilling to accept the taken-for-granted components of our reality and the "official" accounts of how they came to be the way they are. (1994, p. 4)

According to Seidman, poststructuralists such as Derrida begin to emphasize the "politics of language and knowledge" because "meanings have social
and political significance" (1998, p. 222). He argues that for Derrida

> whenever a linguistic and social order is said to be fixed or meanings are as-
> sumed to be unambiguous and stable, this should be understood less as a dis-
> closure of truth than as an act of power, the capacity of a social group to im-
> pose its will on others by freezing linguistic and cultural meanings. (1998, p.
> 222)

While reclaimers may not use the language of poststructuralists, I argue
that in many ways they engage in the deconstruction of linguistic and cultural
meanings surrounding Native peoples and Nativeness that have previously
gone unquestioned. By doing this, they challenge dominant, white conceptions of Nativeness, notions that previously went unchallenged. In this chapter, I look at the various arenas in which reclaimers engage in such challenges. "Deconstruction aims to disrupt and displace the hierarchy, to render
it less authoritative in the linguistic organization of subjectivity and society.
Subverting hierarchical oppositions allows marginal or excluded signifiers
and forms of subjective and social life to gain a public voice and presence"
(Seidman 1998, p. 224). Reclaimers subvert the racial hierarchy and its designation of indigenous peoples to the lowest rungs of that hierarchy, through
their challenges in educational institutions and popular culture. In this way,
they engage in a poststructuralist enterprise similarly found in Lyotard's
work, as Seidman describes, "social conflicts in postmodern society are contested and local. . . . Educational institutions, hospitals, psychiatric clinics,
prisons, and the mass media are major sites of conflict. . . . [There exists] a
kind of generalized revolt against centralizing authorities by marginalized
and excluded groups" (Seidman 1998, p. 228).

By challenging the historical meta narratives that are presented as the historical truth, reclaimers engage in an attack on the "notion of a unified science and have made claims for a plurality of theories expressing different perspectives on the world. . . . [T]he location and special needs of such groups
make them experience reality differently and that this perception is ignored in
mainstream social science. . . . [I]n a complex world, many truths are possible" (Joseph 1998, p.100). The deconstruction of historical meta narratives is
welcomed by many in academia as many scientists now recognize that "the
wisdom embodied in indigenous systems should be preserved for the world.
. . . The claims of any particular group, society or civilisation to represent the
progressive forces of history were also questioned" (Joseph 1998, p. 91). Yet,
while some academics work to preserve indigenous knowledge and embrace
the idea of multiple "truths," the deconstruction of scientific and historical

metanarratives is still perceived by many as a threat to the current social order. One woman reclaiming her indigenous heritage subtly acknowledges this threat while describing the necessity of reclaiming indigenous knowledges in this way: "It's important to have multiple voices come in . . . creating the music that we learn from . . . rather than one voice, um, that has been the dominant voice for a long time. And—we still need that voice. That voice should exist but we need to have the other voices coming in, too, entering into a chorus instead of a solo." I ask her why she thinks the "chorus" is so important, and she elaborates,

> Because—because, well, we all lose. . . . I mean, there's a reason that people were spread out across this planet. And there's a reason for us to come in with our different experiences and cultures and ways so that we learn from each other so that hopefully one day we can be more harmonious together. Um, but, um, for now, I'm just . . . I'm trying to be . . . maybe . . . take a conductor role. So, taking away the solo. [Laughing]

This chapter emphasizes how, despite the presence of diversity, multicultural education, the development of the "new" social history, poststructuralism, and all the various ways scientific and historical metanarratives are being challenged, the story of the elimination/assimilation of Native peoples still perseveres and is being perpetuated throughout educational institutions. Additionally, I emphasize that this metanarrative is racialized. At its core, it is a story about the dominance of one racial group and the subordination of others. Therefore a challenge to this metanarrative is a challenge to white racial hegemony.

Reclaimers engage in various actions that challenge the racial historical metanarratives. "For Foucault, power is all-pervasive in society, embodied in institutions and practices—dominating, co-opting, negative. Knowledge, then, cannot be outside power. Rather, it should be understood as an effect of power. . . . [P]ower is discursively constructed and . . . a primary level of politics is about contestation of meanings" (Joseph 1998, p. 13). By challenging educational institutions and institutional practices, reclaimers are contesting knowledge claims, destabilizing the power relations on which the racial hierarchy has been built and is perpetuated. "What makes power hold good, what makes it accepted is . . . that it traverses and produces things, it induces pleasure, forms knowledge, produces discourse. It needs to be considered as a productive network which runs through the whole social body" (Foucault 1980, p. 119).

The academic practice of challenging historical metanarratives is partially enacted in the form of multiculturalism and diversity education. Both are seen as necessary trends within educational institutions because of significant demographic changes resulting in the increasing presence of racial and ethnic minority students in schools. Banks (1992) defines multiculturalism as an approach that recognizes and values cultural differences and attempts to include all racial, ethnic, and cultural groups in classroom examples and content and to teach history, literature, and other subjects from the perspectives of multiple groups rather than just the dominant group. The emergence of multicultural education in schools is a result of goals set forth

> by African Americans and other racial and ethnic groups in the early 1960s. During that time, advocates of multicultural education challenged educational institutions to reform their school curricula. . . . [T]heir challenges to the educational system were also seen as challenges to the existing ownership of knowledge and to the larger issues of the distribution of power and wealth in our society. (McIntyre 1997, p. 653)

The objective of multiculturalism is to emphasize cultural pluralism rather than cultural assimilation (Farley 2005, p. 398). Multiculturalism is not without its critics, however (e.g., Bloom 1987; D'Souza 1991; Bernstein 1994; Schlesinger 1991). Many argue that multiculturalism goes too far when it questions our common national history, leading to societal divisions rather than what they view as a necessary cohesiveness.

I would add a very different criticism to multiculturalism and diversity education operating in educational institutions today. One could take a perspective similar to Escobar's (1995) analysis of the history of development through an analysis of the transformations of discursive regimes. He argues that incorporating peasants, women, and the environment into the development discourse, instead of creating conditions for new discursive regimes to emerge, is really an apparatus of social control (1995, pp. 154–55). "To bring people into discourse—as in the case of development—is similarly to consign them to fields of vision. It is also about exercising 'the god trick of seeing everything from nowhere'" (Escobar 1995, p. 156). In other words, while it may appear progressive to suddenly incorporate the previously invisible into the discourse, it actually is simply another way to control them, because one is able to control *how they are represented.* Therefore, as long as dominant groups control educational institutions, simply the presence of multiculturalism is not enough. Frankenberg makes a somewhat similar argument:

> In practice it has proven to be extremely difficult to establish multiculturalist or pluralist approaches to curricula or media in the context of continued structural and institutional white leadership. Proposals for the development of pluralist or

multiculturalist curricula are often "watered down" in their pathways through institutional bureaucracies. (1993, p. 15)

One of the most significant ways multicultural education is watered down is through an avoidance of discourse surrounding whiteness and white privilege in schools of education (Fitzgerald and Jones 2001). According to McIntyre:

Though educational literature is inundated with new and improved suggestions for training teachers about multicultural education, what the literature lacks is innovative research into the relationship between white racial attitudes, beliefs, and how white teachers make meaning of whiteness and its relationship to multicultural education. (1997, p. 18)

The fact that so many of the battles Native reclaimers are fighting occur within educational institutions or over school curricula leads one to question the emancipatory potential of multiculturalism in its current form. One reclaimer, a woman who had just recently earned a master's degree, supports this point with the following comment: "I found it a hostile environment; graduate school was very difficult. . . . I felt like there's a lot of talk about cultural diversity and embracing diversity but it's all talk. When it comes down to the reality, they are not willing to bend the program to meet the cultural needs of anything but short, fat, white boys. You know?"

Similarly, Foucault "investigated the *social effects* of these [subjugated] knowledges. He asserted that discourses that aim to reveal the truth of the abnormal personality or human sexuality or the criminal help to create and control the very objects they claim to know. Scientific knowledge functions as a major social power" (Seidman 1998, p. 236). In this way, academic attention to indigenous peoples, diversity, and multicultural education can assure how such subjects are broached. For instance, one can recognize the plurality of cultures emphasized in multicultural curricula, yet fail to find a critical interrogation of the role of the dominant group in subjugating indigenous knowledges in the first place. It is also important to acknowledge the contentiousness of multiculturalism in academia. While some have leveled scathing criticisms upon academia for presumably embracing multiculturalism at the expense of the classics, many institutions still cannot come to an agreement on what should count as a multicultural requirement or if undergraduates should even have a multicultural requirement.

Author Joseph Rhea emphasizes the role minority group members have played in their own emancipation from oppressing cultural images. He argues that we should think of the work minority group members engage in, where they demand their inclusion in the dominant culture, collectively as a race pride movement. These "assertions of minority identity since the mid-1960s" happen among Native Americans, Asian Americans, Latinos, as well as African Americans (1997, p. 4). His argument is that minority activists since the 1960s have focused on the cultural sphere rather than the political sphere, which is the primary objective of the civil rights movement. Part of their work emphasizes demanding "public recognition of . . . injustices" the groups have faced (Rhea 1997, p. 1) and recognizing that they have had to fight for such recognition rather than viewing increasing diversity and minority cultural representation as all part of a growing multiculturalism that is being led by dominant group members. His work demonstrates "that recognition of the role of minorities in American history has increased not because of a general drift toward cultural pluralism, as is often believed, but because of concrete actions [by minority group members] which can be documented" (1997, p. 7).

My initial interest in political activism is, I discover later, rather narrowly defined. I ask all my interviewees if they consider themselves to be politically active, if they work politically on behalf of Native issues, or if their newly reclaimed Nativeness in any way influences their political views and actions. These questions tend to imply traditional notions of political activism such as voting, running for office, or working in some way to influence the government's agenda. If I had remained with such traditional notions of politics and activism, I would have walked away from this research with the assumption that there is not much of a connection between racial/ethnic reclamation and political activism. However, it begins to occur to me that I am defining political activism too narrowly and, thus, possibly asking the wrong questions.

Two reclaimers from my sample do think of themselves as politically active in this traditional sense. However, most do not. What I came to conclude is that cultural activism can be thought of as political. It is important to operate from a

> broad-based notion of "doing politics" that included any struggle to gain control over definitions of self and community, to augment personal and communal empowerment, to create alternative institutions and organizational processes, and to increase the power and resources of the community workers' defined community. (Naples 1998, p. 180)

In this spirit, I define cultural activism as reclaimers' efforts to live their Native culture, particularly in the form of participation in traditional ceremonies, learning Native languages, dancing at pow-wows, and such. This can be thought of as activism because it denotes a direct challenge to white cultural hegemony. By referring to these activities as activism, I am implying that there is something subversive about participating in and working to keep alive subordinate cultures, cultures whites have actively attempted to destroy.

In casual discussions at pow-wows, I find that many political activists are intolerant of such cultural activists. For instance, I spoke to an AIM (American Indian Movement) activist working an information booth at a local pow-wow who clearly views his contributions to Native culture as more significant than that of cultural activists. He comments that some people "just want to dance around. But they know this [the political activism] has got to be done. And it can get ugly." Another reclaimer makes a similar comment, snickering at those who "just dance around." He works as an editor of a tribal newspaper, and he explicitly uses this forum to advance Indian rights, specifically by working to get Indians behind mainstream political candidates that work for Indian interests. From his perspective, cultural activism is not as significant as traditional political activism. Cornell (1988) postulates that it is cultural activism that leads to political activism, and intertribal gatherings such as pow-wows help create the supratribal consciousness that he believes generates renewed insurgency among Native peoples. I speculate that the process is self-perpetuating: cultural activism results in renewed political activism, which in turn creates an environment where cultural activism can flourish, and the cycle repeats. The fact that one can find AIM booths set up at pow-wows exemplifies the interconnectedness of the two, that cultural activism and political activism cannot be neatly and easily separated.

Throughout interviews with reclaimers, I find ample evidence of their fight for cultural inclusion of Native perspective[s] in educational institutions and in popular culture. Rhea argues that "the race pride movement generally had to address institutionalized cultural exclusion one place at a time" (1997, p. 5). I think the battles these reclaimers choose to fight, many of which non-reclaiming Natives are also fighting, contribute to the race pride movement that Rhea speaks of. In numerous ways, reclaimers are challenging the racial hierarchy by demanding corrective, inclusive history. For many reclaimers, these battles are waged within their children's schools as they contest subject matter, Native representation, and holiday festivities, among other things. Additionally, many reclaimers from my sample are in higher education, as students or faculty, and they actively challenge their colleges and universities on cultural grounds—issues such as repatriation, underrepresentation of Native students, and cultural events such as pow-wows are insisted upon. Such challenges within educational institutions are significant because, as Foucault emphasizes, knowledge cannot be outside power. In addition to educational challenges, reclaimers provide more generalized cultural challenges. For instance, American mainstream values of materialism, consumerism, and individualism are challenged through native reclaimers' embrace of environmentalist ethos, explicit anti-consumeristic attitudes, and an embrace of collectivist thinking over individualistic thinking. And finally, the challenge over the misrepresentation of Natives in the form of team mascots is a battle numerous reclaimers from my sample are engaged in.

These challenges are significant because they are evidence of a challenge to white cultural hegemony. According to Foucault, "Truth isn't outside power. . . . Each society has its regime of truth, its 'general politics' of truth: that is, the types of discourse which it accepts and makes function as true" (1980, p. 131). Reclaimers challenge the general politics of truth regarding race in this country by reclaiming a denigrated racial heritage and by redefining Nativeness on their terms rather than allowing the dominant group to define it. While many non-reclaiming Native Americans actively challenge the dominant white culture and have struggled to keep Native cultures alive through centuries of attempted cultural genocide, I think it is significant that reclaimers, individuals who have race privilege, who through assimilation have access to the privileges accorded members of the dominant racial/ethnic group, explicitly reject these and instead struggle for cultural representation for themselves as *indigenous peoples*. While such challenges contest the hegemony of the dominant culture overall, again, my argument is that the dominant culture is racialized. Therefore, their actions are a direct challenge to *white* cultural hegemony, and thus, their actions are inherently political.

Rhea states, "For significant change to take place in the status of Indians, general cultural attitudes about Indians would have to change. Since the 1960s, they have fought, like other minorities, to change the national recollection of their history and thereby alter the national attitude toward living Indians" (1997, p. 9). While Rhea looks at Wounded Knee, a reinterpretation of Custer at the Custer Battlefield, and the Little Bighorn site, the reclaimers I speak to struggle with local issues such as misinformation relayed to them in educational institutions, whether in colleges they attend or have attended or in their children's schools.

Educational institutions have long been critiqued for their perpetuation of race/class/gender privilege. Marx speaks of the role of the dominant class in controlling institutions so that the interests of the dominant group are presented and accepted as operating in the best interests of all. Social reproduction theorists working within a Marxist framework, for instance, focus on how schools reproduce the social relations of capitalism (Bourdieu and Passeron 1990; Bowles and Gintis 1976). Subordinate groups are sometimes portrayed as resisting the imposition of dominant group ideology, yet through such resistance, they are perceived as maintaining the class hierarchy (Ogbu 1974; Willis 1977).

All of the preceding schools of thought focus on the reproduction of the class structure and, with the exception of Ogbu, tend to downplay the reproduction of the racial hierarchy. Researchers Feagin, Vera, and Imani (1996) address this theoretical void with their analysis of the struggle black students face in predominantly white colleges and universities. One of their primary arguments is that such colleges and universities, while attempting to portray themselves as race neutral and as, in fact, actively encouraging racial/ethnic diversity within their student body, are actually racialized spaces, which they define as "specific areas and territories [designated] as white or as black, with the consequent feelings of belonging and control" (1996, p. 50). In other work, I focus on the reproduction of the white racial hierarchy in a teacher education program, through its failure to deconstruct the notion of whiteness, and an avoidance of discourse surrounding whiteness and white privilege, despite a commitment to multiculturalism and diversity education (Fitzgerald and Jones 2001). The very existence of and objectives behind the formation of Bureau of Indian Affairs (BIA) schools are evidence of the perpetuation of white racial hegemony in education:

> Education had long been considered the Indians' pathway to civilization. . . . Boarding schools were the preferred institutional setting because they removed the Indian child from the daily reinforcement of tribal custom and language . . . like all schools for Indians, but more intensely than most, they fostered the spread of English. . . . [M]ost of these schools . . . worked hard to discourage tribal ties and indigenous cultural activities. (Cornell 1988, pp. 114–15)

Reclaimers challenge white racial hegemony through their challenges in educational institutions, whether dissenting against curricula; Native representation or Native invisibility; materialistic, individualistic, and consumption-oriented society; or their cultural representation in the form of team mascots. These actions are inherently political in that they are efforts to deconstruct the racial hierarchy and can be thought of as part of the race pride movement that Rhea (1997) speaks of.

CORRECTIVE HISTORY LESSONS

Forcing Native recognition and accurate representation in educational materials and educational institutions is one way reclaimers challenge the white racial hegemonic structure. A standard complaint I hear out of many reclaimers is how Natives are invisible or even misrepresented in history books and how they are actively challenging that. To hear such a complaint during this era, after over a decade of emphasis on multiculturalism and diversity in schools, is intriguing. One woman expresses her feelings this way: "A lot of times . . . you know, American history books in American society tend to show the European view of things. You know, my contemporary U.S. history book in high school had a whole paragraph to cover the American Indian Movement and the stand-off at Wounded Knee. . . . I'm like, a paragraph doesn't quite cut it." She explains that one of her goals is to open "people's eyes to what has gone on and what is going on. . . . [Y]ou have all this poverty on the reservations. . . . I'll talk about that every chance I get with people 'cause a lot of people just don't understand." As a college student, she challenges her history professors to recognize the Native side of things. She says that she is operating from what she refers to as a biased perspective, but justifies this by saying, "I tend to be a little biased toward the Native perspective of things . . . but . . . it's been a perspective that has been silenced so long that I think that, you know, it needs to be heard. Um, and you know, it deserves some attention."

This, however, is not as simple as it sounds. Who decides what a Native perspective is? There are over five hundred Native tribes indigenous to this continent, and "cultural or historical homogeneity did not exist" (Bonvillain 2001, p. 1). There is not even agreement on what constitutes indigenous cultural knowledge, and the contest surrounding such definitions often simply represents current power relations. As Cornell and Hartmann argue (1998),

> [V]irtually every people in the world's history has engaged in some sort of contact and interaction with other peoples. . . . They have traded not only goods but also words, ideas and practices. They have adopted what they found useful and ignored the rest. At what point in that long process of exchange and adaptation have the cultures and identities involved been "authentic," and at what point did they lose their "authenticity?" (p. 94)

Several reclaimers from my sample explicitly connect being a parent to their reclaiming process. Many women find themselves addressing Anglo-biased curriculum in their children's schools, for instance. These women's activities surrounding their Native reclamation resemble what sociologist Nancy Naples refers to as activist mothering. Naples defines activist mothering as "political activism as a central component of mothering and community caretaking of those who are not part of one's defined household or family" (1998, p. 11). Similar to this work, most of the reclaimers who engage in reclamation at least partially on behalf of their children do not see themselves as activists, and even Naples was slow to recognize what they did as activism. She explains, "As I reexamined the activists' personal narratives, I recognized how a broadened definition of mothering was woven in and through their paid and unpaid community work which in turn was infused with political activism" (1998, p. 113).

One woman explains that she is pursuing her Cherokee heritage because "what's important for me right now is that the future generations, my children . . . [are] taught about their culture and brought up with it, you know, [so that] it will still live." Another woman describes becoming interested in her Native heritage when her oldest daughter was born:

> When she was born, it become more of a . . . I was more curious and interested in investigating and looking around . . . 'cause I wanted to be able to pass on something to her that I hadn't truly identified with. . . . I want to reclaim what was lost before they [whites] came in and pushed everybody around, you know? . . . [A]nd that's part of what I am teaching my kids, too.

As one mother of two grade-school-aged children explains, "I teach at the school every chance I get," adding,

> The school system has invited me every Thanksgiving to go talk. . . . I do a grade-school program. . . . I talk to them about what is was like when people came here and how they dressed and how they ate and how they nearly starved to death. I bring 'em wool and show them what it feels like when it's wet and it won't dry and you know, the diseases hold . . . the difference between wearing leather and how resilient that is, how dry it keeps you. And the food, what food spoils and rots and gets worms in it. The difference in how we [Native peoples] did things and how, basically, Thanksgiving was Abigail Adams's invention. It didn't exist. . . . [T]here were no Thanksgiving feasts. They base it on a time when pilgrims were here and they were starving to death and the Indians saved them.

In this quote, this mother is doing a number of things. First, she is explicitly challenging the portrait of history that most students are still being taught, which is that whites brought "civilization" to the Natives and were more advanced than them. Second, she is challenging part of our sense of nationhood by openly acknowledging that a national holiday such as Thanksgiving is actually a social construction, an invented tradition. Eric Hobsbawm speaks of the "invention of tradition" as part of the establishment of a sense of nationhood, "'a set of practices, normally governed by overtly or tacitly accepted rules, and of a ritual or symbolic nature, which seek to inculcate certain values and norms with the past'" (Callinicos 1988, p. 171). The objective, according to Hobsbawm, is to establish obedience and loyalty, and to get individuals to see themselves as sharing the same identity (Callinicos 1988, p. 171). What Hobsbawm is emphasizing is the social construction of national identities that is partially achieved through the invention of traditions like national holidays. Finally, this reclaimer is presenting a highly critical portrait of white America through this sort of reconstructed history.

Later in the interview she adds,

> Thanksgiving is actually a facsimile of the Green Corn Festival. . . . We celebrate . . . the bounty, you know, we have a big garden and we celebrate that and it's a

lot more simple. I don't do Thanksgiving. It's a fantasy of Abigail Adams, you know. She just made that story up. There was no sit-down dinner . . . that was created. It's just a fantasy image to create a holiday.

She also explains that instead of taking on only the school to clear up such inconsistencies, she offers her children what she refers to as

corrective history lessons . . . when they come home with images, um, my daughter brought home a word puzzle with the word *squaw* in it . . . and I took it to school and I said, "Are you aware that the English facsimile for that word is *cunt*? You really need to have these things looked at before you send them home." . . . It's a derogatory word, it's not a complimentary term.

She says that the teacher expressed appreciation and was not aware of the offensive meaning of the word. Another woman expresses similar sentiments in regard to the Euro-American education her daughter is receiving in their local public school system: "Oh, we have lots of fun with Thanksgiving. . . . My daughter got in trouble because I told her a joke about, um, Thanksgiving is celebrating the going-away party we held for the pilgrims, but they never left [laughs]. Her teacher didn't think that was very funny!"

While the former reclaimer encounters a teacher whom she perceives to be open to such challenges to white hegemony, the latter perceives the teacher to be less open to such a cultural challenge. I think it is worth taking a moment to interrogate the range of responses by these teachers. How well are teachers prepared to address issues of multiculturalism and diversity education? In other work (Fitzgerald and Jones 2001) I analyze how white privilege and the racial hierarchy are perpetuated in a teacher education program. I find evidence of this in four distinct sites: in pre-service teachers' discourse, in curriculum design, in texts, and in the pre-service teachers' field placements. In all, there is a negation of whiteness as a racial identity, a denial of privilege among white pre-service teachers, and in some there are explicitly racist comments. It is important to recognize the influence teachers have over students and their development of self, as well as how well teachers are educated to deal with multiculturalism and diversity education.

One male reclaimer's story exemplifies the significance of teachers. This young man's reclaiming story is particularly enlightening because he reveals a process of forgetting his Native heritage and rediscovering it at his high school graduation. He describes a grade school teacher who profoundly influenced his life. Not normally prone to exaggeration, he describes her as "the best teacher in the world." This woman apparently is a very controversial teacher, and as he describes, she throws out the books and traditional teaching methods and instead teaches through stories, having the early grade-schoolers listen to stories as well as write their own. Due to her alternative teaching methods, she is fired at the end of the school year. She returns many years later, however, to celebrate the high school graduation of her former class. Upon graduating, she hands back to each student a story they had written in her class years before. This reclaimer describes going home, reading the story, and crying. He had written about being Indian, his feelings of being different, aspects of his culture and identity he had long since forgotten. This recognition that something that had meant so much to him, that was such an essential part of him, had successfully been erased through his years of formal education overwhelms him. It is at this point that he decides he needs to reclaim the parts of himself that have been destroyed.

It is impossible to gauge what interpretations school children decipher from such contestations of meaning, but the important point for the women of my sample is that the children at least get to hear contrasting opinions. There is then potential that the children will question the historical metanarratives they will presumably continue to be exposed to throughout their lives in educational institutions. It also has the potential to make teachers question their own locatedness and the supposedly objective knowledge they are passing on to their students. The reclaimer who relates the earlier story about the word puzzle with the offensive word in it is somewhat understanding of the ignorance of her children's teachers when it comes to Native issues:

> There's so much ignorance. The Columbus Day thing, you know, they're making him out to be a hero . . . and he makes Adolf Hitler look like a Boy Scout. . . . [H]e was a butcher. He annihilated an entire tribe . . . thousands and thousands and thousands of people he butchered for gold he never found. You know, he was a monster. And we celebrate him as some sort of hero. And they say he "discovered" America. Excuse me, Turtle Island [the term Native peoples had for the United States] was here 10,000 years before that idiot came here, you know? A civilization with cities and commerce.

Another interviewee lodges a similar complaint against such standard American history lessons. She does not have children, so she does not go into schools to challenge Native representation, but she describes one way she challenges Native representation in history—through talking to people every chance she gets:

> I'm real big with getting people to see the other side of things. The whole Columbus thing is a real peeve of mine. Why do we have this whole day, you know, celebrating this idiot that landed on the wrong continent and called it the wrong thing . . . and then started the genocide of, like, so many people. That's my other thing. The whole genocide issue. The fact that, you know, from Columbus's settlement to the beginning of this country on through, it's classified as genocide.

With the definition of genocide being the deliberate, you know, the attempted deliberate extermination of [an] entire race, class, you know, ethnicity, whatever. That's what the U.S. government did! They said, we're going to kill the Indians, or assimilate them, and everything. . . . [T]he Bureau of Indian Affairs started out under the War Department!

Her concluding point here is worth noting. I am not sure if she is conflating killing the Indians with assimilating the Indians, or if she is pointing out two separate practices the United States government engaged in in relation to Native peoples. My hunch is, it is the former. However, I think it is at least intriguing to think about the conflation of "killing" and "assimilation" since colonization has had such devastating affects on Native peoples.

One mother I interview describes another school event that, through her insistence and willingness to participate, eventually includes a Native perspective as well. Her children's school has what they call a Prairie Days program,

. . . and the kids dress up in little prairie dresses and go to school and re-enact what is was like to be—they don't have any lights on in the school and they have different programs about different things and ways they did things and little craft projects and stuff. And I said, "You know, Indians were kind of a part of Prairie Days, too." And so I got to do . . . one of those.

This aspect of reclaiming appears to be gendered, which is why I find it similar to Naples's activist mothers. Of the reclaimers I spoke to, both males and females challenge educational institutions in terms of Native representation, yet they do so differently. The men, for instance, do not describe their activities as enacted in the name of their children. One young male interviewee, in his early twenties, describes how he would go to elementary schools to teach about Indians, which earned him extra money while he was in high school. Another interviewee, also in her early twenties, offers a similar story. She says that she remembers her grandfather coming to her grade school to share their Cherokee culture with the class. She went to a small Catholic school and, according to her own description, was one of the few students of Native heritage in her school (despite the fact that it was in Oklahoma, a region perceived as "Indian country" by whites and Indians). She explains, "I have memories, when I was in grade school, early grade school, of my grandfather coming to classes and, like, he would dance for us . . . or he would tell stories or he would . . . he would talk about the Cherokee culture." Other than this, she did not really grow up with much of a celebration of her Native heritage, and her grandfather at some point stopped visiting her school to teach about their Cherokee culture.

The fact that he went to her grade school to teach something about Cherokee history is also interesting from the standpoint that he is a product of BIA

(Bureau of Indian Affairs) boarding schools. According to this reclaimer, he does not speak of this period of his life since "there are a lot of wounds there." Another female reclaimer speaks similarly about her relatives' experience in boarding schools:

> One [cousin that attended boarding school] that I've talked with about it doesn't want to talk about it, um, he's an older fella and he was beaten for speaking Cherokee and for being homesick. . . . He cried and he got very ill. And, um, finally his dad, my uncle, went and got him, and, um, I think he was there two and a half years. He doesn't like to talk about it.

While she accepts that he does not want to relive the experience by talking about it, she says, "I wish more people knew. . . . I don't know that any good would come of people knowing, but it was a terrible misjustice [sic] that has been done to these poor people that have to deny who they are. . . . To take these children from their families was like the ultimate in desecrating them as people."

Another reclaimer relates a story her father told her when she was little that challenges some very significant American history lessons she was learning at the time. She describes her father as someone who loved to tell "tall tales" in which she says he was "actually weaving—this is very traditional for Lakota people—weaving truth into, uh, what would be considered a fictional story . . . later on you would understand it." She describes a particular story as an example:

> An example of that is that he told me, um, when I was little that one of our relatives killed Abraham Lincoln and it wasn't John Wilkes Booth at all because Abraham Lincoln was a bad man. . . . And so then I went off to school and, you know, here I am, I'm little—I mean, the only Indian kid in my entire school. . . . This is the 1970s. So, I'm in there, I'm like, "Well, my family killed Abraham Lincoln." Everybody's like, "Abraham Lincoln was a good man. You suck." . . . I'm like, "Nooooo. He's a bad man." Of course, people are finally beginning to figure that out. . . . But, actually, it's interesting now 'cause, um, looking back . . . why would my dad even tell me something like that? . . . I think it was only like a few days before he [Lincoln] was shot he hung like thirty some-odd Lakota men, which is the largest hanging in American history.

As an adult reflecting back on this story, this reclaimer, whose father has already passed away and cannot explain his intentions, interprets a larger meaning into her father's "tall tale." As a member of the Lakota tribe, he does not want her to uncritically lavish praise on this former American president. Despite the favorable view white historians have of Lincoln in terms of ending slavery and oppression for blacks, he is clearly no friend to the Indian, and this is the message she is supposed to get from the "tall tale" he told her as a child.

The aforementioned examples are interesting because we do see multiculturalism at work in that many of these individuals are invited to the schools to present the Native point of view. This is not something that would have been considered necessary or maybe even acceptable in elementary schools prior to the 1970s. However, the presence of such instances is not entirely unproblematic. One is the reliance upon Native people to teach Native history and culture, rather than on the non-Native teachers themselves to learn this aspect of history as part of an inclusive understanding of American history. If there are not Native children in the class, will the perspective remain unspoken? Is multiculturalism "for" minority children, to help them feel more comfortable in the classroom, by providing them with a slice of "their" history, or should it also be "for" white children, to help them understand the diversity within American history and culture? The young man identified earlier who goes to elementary schools to teach about Native Americans expresses what he perceives as another dilemma with this: "I used to go dressed up [in regalia], but then I realized that that was kinda perpetuating the stereotype . . . with the little kids, they're like, 'Well, he's an Indian, look at the way he's dressed.'" The stereotype he is referring to is that Native people are no longer part of American society, so we tend not to think of them as wearing jeans and living among non-Natives. We tend to instead think of them as part of history and as dressing in traditional tribal regalia only. As someone educated in the white, mainstream culture, it is possible that this reclaimer initially felt the same way. When he goes to teach grade-school children about Indians, he initially unquestioningly wears his tribal regalia. After reflecting on his own actions, he begins to question what message he is sending to the children.

One woman's story of how the Trail of Tears is presented in her daughter's junior high school American history class is evidence that multiculturalism, as currently operationalized, is not enough. As she explains,

My daughter was studying . . . history—she was in eighth grade last year and they were doing a unit on American history, and they did the Trail of Tears and she did a little report, and I was looking over her homework and the things she had put in the report were wrong. They weren't true. And I said, "Are you going to turn this in?" "Well, Mom, that's what it says in the book." "But . . . it's not true." . . . The thing that the schoolbook said, and I read it because I couldn't believe they were teaching this in our schools, the thing that the schoolbook says, that the Native Americans were rounded up and kept in camps until a better time to travel. They were rounded up in June and July, kept there until October when the weather was turning foul and then they left. October is not a better time to travel than June and July.

Her response to this is to call the teacher saying, "You're teaching this to my children and she thought of this information as fact and it is not. *My* children know that it's not, but there are people in her class who do not know and I think that's wrong." This incident leads her to go to the school and try to teach something about Native Americans. She says that a lot of the children think her regalia is "cool," but the important thing for her is that she made them question the historical metanarratives they are being presented. "I don't know how many of them thought the information in their schoolbook they receive might not be accurate. Um, a couple of the girls said, 'Oh . . . I didn't know that.' And so, maybe they'll do a little more thinking before they swallow everything that they're told."

An even more extreme example is one woman's challenge to the dominant culture through her conflict with the Pledge of Allegiance and her resulting "alternative" to it:

> We have a conflict with the Pledge of Allegiance, and they [the schools] teach them the Pledge of Allegiance. They make the kids pledge allegiance to a piece of fabric from an occupying force and I object. It's not my flag. I am proud of this country, but it's not my flag. . . . We write our own Pledge of Allegiance . . . . I write the Pledge of Allegiance to support the planet I live on, not a piece of fabric.

She admits that such an extreme perspective possibly makes it difficult for her children at school:

> So, you know, my children hear me preach this at home, that's not our flag, and they go to school and refuse to stand for the Pledge of Allegiance, what do you think is going to happen to them? So I say, you stand, you know, show respect for your classmates, but you don't have to say a word. . . . You know how children are—all the family secrets are out. They tell all at school, so when you say these things to them and you teach them, you know, like the Christopher Columbus stuff and the Thanksgiving stuff and I teach them about Sand Creek and Wounded Knee and things that happened in these places and how their ancestors were treated and I have to also couch that in "You can't always talk about this in school, you have to be careful what you say." And I hear myself saying the same things my parents said to me, and I remember the fear that made in me and I hate doing that, you know? You don't want to do that to your children.

She makes an interesting connection here between her experiences as a child when she was told to say she was Italian instead of Indian in order to avoid discrimination and how, despite the fact that she is reclaiming her heritage and providing the culture for her children to grow up in, she feels that today's climate is still hostile to such alternative views.

There seems to be the perception among some, particularly those that decry the presence of multiculturalism and diversity education in schools (e.g., D'Souza 1991; Schlesinger 1991), that today's climate is less hostile to racial/ethnic diversity, yet despite our verbal commitments to diversity and multiculturalism in educational institutions and workplaces, direct challenges to the dominant culture are certainly not always embraced. A comment from one woman shows her recognition of such divergent trends, the presence of multiculturalism in popular culture as well as Native invisibility:

> I've become more aware of, there seems to be a lot more interesting things that I've not seen before . . . I see things on TV or this or that, that wasn't there before . . . multicultural things like, like more TV shows, movies . . . about how our society is becoming more multicultural. My children watch Nickelodeon and Disney and everything like that, I am just amazed at the increase in shows of different cultures. You've got the Latin people now have a show, the Spanish have a show and these are kids shows. . . . Now, there's not an Indian one out there.

Interestingly, this woman describes how her children's school embraces diversity by having a Jewish rabbi come speak to the class and later a parent of a Muslim child came to speak about their culture, yet,

> their year went and there was no one to talk about Christianity at Christmas . . . . I had a teacher say, "I know your faith is very important to you. Could you come and talk to these kids because they have all this coming in but there's kids who don't have anybody to identify with." . . . And these kids were so hungry to identify with something because our society is so multicultural they don't have anything to identify with.

This comment shows how the dominant culture, in this case, the dominant ideologies of Christianity, appear invisible because there is an unspokenness surrounding its normativeness. A grade school would have Muslims and Jewish rabbis visit because there is an assumption that these are religions that most students are unfamiliar with. However, the fact that no one came to visit and talk about Christianity is then viewed as problematic, and ironically, the dominant culture is viewed as neglected.

A lot of the educational challenges that reclaimers engage in occur in higher education. One, a college professor of social sciences, explains, "I have a lot of fun in American history classes! I just start talking about treaties and I see their eyes roll back into their heads and they're thinkin',

'Come on! Let's talk about white folks' history for a while.' My response to that is, 'You've been talking about that your whole life. Let's talk about something else.'" As an Indian instructor on a predominantly white, Midwestern college campus, this man sees himself as a role model for Indian students in higher education. He jokes that "Indian students follow me around all the time." While he presents this as a joke, he does serve as a role model for Native reclaimers. Another interviewee I met with several years after this reclaimer made that comment, explains how her reclaiming process was triggered, citing his influence:

> Well, I was taking—my professor at the time . . . he was, actually my history professor was an Indian and he shared, that, um, I think he was teaching about how he didn't really know until he was an adult that, um, why being Native was a problem, that he didn't really understand until he was an adult that being Native was something to be proud of. He shared his own history and his own experience of discovering that it was okay to be Native and nobody was going to lock you up or do something like that. That set the wheels in motion for me. So I started asking. I told him that my grandfather was a full-blooded Indian and, um, we were told not to talk about him. He said that was very common and that there were hundreds of stories that he's heard of—of people that don't realize until their ancestors are gone . . .

Again, the presence of poststructuralism, multiculturalism, and the new social histories in academia leads one to suspect that institutions of higher education are more tolerant than elementary schools, primarily since they are accused of operating from a liberal bias whereas there is considerable state influence on elementary school curriculums. Yet, reclaimers relate numerous challenges in these arenas as well. One woman comments on Native invisibility in subject matter of her college classes:

> The omission of, uh, information about Native people in this country makes me very aware of my heritage and who I am. . . . I mean, like, you know, when—when I go to classes and they're talking about race/ethnicity, Native people aren't in there! That makes me very aware of—of wanting to get that information out there.

Two other interviewees are pursuing graduate studies in order to teach college, one in counseling psychology and the other in Indian studies. Both perceive their recently reclaimed Nativeness as a significant influence on their choice of degree programs and career paths. The woman pursuing her Ph.D. in counseling psychology explains her future research agenda this way:

> One of my areas that I—that I plan to pursue in psychology is looking at normative behaviors for Native people. . . . [T]he whole thing in psychology . . . almost all of the information that's available about Native people is on pathology . . . the drug use . . . the alcoholism . . . suicide . . . that's all we see. And so that kind of paints a very dark picture of, um, what is going on in Native communities today. . . . It's kind of perpetuating that kind of—the colonial myth that Native people are dying out. And what I want to do is, I want to come in and kind of infuse the information that's out there, uh, with the idea that Native people are surviving . . . rather than being exterminated.

She also adds that there are many arenas in which Native peoples must wage battles and all are important, but she perceives her role as involving

> . . . education and, and talking with people. Um, and um, hopefully doing some research and publishing. And teaching. And talking. . . . I wanna teach from a Native perspective . . . and I also wanna do the, uh, make sure that there—make sure that when we're teaching multicultural issues, uh, in psychology that we include Native people.

Another college student reclaimer complains that white people in her classes often expect her to speak for all Indians. "Oh, yeah, in classes in graduate school I was always asked, 'How would Native Americans feel about that?' I can only speak for me. You know? How would white people feel about abortion? Answer that for me—you're a white woman, don't you know? I mean, what a stupid question. I can't answer for all Native Americans. I can't even answer for all Cherokee." This is a complaint I hear several times during campus Native American student organization meetings. Students of Native descent are asked to provide dominant group members with a "Cliffs Notes" version of the Native experience, and this is something they resent. Lorde (2001) makes this argument along gender lines, although it is certainly applicable to all dominant and subordinate group relations. She argues that this is an intentional ploy on the part of dominant group members: "Women of today are being called upon to stretch across the gap of male ignorance and to educate men as to our existence and our needs. This is an old and primary tool of all oppressors to keep the oppressed occupied with the masters concerns" (2001, p. 24). As members of the dominant group, whites, have the privilege of our group's history being presented to us in classes. Members of subordinate groups must work to find information on their people and history, in addition to being forced to learn white history as part of their educational curriculum.

As this chapter argues, reclaimers attempt to alter mainstream educational institutions in order to present the Native perspective from a Native point of view. Yet, one can also question the effectiveness of attempting to alter educational institutions through such alternative histories. To what extent will this inspire cultural change? For the reclaimers I speak to, that seems to be the agenda in this arena, to alter curricula and the way Native peoples are presented in order to force cultural change; to make the culture more open to Native perspectives, to have Native perspectives validated in this society. However, such cultural change may not necessarily follow from an infusion of Native peoples and ideas, whether reclaimers or traditional non-reclaiming Indians, into educational institutions. As Lorde points out, *"The master's tools will never dismantle the master's house.* They may allow us to temporarily beat him at his own game, but they will never enable us to bring about genuine change" (2001, p. 23, italics in the original). If educational institutions are under the control of the dominant group, should Native peoples want to be let into these institutions, as "alternative" subject matter to the dominant discourse, or would the creation of alternative institutions be more fruitful?

Additionally, reclaimers have spent their entire lives in these white-dominated educational institutions. What effect does this have, if any, on their perceptions of these institutions? Do reclaimers perceive them as salvageable? To what extent is reclaimer concern with educational institutions a result of the very power of the dominant group Foucault speaks of? "What makes power hold good, what makes it accepted is . . . that it traverses and produces things, it induces pleasure, forms knowledge, produces discourse. It needs to be considered as a productive network which runs through the whole social body" (Foucault 1980, p. 119). We see here evidence that reclaimers accept, to a certain extent at least, educational institutions as sites of legitimate knowledge production. Does this work in the interests of Native peoples or in the interests of the dominant group?

Best (1995) states that for Foucault, "a key goal of genealogy is to show how science is employed for purposes of social control. This analysis is directed against positivist and Marxist theories that see knowledge as neutral, objective, or unproblematically emancipatory" (p. 211). The reclaimers I speak to seem to be taking a modernist, critical perspective of educational institutions, recognizing how they may operate as tools of the dominant group but that there is also emancipatory potential within them. For poststructuralists like Foucault, as institutions where science is produced (higher education) and institutions where scientific knowledge is employed (elementary and secondary institutions), these institutions still need to be recognized as apparatuses of social control rather than as sites with emancipatory potential.

REPATRIATION BATTLES

Another type of struggle involving Native representation occurs at the university three reclaimers attend. The university has possession of Native remains and this became a point of contestation between the campus Native American student organization and the university. Repatriation battles are being fought by Native peoples throughout the country, specifically since the passage in 1990 of the Native American Graves Protection and Repatriation Act (NAGPRA) "that empowered Indians to reclaim the burial remains of their ancestors and objects found in grave sites. . . . Items presently in museums, galleries, and other institutions must be returned to Native American groups upon application and demonstration of 'rights of possession'" (Bonvillain 2001, p. 27). This is the one significant area of overlap I find between actions my reclaimers are engaged in and Rhea's examples of Native actions that collectively, with other people of color, form what he refers to as the race pride movement. He points out,

> Under NAGPRA, museums will have to take contemporary tribal definitions seriously, precisely because those tribes are now empowered to seize objects from their collections. . . . [T]his new law also carries with it the expectation that Indians will define their heritage. (Rhea 1997, pp. 35–36)

This campus student organization was formed in 1987 and actively began protesting the ancestral remains of 1800 Native Americans being held by the university. Their activism was part of nationwide activism that resulted in the passage of the Native American Graves Protection and Repatriation Act (NAGPRA). This was a major issue for over ten years, as students petitioned the administration and protested such policies and practices. Repatriation is a significant issue among Native peoples because, as one reclaimer with plans to attend law school and pursue federal Indian law explains, "If you talk to a lot of the old spiritual guys, their view is to not become settled until we get our ancestors buried and, you know, then it will come. It's not going to come if they're sitting in a warehouse. . . . [T]hey see repatriation as important." And because the elders see repatriation as so important, this young man feels a lot of pressure to succeed in law school: "A lot of the guys are putting a hell of a lot of pressure on me [to succeed]." He explains that there is a need for more Native lawyers working on the issue. His mentor, a man he refers to as an uncle, works on repatriation cases and pays his own way traveling around the country meeting with different tribes. "So, a lot of those guys are depending on me to get out [of law school]. . . . [T]hat puts a lot of pressure [on me] to make sure that I'm good 'cause I don't want to show up at a repatriation meeting somewhere in this country and see all those guys . . . and, yeah, I'd rather just fall on my face than to look at all those old guys and tell them that [I failed]."

During the period of their repatriation battles, the student organization invited Osage elders to campus to decide if the bones were theirs (since the Osage, while currently in Oklahoma, are indigenous to the region). According to newspaper reports, the Osage elders could not be sure if the remains were theirs or not. This is a significant issue because not all tribes maintain the same burial practices and customs, so it matters to which tribe the remains belong. As Rhea points out, "There are challenges for both the museums and for the Indians in this act. . . . [F]or the Indians the verification will be on what is central to their culture, what is sacred. This is a spiritual verification, and much more demanding of integrity and clarity of vision" (1997, p. 35). The student pursuing federal Indian law in law school explains some of the challenges with repatriation, despite the presence of the NAGPRA. He says, "As far as repatriation goes, because the state government doesn't even know what the federal laws are in repatriation, they screw it up all the time. The university screws it up more than anybody I know. . . . Tribal representatives are supposed to be notified when their remains are encountered and stuff like that, and they never are." Later he adds, "Even though the law says that the government entities need to call people [when a violation of NAGPRA is discovered], you know, a lot of it is found out on our own."

I think there is significance to the repatriation battles in which Native students, many of whom are reclaimers, are engaged in because, first, they are challenging the right of science to take precedence over cultural beliefs and practices. Second, they are challenging the racism behind the actions of scientists. And third, the media coverage repatriation issues generate allows some Native cultural practices and beliefs to infiltrate the dominant, mainstream culture, which is, again, a challenge to white cultural hegemony. Because Native students protested actions by their university and challenged the presumed right of "science" to take precedence over cultural beliefs and practices, they engaged in powerful counter-hegemonic actions. Despite the presence of poststructuralism, where unified notions of science are challenged and the idea of a plurality of "truths" is emphasized, it is clear that traditional notions of science that emerge out of the scientific revolution and inform the modern era are still the dominant ideologies within the university. It is hardly surprising that anthropology departments presume their right to knowledge production takes precedence over the cultural beliefs and practices of Native peoples. The students' repatriation demands, not surprisingly, met with considerable resistance from the administration. The students' actions were perceived as radical. Nagel points out that, "The use of history as a mechanism of community reconstruction might involve the recovery and preservation of historical materials, sites, or knowledge; . . . the repatriation of Indian artifacts and burial remains to tribal museums and burial grounds . . . [is about] redefining the ownership and the meaning of these objects" (1997, p. 11). In her view then, the actions of the students were pretty controversial, especially at a university. The racism of scientists is evident in the fact that the bones of Native Americans are argued to be essential to scientific knowledge, yet the bones of our white ancestors are not viewed as essential to science. This issue received a considerable amount of news coverage in the campus newspaper and in local papers. This coverage alone generates an awareness of Native American cultural practices—specifically, according to one interviewee, around the idea that reburial is necessary because the ancestor's soul must come full circle and rest in the ground, and that such a return to earth is an essential aspect of Native belief systems.

An additional battle some student reclaimers fought on their college campus was the right to hold an annual pow-wow to raise funds to support a Native American student scholarship. As the student in charge explains,

> I started the pow-wow at the university here, and the whole reason I started that is because I walked into . . . the vice provost's office and I told them, you know, for years I've gone to universities all over the Midwest to go to pow-wows and I'm like, we ain't got shit. And I originally started that to try to be an educational tool for the campus and a recruitment tool because Indians don't just attend a pow-wow in their own town, they travel everywhere for those.

This pow-wow has remained an annual campus event for six years now (the first one was in November of 1996). The students involved in organizing the first pow-wow express pride in their accomplishments, stating that numerous goals were achieved in that this event showed Native Americans as families, as extended families, working together, celebrating together, living their culture. Hosting a pow-wow is also viewed as a way to give back to Native American communities.

Such an event challenges the "racialized space" of this university campus (Feagin, Vera, and Imani 1996). It forces a Native presence in an area that is not perceived to be "Indian country." In fact, even an Osage tribal member I spoke to at the first campus pow-wow complained that there should not have been a pow-wow here because "there's no interest here for it. . . . Sure, the Osage have a connection with this land because we used to be here, but we're not here anymore." This comment seems to accept the dominant group's definition of what is and is not Indian country, where Indian culture should be practiced and where it should not. This comment exemplifies white cultural hegemony, in that even many Natives feel that certain areas of the country (the West) are appropriately labeled "Indian country" (Brayboy 2000). This is intriguing because it ignores the obvious historical fact that Native peoples inhabited every region of this country prior to white intrusion and the Indians' eventual forced relocation. I attribute the Osage tribal member's comment to be a result of his having grown up on the reservation in Oklahoma and the tension he feels toward reclaimers, many of whom he describes as "wanna-be" Indians (see chapter five).

Reclaimers actively engage in another type of challenge to educational institutions, which inevitably results in larger challenges to the rights of science as well. Several reclaimers I spoke to engage in repatriation battles with the university they attend. Repatriation battles are being fought nationwide by Native peoples, reclaimers and non-reclaimers alike, and are direct challenges to white cultural hegemony. Reclaimers challenge not only Native representation in educational institutions, however. They also actively challenge the mainstream, dominant cultural values on environmental issues, consumerism, and individualism.

EMBRACING AN ENVIRONMENTALIST ETHOS AND CONFRONTING CONSUMERISM

Another arena where Native reclaimers challenge the hegemonic culture is in terms of their embrace of an environmentalist ethos and anti-consumeristic values, both of which are contrary to mainstream American cultural norms and values. This can also be perceived as a challenge to white racial hegemony when one looks at poverty rates among racial minorities. While 13.7 percent of the United States population fell below the poverty level in 1996, 32 percent of American Indians were living in poverty (Farley 2000, p. 267). Several of my interviewees comment on the impoverishment of Native peoples on reservations, with one specifying, "There's nothing . . . people do not understand that there are still reservations out there that don't have running water. And, you know, don't have adequate electricity. I mean, you're talking about what we as the American people would call the Dark Ages, and it still exists." In the United States, people of color are disproportionately impoverished, and they therefore have difficulty living the American, consumeristic dream. Instead of bemoaning that fact, reclaimers challenge mainstream cultural values of consumerism. While several of my interviewees describe their childhood as impoverished, many are from middle-class or working-class homes and now have college degrees or are working toward college degrees, and many are professionals and therefore can participate in our consumer culture, if they choose to (again, this is an option most reservation Indians do not have). Over half of the reclaimers I spoke to expressed antagonistic attitudes toward our mainstream, consumeristic society, having embraced instead an environmentalist ethos—an astounding number considering none of my initial interview questions are directed toward this theme. It is significant that so many *choose* not to live the American, consumeristic dream, especially since trying to maintain a non-materialistic lifestyle while living in mainstream American society is a difficult endeavor, especially for those reclaimers who are raising children.

One college-educated female reclaimer elaborates on how her ethnicity influences her daily life with a description of the way she is trying to raise her children:

> I try to teach my children respect for creation and for the environment. The seven-generation rule—anything you do, you should consider seven generations beyond yourself and how that will affect them, you know? You don't discard, you don't waste. We have to have respect for the things that are given to you. I try not to make them materialistic. That's kind of a losing battle. [Gives an exasperated laugh over her last comment.]

She also explicitly connects her Native heritage to her self-proclaimed "tree hugger" beliefs: "A lot of tribes think that that's our role now—to teach people how to take care of the earth because it's not been done well." Another reclaimer also mentions the seven-generation rule, even though she is reclaiming a different tribal culture. She spoke of her work with Native peoples as "giving to the next seven generations . . . because there was a lot of struggle that got me to be where I'm at and there was struggle that kept me alive. . . . It's very important for me that I'm doing something that's purposeful . . . involving Native people." She expresses concern at what is happening environmentally:

> What's going on with the land . . . when I see what we do to this—to—to the— to the lands. I mean, just to the earth in general, but also to the land, because I know that that land is held sacred to someone—to me, but also sacred to somebody else who maybe just had ceremonies or something with those areas, and it's just so painful because then it's just—it's plowed over and—and made into condominiums or shopping malls and, um, those things really hurt. . . . [I]t's so deep rooted that the pain never goes away for me.

Another reclaimer says her Nativeness informs her political ideologies and activism. Specifically for her, being Native influences her attitudes toward "environmental issues. . . . I'm what they call a tree hugger. . . . And the animal thing. My husband calls it 'Stacey's home for handicapped animals.' . . . [A]ll kinds of strange critters out here. We try to treat things right. They come our way—and they deserve an existence and respect, too." Another woman claims, "It's important for people to understand that we're killing what's most precious, and that's life. There are so many homes going up today all over the place and so many wild animals being [displaced]. . . . We have torn up all of their habitats. We're killing the earth and nobody cares." Another reclaimer makes a similar comment specifically in terms of battles reservation Indians must contend with: "There's environmental fights all the time 'cause there's people trying to build, like, nuclear power places next to reservations and then dumping the waste into the water supply, you know?"

Other reclaimers make similar points about their fondness for nature, animals, and the outdoors and see this as an extension of their Native identity and heritage. One reclaimer simply explains, "Outdoor activities always gave me something to relate to, to feel like I belonged. . . . I was in Girl Scouts and I started camping a lot. Um, going with my dad in his boat and doing a lot of nature activities instead of hanging out with kids in the school . . . 'cause it became more of a way where, like I said, I fit in." A young male reclaimer says, "Whenever I look at Native Americans, they've always had that kind of peace, that kind of being one with nature, an emphasis on harmony. . . . I guess that is what I try to identify with." Interestingly, this young man speaks of Native Americans in the third person, when most reclaimers refer to Native Americans in the first person. I attribute that to the fact that he has only recently begun reclaiming his indigenous heritage (a little over a year prior to our interview).

Another female reclaimer speaks fondly of childhood memories with her grandfather:

> And one of the things I would treasure is, we would go out fishing and we'd run down—well, I would run, he would walk, he was a very tall man . . . to the river and just fish and talk, and he would talk to the animals and he would tell me stories that now I wish I could remember more of them. I remember once I stepped on a wasp, 'cause I was always barefoot, and he grabbed something, a weed, up out of the ground, chewed it up with the tobacco that was in his mouth, and put it on my foot. . . . It never did burn, never did sting. . . . I have no idea what it was. I wish I knew.

She also describes another nature-related lesson her grandfather passed on to her. She says, "Grandpa used to say that anything you're troubled about, anything you're fussing over, trying to figure out . . . compare it to a walk in the woods. If it makes sense like a walk in the woods would, then it makes sense. . . . [In the woods] you kind of know what's right and what's not . . . what's in balance . . ."

Another woman explains that she feels the earth puts forth a positive energy that many of us choose to ignore, but

> . . . you can pick up on what Mother Earth is trying to give you along with the trees and the rocks and actually learn to be more like them. More stable. Is it a Native thing? They definitely speak of it eloquently and they probably are more

in tune with it than anybody I know. But, I also believe that anybody who's willing to try, whether they're Native or not, can do the same thing—it's just a matter of whether or not they listen. . . . Um, so is it a Native thing? No, not really.
It's just that they're more in tune with it, if that makes any sense.

LaDuke comments on Native people's connection to the land, nature, and the
environment: "Our relationship to land and water is continuously reaffirmed
through prayer, deed, and our way of life. Our identity as human beings is
founded on creation stories tying us to the earth, and to a way of being . . ."
(1997, p. 251).

A male college professor reclaimer explains his Nativeness as influencing
every aspect of his life, particularly in respect to his anti-consumeristic attitudes. He says that he does not value the "trappings of success" such as a big
house, fancy clothes, and so forth. "I don't feel a great need to impress anyone with my financial success." His comment implies that part of the mainstream approach is to purchase things in order to impress others with your ac-
quisitions. A female reclaimer makes a similar comment: "I'm not
materialistic. I couldn't care less about material objects." Another says,

> I have to live in the mundane world more . . . that is where the conflict arises the
> most. Um, um, you know, the whole commercialism of our society goes com-
> pletely against everything that I truly, honestly want to believe and practice, but
> you have to . . . I have to put gas in my car, you know, get a real job to pay my
> bills. . . . I am not able to completely live my life the way I would like to.

A young college-aged male expresses his perspective in the following way:

> I have a problem with where we're [society] going. . . . I would not say like I'm
> an anarchist or something, but I don't see myself as a functioning part of society
> in the future. . . . I see it as a struggle . . . but it is a struggle well beyond ethnic-
> ity. . . . [I]t's a struggle for anybody if they stop and think about it. I guess it all
> depends on what you want. . . . [I]f you want convenience, a short, fast, life
> [laughing], go eat McDonald's burgers and play on the Internet. I don't know.
> That's not what I want. So, I guess it is a struggle.

Later he adds, "That's one of the things I don't like about capitalism—it has
been oppressive in a lot of ways to a lot of people. So, yeah, it [reclaiming]
has changed my ideas politically." Another woman simply explains, "Most
people, who think that money is everything, are lost. They're lost souls."

One female reclaimer makes her rejection of mainstream materialism and
consumption a significant theme throughout the interview. She begins by expressing her discomfort with the accumulation and ownership of things and
how reclaiming her Cherokee heritage has helped her understand this aspect

of herself that is so strikingly at odds with our mainstream cultural beliefs: "The concept of property and 'this is mine' and you know, ownership and control. That always bothered me. And I didn't realize why, but it made sense after I knew where I came from, I guess." She goes on to describe her grandmother as operating from a similar perspective:

> My grandmother was famous for . . . they had a little restaurant and garage . . . and if somebody came in and couldn't pay for a meal or they were just like a transient wandering through—she fed them, not expecting anything in return . . . . I can remember my parents, they used to be fussing at them [her grandparents] all the time about "Somebody is going to knock you over the head and take everything you own" and her comment would always be, "If they're taking it, I guess they need it worse than I do." And that's a very Native way to live. And I had always been—well, my first husband never understood my knack for giving away. You know, it's just part of who I am, and it makes sense knowing the way the Cherokee live because they—ownership and collecting things is not the Cherokee way.

She describes another lesson concerning materialism that her Native grandmother taught her: "When I was a teenager, my grandmother's house burned . . . and I went down and I stayed with her for a while and helped her clean up and I was thinking that she would be grieving over the stuff that had burned . . . and she said 'Oh, it's just stuff and it all burns.' And everybody around her was upset and bothered, but it really didn't bother her." She later relates another story concerning her grandmother's influence concerning materialism on her: "I had an old van that I was getting ready to get rid of and, um, I asked her what I should sell it for and she said, 'Why would you sell it? Don't you know anyone who needs a vehicle?' That you don't find. And I gave it to a stepsister who was struggling and going through a divorce and really needed one."

A similar story is told by another reclaimer. She says that she was raised with Lakota values, despite the fact that she was raised in the white mainstream society. For instance, she says,

> Our family was very generous, even though we didn't have much at all. Uh, and I carried that into my life. . . . I noticed, um, the friends I made, who, for the most part were of European ancestry—straight-up American, um, people are always surprised by my generosity. Um, which is always strange to me because it seems very normal for me.

The previously mentioned woman who is reclaiming her Cherokee heritage describes trying to learn and live the "old ways," what she considers to be the ways of her Cherokee ancestors. I ask her what she means by this, or what the "new ways" are that she avoids. She answers simply that the new ways are represented by "the greed and the give me, give me, give me. Um, doing things for gain, for profit, for show. The old ones don't think like that and weren't like that." She later adds,

> Being Cherokee means being willing to give up greed. Being willing to struggle through, find who you are. . . . [T]hat is a struggle, you know, in a busy world where it is dog-eat-dog. . . . So, to me, being Cherokee means being willing to live that, not just to talk about it, but to live that.

For this woman, living according to the old ways means, "It's a lifestyle and a philosophy and a way of living and thinking and being that is very, um, it comes up against almost everything we're taught growing up in school . . . the American dream, what it means to get ahead, and to, you know, keep up with the Joneses, and that's just not Cherokee." If she has to choose, between the white world and the Native world, she would definitely choose "oohhh, Native." I ask her what a Native world looks like and she provides a description:

> Living in a Native world . . . there's a lot of balance and harmony, which sounds like a lot of really nice words, but living that looks like everybody has a place, everybody belongs, um, nobody is better than anybody else. We're all related. We're all related, the trees—the grass, the rocks . . . all the two-leggeds and all the four-leggeds . . . we're all related and we all have a place and we all belong.

Even though this woman describes the "Native world" and the "white world" as if they are distinct and separate, some of her comments display her recognition that there is more fluidity to the boundaries between the two. For instance, she talks about how reclaiming her Native heritage has changed her. She still lives in the "white world," but she has altered her life significantly since beginning her reclamation process:

> When I first started reading about my Native heritage, I was verywhite. And very into working too hard, spending a lot of time at a job, and I think my kids, um, saw a very obvious difference, 'cause when I began to realize that what I wanted to be was what my grandfather and grandmother had taught me and, um, it made a difference in life choices that were very difficult and hard for the world to understand, but that were more important. Um, I was working at . . . [a major insurance company], um, making quite a bit of money and my kids were home alone in the summer with no one there . . . and one day my son told me about one of his friends and something they had done only two weeks before and I thought, "Where was I?" And that's when it hit me—this is not the way I am supposed to live.

She quit her job and faces serious financial struggles as a single mother of two children, but believes she made the best choice, explaining, "That summer I came to know my kids better . . . even though financially it was terribly difficult. . . . We learned to live a much simpler kind of life where money wasn't as important." She says the financial strain is difficult for her children, but that they learned a valuable lesson about what really matters in life. "But, when I was with them in the middle of the week and we were playing in a river just on a spur of the moment, it gradually . . . enough of those experiences came into play and they thought [positively] about it . . . and I'm hoping they will carry that with them into adulthood, that there are things more important than getting ahead and collecting stuff."

Some reclaimers in my study are explicitly critical of the effect greed and materialism is having on the earth as well as the cultures of the earth. As one woman explains,

> The white man did ruin it [the earth]. The white man came in with his greed and his, I mean, in all of history no matter how you cut it, when the Indians took something, they took it with permission. They asked before they ever took. They asked the tree, "May I cut you?" "Thank you so much for your spirit in doing this." . . . Trees do talk if you're quiet enough to listen. And what they would tell you is, the white man did destroy it, they came over, they, uh, invaded, they were money grubbing, they destroyed completely, wiped out over a hundred tribes.

She continues with an explanation of her belief that Natives are the keepers of the earth: "They're the ones who understand and have the knowledge that whites never understood. It's not to say that the whites can't understand, it's just that they never have. They were too busy with the 'I have to get this-and-this-and-this.'" Later she adds, "If you stop and think about things like that and the Trail of Tears and what they did to the Native Americans, it is pretty sad. You figure we lost over a hundred tribes for no reason other than greed." Another reclaimer similarly comments, "A lot of tribes think that that's our role now—to teach people how to take care of the Earth because it's not been done well. Hopefully it will happen."

This particular reclaimer does not feel that Native people are immune to greed and materialism. She instead perceives white culture as influencing such characteristics in Natives, as luring Native people from the "old ways." She is critical of her brother, for instance, because his interest in reclaiming their Cherokee heritage revolves around pecuniary gains he hopes to make. As she explains, "My older brother is very interested in getting it all proven and all of the paper and documentation done because he is looking at it financially—housing and school for his kids—and he has the kind of greed

. . ." I ask her if this bothers her, and she replies, "Yes, it does . . . it's just so not-Indian and those are the people who are proving, documenting, and getting benefits of being Indian, but those are the people who don't behave [according to] the old ways."

She goes on to explain that living according to the old ways is difficult for many reasons, one of which is that "there aren't a lot of the old ones who are teaching what it means to be and think and feel and live the old way. People are kind of clueless on what that looks like or feels like and it disturbs me that there are more of the Indians who are greedy, the sort of 'give me, give me' sort of people and not taking care of doing things the way they should be done." Additionally, as mentioned earlier, even indigenous knowledges are contested, so assuming there is an "old way" that can be passed on is painting a far too static picture of Native cultures than is realistic. She says that she views this greed and materialism, not living according to what she perceives as the "old ways" a lot among Natives, both those who are reclaiming and traditional, non-reclaiming Indians.

Another reclaimer says that her mother contacted her after she heard something about some Natives receiving some money, and she felt she had to correct her mother by saying, "You know that we're not in this for the money . . . . It's not about the money." Similarly, Native casinos bother her. She talks about a reservation she visited and adds,

> There's a casino there and the old ones won't go near the casino, um, just because it's all about money and greed. . . . Some of them justify working there or letting their kids work there because they think there's some balance somehow in that—so much has been taken and it's a way to take back. You know, lure the white people in and take their money and that's okay because they've taken so much from us . . .

Her opinion differs, however:

> I think anything, like . . . that takes advantage of people . . . the thing I saw [at the casino] was people with walkers, people who were poor, not dressed well, people who were hoping against hope that this was going to be their lucky day. Spending everything they had, that should've gone toward food, on gambling. So, that just left a real bad taste in my mouth. I think gaming . . . is just not something that people ought to—I think it really upsets the balance of things.

Nagel argues that the renewal and revitalization of Native communities is especially intriguing because it is primarily "not the result of economic growth" (1997, p. 6). Despite the presence of gaming on some reservations, most Native American reservations face extreme poverty, some of the worst conditions in this country. The fact that so many of the reclaimers I spoke to reject mainstream values of consumerism and materialism, and reject middle-class American aspirations of financial success, is an intriguing challenge reclaimers make to the dominant, white culture.

INDIVIDUALISM VS. COMMUNITY MINDFULNESS

Another aspect of Nativeness that many reclaimers speak of embracing that challenges dominant, white cultural values pertains to their emphasis on community, or the collective, however they define that, over the needs of the individual. The emphasis on individualism, part and parcel of the idea of American exceptionalism in political theory, has a long history (e.g., Lipset 1990; Quadagno 1994). This theory explains American political uniqueness in terms of the influence of specific cultural ideologies on the development of political institutions, particularly those pertaining to an individualistic ethos and the sacredness of private property, which ultimately distinguishes our system from European cultural and political institutions (Quadagno 1994, p. 5).

One reclaimer speaks of how her Nativeness informs her parenting and her efforts to explicitly teach her children that they are part of something larger than themselves. She says, "Taking responsibility for one's actions and, um, how your behavior affects the entire family, reminding them that they are part of a family unit. Making them feel connected with everything, connected with their classmates, connected with their family members . . . teaching a group mentality . . . and a sense of self."

The reclaimer studying counseling psychology with the objective of teaching and doing research from a Native point of view explains that going to graduate school is more than simply a path toward personal advancement:

> That's really important for me, um, to be working within the community while I'm also on campus because I'm not doing this for myself. . . . I'm doing this to hopefully give back because there's a reason that my life has led me in the path that it has gone, um, to get me to the point that I'm at now. And this is not about me. This has never been about me. And it's when I came to recognize that this isn't about me that my life started to go really well. . . . I think it's kind of based on, um, some spiritual kind of beliefs that the ancestors have kind of come in and helped nudge it along.

In this narrative, she sees herself not only as part of a living Native community, to which she wants to contribute, but also as part of an ancestral community, with her ancestors nudging her along. Later she adds, "When I made that decision, then my life kinda started to go in the right direction . . .

because the ancestors really want me to go in the direction that I'm going into. They brought me back to my family. Or rather they brought my family back to me. And it's so wonderful."

Another reclaimer also speaks of emphasizing a group mentality in her children. As she explains, "I try to teach them to respect other people and to understand that that isn't always returned." And she emphasizes how different Native culture is from white culture:

> Well, Native culture is very different from the dominant culture. The Western culture is a competitive culture, the capitalists . . . everything is bottom line, everything is "What can I get?" . . . individualistic and profit-oriented. And the Native culture is very community minded: "What's good for the community?" Uh, how do we . . . get a consensus, you know? And teach the children to be co-operative and compliant. And you put them in a public school system with people who eat them alive, you know? 'Cause it's the competitive model. . . . So, it's just a very different way of thinking. The cooperative model has been proven over and over to be a better model for children to learn under. It produces much more community-minded people who care about their earth and fellow man. But, we continue to promote the competitive model in all our public schools.

She later adds how difficult she believes it is to be bicultural, Native and European American, because these two cultures are so drastically opposed to one another. She speaks of this as

> cultural schizophrenia—where you have to live in two different cultures, in or-der to survive you have to understand the dominant culture and the competitive model if you want an education. But, if you live in the traditional Indian system, it's a cooperative model, so you have to be able to walk in both worlds in order to survive, and most can't.

She says she is very conscious of teaching the cooperative model to her children at home, yet she is also conscious that the schools are teaching a competitive model. She feels this creates tension for her children in school.

While only a few reclaimers whom I spoke to brought up this tension between individualism and community orientation, I think it is a significant cultural clash between Native and white communities. I think it is also implied by other reclaimers, for instance, when speaking of their generosity and giving things instead of selling things to others because it implies a concern for others in your community, not simply individual gain.

MASCOTS

Another arena in which traditional Native American activists and Native re-claimers express discontent pertains to professional and college mascots. As one young man explains to me,

> What if your mascot were Sambo eating watermelon, you know? Or the Frito Bandito wearing a sombrero? I'm like, these are all images that have been done away with, and Indian people helped get rid of them. But, I'm like, now you're slapping us [Indians] in the face by keeping our images going [wearing a Braves hat or the like]. . . . You know? You wouldn't dare see a Kansas City White Trash t-shirt, you know?

He also gets frustrated with other Indians who do not feel offended over the mascot issue, explaining, "You know, a lot of the younger generation don't give a shit. It pisses me off when I see a young Indian kid at a pow-wow wearing a Cleveland Indians hat. You know, it makes me mad." He says that he participated in a pow-wow and "one of the guys sittin' there had a Kansas City Chiefs shirt on. . . . They give the impression that it's okay because this Indian is wearing that. It just goes against everything."

An Osage reclaimer explains his rather contradictory feelings concerning the mascot issue:

> To me, yes, it's offensive. But, I also have many other things to worry about . . . . I would like to watch the game instead [of protest a Braves versus Cardinals baseball game] and so, it's a personal choice. Yes, the Red Skins, the Braves, all that. . . . Red Skins is really offensive. . . . I think Red Skins is awful . . . because it was used in a derogatory way back when they used to use it as an insult.

One female reclaimer explains what she finds offensive about mascots as follows:

> The mascot [issue] makes me very aware of [her Native heritage] and hurts me a lot . . . horribly. . . . I feel awful. . . . The one in Illinois is the worst because he's in Lakota dress and . . . it's so aggravating because then you hear people and their incredible . . . bigotry and racism when they talk about the need for the mascot and how they should keep the mascots because they're honoring the In-dian people by doing that.

When asked how she feels about the mascot issue, another woman ex-claims, "If it were the New York Niggers, how would you feel? Would that be acceptable? Jersey Jemimas?" One young man is critical of the battles AIM (the American Indian Movement) is fighting but supports their work on the mascot issue. He explains, "I don't even know what they're fighting now. They're still really hung up on the mascots, which I'm all for that. A race of people shouldn't be halftime entertainment."

Protesting the use of Natives as mascots is an issue many reclaimers and traditional, non-reclaiming Natives engage in and is a way Native people fight to control Native representation. This battle is evidence of their challenge to white cultural hegemony because indigenous peoples are not simply acquiescing to racialized images of Native peoples in popular culture. Another key aspect of this fight that warrants notice is that they are fighting Native invisibility by fighting what are, arguably, the most visible images of Native peoples nationwide. As one reclaimer says, we no longer stereotype other racial/ethnic groups in the form of mascots, so why is it acceptable that we continue with such demeaning Native portrayals?

CONCLUSION

This chapter analyzes the various ways the Native reclaimers I speak to challenge white hegemony and the racial hierarchy. Through challenges to Native invisibility, stereotypical portrayals, and Native representation in educational institutions, to their challenges to American mainstream values of consumerism, materialism, and individualism, and the use of Native images as team mascots, the reclaimers I speak to are actively engaged in the deconstruction of the historical and current dominant group construction of Native peoples.

While I may have entered this research with a rather narrow definition of activism, understanding it in the traditional sense of political activism, the reclaimers I speak to challenge me to rethink my conceptions of politics and activism. They are engaged in cultural activism, expanding activism beyond "the concerns of politics to the social, to the terrain of everyday life" (Omi and Winant 1994, p. 97). Racial minority movements of the post-1960s period have as their greatest achievement their "ability to create new racial 'subjects'" (Omi and Winant 1994, p. 99).

> Social movements create collective identity by offering their adherents a different view of themselves and their world; that is from the worldview and self-concepts offered by the established social order. They do this by the process of rearticulation, which produces new subjectivity by making use of information and knowledge already present in the subject's mind. They take elements and themes of her/his culture and traditions and infuse them with new meaning. (Omi and Winant 1994, p. 99)

While it is important to point out the significance of the actions reclaimers are engaged in, and specifically to recognize them as a direct challenge to white cultural hegemony, it is also important to critically interrogate their actions as well:

> There is much that is liberating about this, as Western modernity abandons its imperialist arrogance towards those "primitive" cultures which surround it; but there may also be a "freezing"of history, a loss of imagination and thus of the practical possibility of radical social change. The styles of the past may be welcomely reinvented, but only perhaps as one-dimensional images in the "heritage industry" of an eternal present. (Outhwaite and Bottomore 1994, p. 391)

To what extent are reclaimers "freezing" images of Nativeness in the same way dominant groups are accused of freezing history? This appears to be a challenge to the reclaimers I speak to. Many of them voice concern over the mainstream stereotype of Native peoples as a thing of the past rather than active, living communities today. Yet, to what extent do their conceptions of authentic Nativeness have the same effect? To what extent does upholding dichotomous understandings of Native versus mainstream society represent reality and to what extent does it reinforce historical conceptions of Nativeness? To what extent is this phenomena the effect of establishing Native identities outside of Native communities?

The Native reclaimers whom I spoke to challenge white cultural hegemony in many ways, from challenges in educational institutions, to challenges to mainstream cultural values of individualism, materialism, and consumerism. In the process, they are deconstructing the cultural meanings of Native peoples and Nativeness previously constructed and perpetuated by whites. Beyond these cultural challenges, the next chapter analyzes the individual ways reclaimers express their resistance to the white, dominant culture and their embrace of their Nativeness. The next chapter also looks at the ways Native reclaimers perform or enact their newly reclaimed racial/ethnic identity.

Chapter Three

Reclaimer Practices:
Religion, Spirituality, Language,
Family, and Food

One of the fundamental questions intriguing me when I begin this research is how reclaimers practice, enact, or perform their newly reclaimed Nativeness. In other words, what rituals do reclaimers engage in that are directly related to their racial/ethnic reclamation? Enacting cultural practices is a way of performing one's identity, and particularly in this case, I argue, performing a newly reclaimed identity carries with it a certain intentionality. As Victor Turner points out,

> In the sense that man is a self-performing animal—his performances are, in a way, reflexive; in performing he reveals himself to himself. This can be in two ways: the actor may come to know himself better through acting or enactment; or one set of human beings may come to know themselves better through observing and/or participating in performances generated and presented by another set of human beings. (1979, p. 72)

Barbara Meyerhoff describes the significance of rituals for the Eastern European Jewish immigrant elderly community members she studies:

> Always, self and society are known—to the subjects themselves and to the audience—through enactments. Rituals and ceremonies are cultural mirrors, opportunities for presenting collective knowledge. . . . The means . . . people use to "see" themselves. Because their invisibility was so painful to them, and they struggled to find opportunities to appear in the world, thus assuring themselves that indeed they existed. (1978, p. 32)

Reclaiming is an active process; these are individuals who are actively seeking a culture previously denied them. They work at learning their heritages and they embrace Native rituals and cultural practices as a way to perform their new racial/ethnic identity as well as a way to participate in a wider cultural resurgence. Culture, according to Hall and Neitz (1993), "comes from the Latin for 'cultivating' or tilling the soil. Culture, in this sense, amounts to the ways of taking care of things" (p. 5). Again, Meyerhoff elaborates on the significance of rituals: "Enacted beliefs have a capacity for arousing belief that mere statements do not. 'Doing is believing,' hence ritual and ceremony generate conviction when reason and thought may fail" (1978, p. 32). While I find incredible variation in terms of the ways reclaimers practice their new cultural heritage, there are four significant themes relating to this that emerge from my interviews: an emphasis on religion and/or spirituality, learning Native languages, an embrace of foods associated with indigenous peoples, and an embrace of nontraditional family arrangements. This chapter, then, relates reclaimer practices that set them apart from mainstream, non-Natives and that also often distinguish them from their previous, non-reclaiming selves.

Despite the fact that the reclaimers I spoke to discussed practices they engage in that set them apart from mainstream, non-reclaiming Natives, there is an identity/practice tension evident in their narratives. As is evident in the following discussion, many reclaimers describe cultural practices that they intend to engage in but, for whatever reason, have not successfully engaged in. One male reclaimer I spoke to, for instance, bemoans the fact that he wants to pursue traditional cultural practices but, as a member of the Eastern Cherokee Nation, these simply are not available to him in this region of the country. He cannot, for instance, participate in the traditional ceremonies tribe members incorporate into their lives, and there are not tribal elders here to pass on the necessary tribal knowledge; therefore he describes facing a continual struggle to maintain a balance between the Anglo, mainstream culture and his Native heritage. He explains that he does his best to participate in Native cultural traditions by attending pow-wows and visiting his tribal reservation during the summer. This identity/practice tension is evident in other reclaimers as well and will be elaborated on in the following sections.

RELIGION/SPIRITUALITY

The significance of religion and spirituality to reclaiming is a consistent theme throughout my narratives. Yet, while all of my interviewees mention religion, the difficulty is in the fact that there is such discrepancy in *how* they speak about religion and spirituality in connection with their reclaiming. For some, religion is synonymous with their racial/ethnic reclamation. For others, it is the questioning of their religious heritage, predominantly Christianity, and their subsequent rejection of it, which contributes to their embrace of their Native heritage. One reclaimer I spoke to interestingly conflates her paganism with her Native reclamation. Many simply speak of Nativeness as a spiritual influence in their life, an embrace of the "mystical" that the dominant, non-Native culture tends to downplay. For some, then, reclaiming is congruous with how they define themselves spiritually, and for others, organized religion is incongruous with their newly reclaimed Native identity. But, for all of the reclaimers I spoke to, religion appears as a significant cultural factor influencing their racial/ethnic sense of self. Additionally, "Spirituality is a powerful force and a unique aspect of Native American people. It is interrelated with their culture, their philosophy, their psychology and their religion" (Brayboy and Morgan 1998, p. 347). Native author Gunn Allen describes some religious practices that are widely practiced among Native people that overlap with the religious practices found in my sample of Native reclaimers: "Among the disciplines widely practiced—and usually considered central to spiritual seeking—were dreaming, vision-seeking, purification, fasting, praying, making offerings, dancing, singing, making and caring for sacred objects, and living a good and varied life" (1998, p. 47).

Christianity, for instance, is so important to one female reclaimer that at one point in her life she became an ordained preacher in the United Methodist Church. However, she explains that during her reclaiming process, she and her family "stopped going to church," opting instead for a weekly family gathering. She explains,

> A lot of the white ways are part of the church and the more I learned about how the missionaries wanted to civilize the Indians and it was a missionary boarding school that children were taken from their homes—I just couldn't be part of that. . . . How do you teach your children that family is important and then be part of something with no family support? I can't do that. I know a lot of people do it, but I can't do that.

Later she adds what she perceives to be another incongruity between Christianity and reclaiming her Cherokee heritage:

> Having the most reverend preacher stand up and tell me that I have to be da-da-da-da doesn't fit with the Cherokee way, not the old way. Um, the Cherokees have a very personal and intimate relationship with their creator and all of creation, and that doesn't come from somebody telling you how to do it. It comes from doing it, living it—from finding that perfect balance. From walking your path.

Another woman similarly speaks of her rejection of Christianity as contributing to her reclamation process. She explains that she was raised in the

Episcopalian faith, which she describes as "one of the worst abusers of Indians there ever was," and she perceives learning more about this religion
proved to be a trigger for her Cherokee reclamation:

> Actually, I bought into Christian principles most of my life and was pretty
> adamant about that and took some Western Civ. [Civilization] classes at . . . col-
> lege and I started doing a lot of reading about Christian history and about Na-
> tive history and doing the comparisons and most of what I learned about Chris-
> tianity is, it's a bunch of bullshit! . . . It was created by a rich aristocracy to keep
> peasants under control. And reading about what their missionaries did to Native
> families and how they were treated and the children—how they were tortured
> and abused at boarding schools and all in the name of Christianity—I basically
> discarded Christianity. "This is bull and I don't want anything to do with this."
> And [I] started researching what my natural history would have been had there
> not been that Christian influence.

I ask her if she feels that her Christianity and her Native identity could co-exist, and she says no, but also recognizes that many people manage to not have
these identities conflict. "Oh yeah, a lot of Indians are very adamant, born-
again Christians, you know, and just as condescending and condemning as
white people were, you know, of one another and of other people." While this
comment is, ironically, rather condemning itself, it also shows how adamantly
she perceives the incongruity between embracing a Native identity while simultaneously embracing a Christian identity.

At another point in the interview, she describes one of her most important
spiritual rituals that she engages in, a sweat. The significance of this ritual to
her is made evident by the presence of a sweat lodge built in her yard. When
she describes a sweat, she does so in terms of its religious significance:

> It's just a place where you can pray any way you want to pray. Any religion is
> welcome. You know, Native people aren't like Christians where they think their
> way is the only way and if you don't do it their way you go to hell [laughs],
> which is basically the Christian premise. Um, it's a very open religion. It's very
> welcoming. It's very comforting. A sweat lodge is a place where you can bare
> your soul and pray for things you need, pray with like-minded people, and it's
> safe. You know, it's not like one of these churches where you shut out the world,
> you know, you don't even let people look out windows, and it's like, cut off all
> creation and focus people! I find those places really cold now and not comfort-
> ing at all.

This woman makes a number of points with this comment, points that I hear
reiterated in the narratives of other reclaimers. For one, she portrays Native
religion/spirituality as something that is incongruous with Christianity. For

her, the primary reason has to do with the rigidity of Christianity and the fluidity of Native spirituality.

Native author Bruchac makes a similar argument:

> The sweat bath [was] labeled as yet another instrument of the devil. Native Americans were extremely tolerant of other people's religions and made no attempt to prevent Europeans from practicing their various Christian faiths. Respect for others and non-interference with their ways are important tenets of Native life. The exact opposite was true of the Europeans, who tried every means from slavery to slaughter to extirpate Native American religions. (1993, p. 25)

Both the United States government and the Protestant and Catholic religious hierarchies oppose the Native practice of sweats, which are found throughout Native North America in some form or another. This ritual is not exclusive to Native North America, as Scandinavians have long engaged in such practices as a form of cleansing the mind, body, and soul. For Native peoples, "The sweat lodge is more sacrament than recreation. It is strongly associated with prayer and preparation" (Bruchac 1993, p. 6). Bruchac goes on to explain that despite the freedom of religion expressed in the First Amendment, most Americans are unaware of the extent of religious persecution indigenous North Americans face. He elaborates, "In 1873, sweat baths were forbidden to all Native Americans by the Federal government. The ban on most Native ceremonial practices including the sweat lodge continued into the 1930s. These laws were actively enforced" (1993, p. 28). The reclaimer who has a sweat lodge in her yard explicitly makes this point: "It was against the law for us to practice our religion, so people watched you to see if you did it. Until 1978, it was against the law from me to practice my religion. I had to keep that private. . . . No freedom of religion for Indians. Carter passed the Native American Religious Freedoms Act in 1978." In addition to sweats, the deeply religious Sun Dance ceremony practiced among Plains Indians was banned by the United States government for sixty-six years (beginning in 1875) in their efforts to assimilate all Indian people (Grim 1996).

A second theme embedded in the previous reclaimer's narrative is the connection between spirituality and nature. For this woman, praying should take place in nature, not be a practice that is cut off from nature. As will be made explicit throughout this chapter, many reclaimers I speak to regard nature in spiritual terms. Such an affiliation between religion/spirituality and nature is recognized as a significant aspect of Native people's embrace of religion. As Holst states, "Native American religions are essentially about symbol and ritual, not dogma. They influence all aspects of a practitioner's life and are centered in the land" (1999, p. 90). Many also differentiate between Native religion, Native spirituality, and the Native American Church. One reclaimer explains her use of terminology in this way:

There isn't really a [Native American] church, I mean not in that sense. It's a way of connecting with the Creator and the creation, and Creator to me doesn't mean an individual; it can be an entity or an event. You know, it's whatever has created what's here. *Great Spirit* is how they translate from most languages into English, and that's not how it should translate. It's more like *Holy Mystery*. That would be more accurate of a translation. It's the unknown. It's not an entity. It's not a man sitting on a throne giving orders. . . . "Burn in hell, by the way, I love you." You know? And there's no hell. Creation is all good, and everything that is created has a purpose.

Despite her initial comment, there *is* a Native American Church; that is the official name of the Peyote religion. The Peyote religion is one of several re-vitalization movements, including the Sun Dance, among Plains Indians. It emerged in the 1870s and was quickly stifled by the United States federal government (Bonvillain 2001, p. 197). Bonvillain explains,

Peyote is thought by believers to be a spirit being as well as a means of obtain-ing visionary messages and absorbing spirit power. It grants people direct con-tact with the spirit world, allowing them to receive knowledge, power, and phys-ical and emotional health. (2001, p. 198)

Gunn Allen points out, "American Indian spiritual traditions are as varied as the lands they live on, as varied as the tribes are from one another" (1998, p. 40). A reclaimer I spoke to also emphasizes the variations in terminology:

Even within the Department of Religious Studies, like, it's kind of, they, there's like a fine line between calling it Native American religion and Native Ameri-can spirituality. . . . A lot of times people . . . use *spirituality*, I believe that's the preference. That's the preference that I use. I mean, I use *religion* interchange-ably as well. . . . There is the Native American Church, which is a combination of Christianity and Native tradition . . . [with] the peyote ceremonies and stuff.

She goes on to explain, "There are stereotypes around peyote ceremonies and stuff. . . . Yeah, Indians out getting high on their peyote and, you know, that's not the case. . . . The abuse of peyote by Native people is virtually nonexist-ent. One of the works I read, you know, basically is comparing it to the wine in Communion for Catholics." Prohibitions against the traditional use of pey-ote during religious ceremonies historically are about religious persecution in the United States.

One young male reclaimer explicitly describes himself as "not Christian" and instead says he and his wife practice "traditional ways." Since she is someone who was raised on a reservation and he is a reclaimer of a different tribe, I ask him to describe what he means by traditional ways. He elaborates,

Well, to different people it means different things. . . . To me it's like, you know, we like, I guess we pray. . . . We do our cedar and sage and stuff . . . and like, give offerings sometimes and small things like that. . . . Like, I'd say we do a lot of the, the praying and stuff like that. And that's something that we do every day, no matter what. And like, a lot of Indian tribes, in my tribe [Osage], there's no word for, like, "religion." There's, like, religious activities and things like . . . ceremonies. . . . It's like we do certain things . . . give thanks for the day and stuff like that.

What is interesting about this comment is that when he describes "traditional ways" he does so in terms of practices rather than beliefs. Again, Holst's (1999) comment applies: "Native American religions are essentially about symbol and ritual, not dogma" (p. 90).

The male reclaimer makes a point to challenge the stereotypes surrounding peyote ceremonies. His wife's family members are part of the Native American Church, "peyote people" according to him, and he explains,

I don't like people thinking of it as a drug. . . . It really pisses me off. I've been interested in that for a little while. . . . It's a mixture of, of like, a conglomerate of traditional and Christianity, and my parents being Southern Baptists weren't, like, real strict on me at all and I didn't really go to church that much, but the influence is there, of course. An, uh, so I kinda grew up with the bulk and that kinda feels like a right way to me and stuff, so I've been kinda learning about that.

This reclaimer rejects Christianity in order to embrace a Native spirituality, yet he recognizes that many Native people manage to incorporate both spiritual traditions into their lives: "See, it's really weird, Indian people . . . to us, doing traditional ways and Christianity, there's no conflict [over the] principles, you know?" He goes on to explain that his wife's grandmother is a good example of this, as she is someone who holds a key to the church (a Catholic Church on their reservation) and also participates in peyote meetings and other traditional rituals and practices. "That's the problem that the, the missionaries had back in history was the Indian people, there was no conflict [for the Indians]. . . . They would tell them, start with your Genesis and stuff like that. Well, for Native people, that was a common thing, that we would go around and share our creation stories, you know?" Ortiz (1999) concurs: "Christianity has not eliminated various elements of Indian religions in Christian worship. Indian spirituality has been and remains an intricate part of the lives of Christian Indians and their communities" (p. 364).

Another female reclaimer discusses how her relatives living on the reservation are also able to mix traditional ceremonies with Christianity. She relates an interesting story exemplifying this:

My family on the reservation is . . . Christian and so a lot of our ceremonies, a lot of the traditional Lakota things that we do are kinda intermixed with daily life. . . . One of my cousins, she, uh, was trying to decorate her house and she went to the graveyard, and she was there at the graveyard and she saw that they were throwing away all the flowers that they had put on the graves, the plastic flowers, and so she thought, well, you know, and nobody has much money and so, she's like, "Wow, I'll get some of those plastic flowers and I'll take those home and put those around." You know, 'cause they're nice, there's color. Well, she takes those home and she brought home some of the spirits with her when she did that and so she had to do some ceremonies to get them out. . . . She had to cleanse her house . . . [and] a lot of offerings [had to be made] and those kinds of things 'cause she really made some people angry. . . . But then this woman is also strongly Catholic. I mean, she's just very Catholic, so for her, for her that wasn't ceremony. Do you see what I'm saying?

Despite her relative's ability to incorporate both traditions into her life, this reclaimer feels that she can no longer embrace Christianity and her Lakota heritage:

I was raised Christian, but I'm not. . . . My problem with Christianity is . . . I mean, I love the humanitarian aspects of it, but, it's um, they leave out the earth and they leave out the animals and it doesn't make any sense to me. I mean and, of course, it's really freakin' sexist and I'm sorry, I'm not somebody's property and my job is not to make somebody's babies. . . . But, I would take some aspects of Christianity into my concept of spirituality. But, no, I wouldn't say that I was Christian.

Despite the fact that "Indians never felt as though they could not incorporate indigenous traditions into Christian worship" (Ortiz 1999, p. 366), it is particularly interesting that the reclaimers I speak to often feel that they cannot simultaneously embrace their Nativeness while remaining Christian. Yet, they are well aware that non-reclaiming Natives often do just that. To me, this is possibly an authenticity issue and signifies a reclaimer's greater need to demarcate themselves from the mainstream and from their former, non-reclaiming selves (i.e., "I was a practicing Christian, but now I embrace Native spiritual practices"). For traditional, non-reclaiming Natives, their Nativeness is less often contested, if at all; therefore, they have the freedom to incorporate dominant group practices into their lives without it jeopardizing their sense of self. Reclaimer reluctance to embrace both traditions might also be, as previous quotes seem to attest, related to the fact that they see the imposition of Christianity on their ancestors as a direct assault on their cultural heritage, as the beginning of the distancing of their people from their Native heritage, and therefore their rejection of it is significant politically and symbolically.

For one male reclaimer, embracing his Cherokee heritage means embracing traditional, non-Christian conceptions of religion as well. He speculates that "95 percent of Cherokees are Christians and only about 5 percent are traditionalists." Ortiz concurs that today Natives are overwhelmingly Christian, although "Christianity has not eliminated various elements of Indian religions in Christian worship" (1999, p. 364). Native author and activist Vine Deloria Jr. speculates that "the Native American Church, famed for its use of the peyote button in its sacramental worship . . . has doubled its membership in the last few years. It appears to be the religion of the future among the Indian people. . . . Eventually it will replace Christianity among the Indian people" (1988, p. 113). For one of the reclaimers I spoke to, embracing the traditional Cherokee spiritual beliefs and practices is partially the result of his engagement with repatriation issues. As a law student, he specializes in federal Indian tribal law in order to effectively challenge in court institutions in possession of Native remains. In addition to his law school education, he also works with a mentor, a tribal elder well versed in the repatriation battles Native people have been involved in. He is told that he is one of the few young people training to enter this line of work, and he works hard to please the older generation, whom he describes as traditionalists in terms of religion. One of the ways he does this is through practicing traditional religion. He says, "I'll admit, I thrive on this attention 'cause all these guys realize that I'm a young dude who will carry on the religion. I'm scared to death that one of my kids won't want it." As he explains, "Some of them old guys [elder tribal members working on repatriation issues], I mean, they think, you know, religiously 100 percent of the day." Native author Gunn Allen affirms this point: "Traditionals live each day in the arms of the sacred, aware that whatever they do will have repercussions far beyond the merely psychological and personal, because everything is sacred or infused with Spirit and Mind" (1998, p. 45).

I ask this reclaimer what specific traditional practices he engages in, and he describes certain gendered rituals between himself and his wife, explaining that these are result of the fact that the Cherokees are a matriarchal tribe:

> A woman's power is seen more than a man's, especially during her time of the month. . . . In that time of the month, it's her power, so that, you know, her power and mine don't come into conflict [she sleeps in the other bedroom]. . . . Someday if we have children, I won't be in the birthing room with her. She understands why. You know, doing things like, she braids my hair every day and in my tribe, we're not allowed to braid our own hair. A guy with unbraided hair is seen as single and braided hair is married.

According to social scientists, this would be evidence that the Cherokees are matrilineal, not matriarchal, because it is more about lineage than true power.

He, however, uses the term *matriarchal* to describe the Cherokee. Additionally, he explains that there are dietary restrictions he follows: "I don't eat shrimp, any shrimp. . . . [T]he only type of seafood I can eat is fish and crawdads. I can't eat fried lobsters, oysters, clams." He gave up alcohol. When asked the rationale behind the dietary restrictions, he says he is unsure and feels it is inappropriate to ask why. He says that his mentor tells him that he will know such answers when he needs to know them, so he does not ask such questions anymore.

Others take a very different perspective on their Christianity and Native heritage, presenting them as compatible identities or, at least, unwilling to refer to them as incompatible identities. One young woman still seems to be struggling with this issue. She was raised Catholic and is still a practicing Catholic and describes her religion as important to her. She explains,

> I still consider myself Catholic, which is kind of an interesting thing, you know. Some Catholic people would say that, you know, whatever beliefs they have as far as Native spirituality would be wrong or whatever, I don't know. But, you know, it doesn't really matter to me. I think they mesh together perfectly well . . . . Some Native people are Christian, some are not Christian but still believe in God. Like, there's that belief in God but not Jesus Christ. . . . So, I would like to learn some more of like the Cherokee prayers and that sort of thing.

She then expresses what she sees as a tension between reclaiming her Cherokee heritage and her Catholicism:

> A lot of Native people do that every day [burn sage as a cleansing ritual]. Some Native people just do it, you know, when they need to re-center. . . . I do have a bundle of sage; I've never burned it. . . . I mean, I don't really practice that sort of thing. . . . [T]he thing is, like, the culture, I think the culture and the spirituality are so intertwined it's really hard to separate them, which is the whole "Christianize the Indians" idea of the missionaries; they wanted to take away their spiritual beliefs, but if you take away their spiritual beliefs, you're seriously harming that culture . . . because you can't separate the two . . . they're so intertwined with daily life.

Despite her exposure to some Native religious practices, practices she learned through a Cherokee woman that she regards as a mentor, such as the practice of "smudging, which is, uh, like burning sage and using the . . . it's kind of like a cleansing with the smoke and the sage. Some tribes use cedar and sweet grass and that sort of thing and . . . prayers," this reclaimer still does not incorporate these into her life. Her preceding quote exposes some tension surrounding such practices. She recognizes that "culture and spirituality are so intertwined," yet she is attempting to embrace Cherokee culture while remaining Catholic, and in the process finds herself unable to embrace certain Cherokee spiritual practices and rituals. She still seems to be struggling with how to balance this. Is this an identity issue for her, an inability to answer the question of what it means to be Cherokee? Are there certain rituals and practices that she must engage in to claim this identity? Is there anything she has to give up of her former self, particularly in regard to her Catholicism, to embrace her Cherokee self? Her current response is that these are congruent identities, but her own narrative exposes a tension with that, a recognition that the issue may not be resolved in her mind. She embraces both a Catholic identity and a Cherokee identity and does not see these as incongruent; however, there are certain Native religious practices, such as burning sage, that she does not participate in. The identity/practice tension is explicit in this reclaimer's narrative. Does engaging in such Native religious practices challenge her Catholic identity? She may very well remain a Catholic Cherokee, but as of yet that tension does not appear to be resolved.

Another female reclaimer I speak to considers her Christianity to be very important to her and when she began reclaiming her Native heritage she says she had to make sure that she was not involving her children in "something that would influence them in a negative way like that, that didn't have the beliefs, the Christian beliefs that I have . . . 'cause that's what is most important to me first. That had to be there or I wouldn't have done it. But, that was there." She elaborates, "When I got into this [Native community organization] my biggest concern was, I was being just like every other white person . . . thinking this has to be a Christian-based thing. . . . But there are still Indians today that practice, you know, non-Christian stuff." While she admits that some Indians are not Christian, the fact that the group to which she belongs is lead by a Christian minister alleviates her fears that it will result in a negative influence on her children. She made another comment later in the interview criticizing gaming from a specifically Christian perspective: "That's one of my other pet peeves as a Christian woman . . . the evil that it's [gambling is] bringing in, that's going to expose my children to, you know, to thinking that they're going to become millionaires by doing evil stuff. . . . [T]hat bothers me." She has a brother who is a Christian minister and is not interested in reclaiming his Native heritage, who warned her of a friend that quit his tribe because "they were doing sweat lodges and that's non-Christian."

Apparently for this woman, there are some Native rituals and practices that she feels are contradictory to her Christianity, but as long as her community cultural group avoids such practices, she is comfortable enough to interact with this group as she pursues her Native heritage. What was important to her, she explains, is "the culture itself. There may be things I may not believe in, maybe in different winged spirits or, um, I don't know . . . " This reclaimer, presumably to maintain her Christian identity, distinguishes between culture and religion, seeing them as separate and distinct where others describe them as intricately wed.

A young male reclaimer I spoke to initially declined to be interviewed by me because he does not think he fits the definition of a "reclaimer" since, as he explained to me, he "doesn't embrace Native American religion." I emphasized that embracing Native American religion is not a requirement, in my mind, for someone to be a Native reclaimer, although at the time I thought this is an interesting distinction *he* makes concerning the validity of reclaiming one's Nativeness. As a Catholic, he explains, "I don't really embrace like, as far as the Native American religion and all that goes . . . but I kind of incorporate a little bit of aspects of that plus what I was raised [with]." He provides an example of how he does this:

> I think that's interesting, especially with the peyote issue. . . . I don't necessarily subscribe to that line of thought in terms of spirituality and mysticism, but I think there might be something to it, to a certain extent. In keeping with the idea that religion is a very personal, spiritual thing. . . . Really the whole basis of Christianity is humility and thinking about others before you think about yourself. I think the Native American religion shares some of that.

As discussed, some reclaimers feel there is a serious incongruency between their Native heritage and their Christian heritage, so much so, in fact, that in order to reclaim, they feel it necessary to reject their Christian heritage. Yet for other reclaimers I speak to, the two traditions coalesce and work well together. This next reclaimer expresses an entirely different perspective. She is a Native reclaimer as well as a pagan, and what is interesting about her story is how she often she conflates the two identities. I ask a question concerning Native reclaiming and she answers with references to her paganism. In fact, she explains that while she knows of her Native heritage she has no desire to authenticate it through genealogy, explaining,

> I *know*, you know? I've grown up with the stories. I know that's just a part of the way I am and I've explored many different types of religions and practicings of faiths and things that I could relate to and this was, you know, getting back to nature and doing what I do now is the closest thing that I've come and I've just related with it and fit right in and it works for me.

Later she says, "I think I'm pretty much, I'm more into my heritage and, uh, um, religious background and all that stuff now, more than I've ever been." When I ask her if other family members reclaim their Native heritage, she answers in terms of religion rather than ethnicity, stating, "My husband doesn't really label himself at all. He has, I think he has a closed mind about religion . . . so, I can't really say that he is denying his ethnicity or anything like that." In all three of her comments, she appears to treat her racial/ethnic reclamation as synonymous with her paganism. When asked if there are any holidays she celebrates in a special way due her Native American reclamation, she answers,

> Um, midsummer is a big one . . . and it all has to do with the harvest and the, celebrating what you harvested . . . celebrating the fruits of your labor and just showing thanks to the spirits of whatever for the, you know, bounty. . . . Some of the other holidays that I celebrate aren't really Native American . . . some of them are, some of them aren't. Some of them kind of go with the Wiccan thing, you know? But, um, the midsummer tradition is real close to the way Native Americans did, and so is the fall festival that we do related to the harvest.

She also is in charge of a children's camp through their church and she finds this to be a "whole new way for me to connect with the Native American thing" because she is having a Navajo Indian come and teach drum making to the children. She explains, "He's going to come out for like an hour . . . to give a drumming class to kind of give a Native American background on drumming because we do a lot of Wiccan-style drumming out there and we welcome all different types of, you know, heritages. Drumming is a big part of dancing and rituals and stuff." There are certainly some overlaps between paganism and the Native conceptions of land and spirituality, but again, for this woman, there is almost complete overlap of these identities and practices.

Another reclaimer was also raised Christian but rejects this religious heritage. "I had been raised Baptist and I was baptized at a Christian church, you know, but it wasn't, I didn't feel connected. I always felt the need to rebel and run away from it. It wasn't something that I had chosen." She also receives the message from her extended family that Christianity is incongruent with Nativeness. She says, for instance, that her mother is very aware of her Native heritage, but that she "doesn't go around telling people that she claims [it]. It might offend her Christian friends, you know?"

And then, of course, there are those individuals who simply perceive their spirituality to be connected to their Nativeness. One woman I speak to explicitly connects her spirituality to her Native American heritage, despite the fact that her indigenous heritage was denied her as a child. For this woman, her spirituality translates into her understanding herself in terms of being Native American. She says,

> Grandma explained to me about my Native American background and how sometimes when a child tunes into more of a spiritual side like I had, then they

are more comfortable in the woods where the trees and flowers can talk to them. They're [the trees and the woods] more of a safe haven. I never approved of the buildings that people put up and go, "These are the churches, you've got to go." You know what? . . . Out there in the country is a church. God made it. I don't have to go to church to be in church.

Despite being raised Southern Baptist, this woman no longer embraces Christianity and expresses clear hostility toward certain aspects of organized religions. She feels that tuning into the energy of the earth is more spiritual than going to a traditional church,

because your preacher is too damn busy yelling at ya, telling you how wrong you are . . . see, I don't believe in the—I know there's probably a devil somewhere and you know, I don't deny the Bible, but I kinda look at Grandfather [God] in a very simplistic way. . . . When you got in trouble, did your father completely condemn you? And neither will he. As long as you do your best to walk a path that is right . . . you're gonna screw up, you're gonna make mistakes . . . but as long as you do your very best to stay within and know that he is there and that he loves you, he's not going to condemn you for anything. A father does not condemn his children.

Interestingly, Native author Ortiz (1999) points out that "the Crow term for 'religion,' 'alachiwakiia,' [translates to] 'one's own way'" (p. 11), exposing a similarity in the understanding of religion across tribes. Later I ask the female reclaimer if she considers herself to be a religious person. She replies, "Yeah, very much so. Um, I don't go to church, not in the formal sense of the word. Uh, my church is the woods. Uh, I find little spots here and there and I do my best to thank God for every day of my life. Life is very precious."

Another woman similarly points out the significance of gratitude as an aspect of her Native spirituality:

There are a lot of little things that you do during the day. Um, part of Native American spirituality is a thankfulness for being alive and, um, the first thing when you open your eyes in the morning, you're thankful for your breath and your life and the things that are coming your way during the day. We [she and her children] say Native blessings and sing Native lullabies at night.

Gunn Allen concurs:

That's why Indians believe that we must all do our daily work and make this life as good as we can. Holy People are more intelligently disposed toward those who meet their ordinary obligations with awareness of the extraordinary nature of mortal existence than toward those who choose to be careless and disrespectful in their daily lives, even if they meditate and pray mightily on occasion. (1998, p. 45)

As earlier quotes express, many reclaimers link their Nativeness and their spirituality to a oneness with nature. Again according to Gunn Allen, "It is reasonably certain that all Native American peoples view the land as holy— as intelligent, mystically powerful, and infused with supernatural vitality. . . . Mysticism among American Indian peoples is fundamentally based on a sense of propriety, an active respect for these Natural Powers" (1998, p. 41). According to one young man, "I don't know any of the dances, songs, or ritual kind of things. . . . So I guess [I practices my heritage by] just going camping for the weekend. . . . I guess in a way, I kind of tie everything together. . . . When I go camping, it can be a very spiritual thing . . . being outdoors, praying or whatever." When asked to elaborate on the connection between his Nativeness, spirituality, and nature, he says, "I guess it would be the idea of a oneness with nature sort of thing." For others, this extends to a holistic perspective on life:

> My understanding of the state of being Native American is that it's all pervasive. . . . It's similar to the whole concept of religion versus spirituality. Spirituality is all-encompassing and all-pervasive in your life; it affects everything. Native American religion doesn't exist, but Native American spirituality does because there are no compartmentalized segments in your existence.

There is also a perception that religion is an aspect of Native culture that whites are trying to appropriate. One reclaimer complains bitterly that "a lot of New Age fruits are taking stuff out of the books and bastardized [sic] it. I am, like, you know what? You've taken enough of that shit, leave the religion to us. That ain't for you." And another woman similarly expresses dissatisfaction with non-Native appropriation of Native religious traditions: "I think there's been a . . . movement in this country for the last twenty years of people trying to figure out their spirituality, and some people have latched onto Native spirituality." These criticisms are not exclusively from reclaimers, as many Natives express similar complaints. Native author Joseph Bruchac writes,

> I have seen continuing interest and involvement in sweats and other traditional Native "religious" practices among non-Natives. . . . Much of what I have seen and read of non-Native practices associated with "sweats" fills me with misgivings. . . . People need to realize that involvement in a sweat lodge, not to mention leading a sweat, is not something to be taken lightly. (1993, p. 6)

Another example of Native dissatisfaction with white appropriation of Native religious practices pertains to what is known of as "white shamanism," which refers to "non-Native individuals who . . . present themselves as actually Native or as authorized interpreters of indigenous thought and action" (Grim 1996, p. 367). As one reclaimer explains, "the sage burning, sweet grass burning and all of that, it's not a joke. . . . It brings the spirits closer to you and unless you know what you're doing, then you have no business messing with it. . . . If you don't know what you're doing or you haven't gotten the appropriate permission to do it, it can turn the tide on you pretty bad."

A critical interrogation of the current white, mainstream embrace of Native religious practices can be explained in terms of what Rosaldo refers to as "imperialist nostalgia," in which agents of colonialism "often display nostalgia for the colonized culture as it was 'traditionally'" when, in fact, what they are longing for is what they have intentionally altered and/or destroyed (1989, p. 69). He continues, "Nostalgia is a particularly appropriate emotion to invoke in attempting to establish one's innocence and at the same time talk about what one has destroyed" (1989, p. 70).

Apart from specific discussions of religion and/or spirituality, reclaimers also embrace what I would call, for lack of a better term, a belief in the mystical. Some describe a mystical experience as "the direct intuition or religious experience of God" (Underhill 1961; Grossman 1999). For philosopher and psychologist William James, "mystical states are more like states of feeling than like states of intellect" (James 1961, p. 371). Gunn Allen describes Native mysticism as follows:

> Mysticism among American Indian peoples is fundamentally based on a sense of propriety, an active respect for these Natural Powers; on a ritual comprehension of universal orderliness and balance; and on a belief that a person's every action, thought, relationship and feeling contributes to the greater good of the Universe or its suffering. Human beings are required to live in such a way that balance is maintained and furthered, and disorder (also perceived as disease) is kept within bounds. (1998, pp. 41–42)

Many reclaimers describe personal experiences, such as visions or dreams, which they perceive as profoundly influential in their lives, yet they hesitate to describe these and the significance they place on them to non-Natives. While the mainstream society tends not to validate such claims, it is clear that they are of great significance to the reclaimers I speak to. Gunn Allen also supports this comment:

> Some of the more bowdlerized accounts of American Indian mystical experiences treat them from a Western point of view, giving the impression that these states are uncommon, eerie, superlatively extraordinary, and characterized by abnormal states of unconsciousness. But tribal testaments indicate otherwise: paranormal events are accepted as part of normal experience—even expected under ritual circumstances. (1998, p. 44)

This embrace of the mystical might be thought of in terms of a broad definition of shamanism, which Harner defines as "reverence for, and spiritual communication with, the other beings of the Earth and with the Planet itself . . . . They are the last ones able to talk with all of Nature, including the plants, the streams, the air and the rocks" (1980, p. xiii). While reclaimers do not use the word *shaman* to describe themselves, they do recognize that talking to the animals and emphasizing dreams distances them from the cultural mainstream. As one woman explicitly states, these are not abilities exclusively Native; however, Native people have been taught to embrace this part of themselves rather than downplay it. For one of my interviewees, being able to embrace this part of himself leads to a "joyousness in knowing who you really are and that you're not really wacky! It doesn't make you psychotic if you talk to spirits!" Another explains,

> I mean, all Natives are more in tune with what's around them than anybody else I've ever known. I mean, they care more about animals. Truth of the matter is, you go to the zoo and you see all these locked-up animals . . . they're not animals anymore. They're displays. Very unhappy displays. Um, but if you walk in the woods and you see a wild thing and you stop dead in your tracks and just relax, you're going to find that it's not going to run because you're not a threat, and you may even get lucky enough to talk to it and get some of its energy that it has to give. The trees will talk; you just got to be quiet enough to listen. The earth talks; you just got to be willing to hear it. Right now she screams.

Many reclaimers speak of dreams influencing their decision to reconnect with their Native heritage. The reclaimer who is pursuing her graduate degree in counseling psychology and hopes to approach the discipline from a Native perspective explains that pursuing this dream is the result of the influence of her ancestors:

> It's kind of based on, um, some spiritual kind of beliefs that the ancestors have kind of come in and helped nudge it along. . . . When you're doing the right thing, you're life kind of fits into place and you find yourself like, as I am right now, um, in a perfect position.

I ask her how she knows it is her ancestors that have put her on this path, and she replies,

> I just always have known. I mean, it's just something I've always known. I mean, I've, some people, I guess refer to them as guardian angels maybe. Or they refer to them as, I don't know, guides of some sort or something. But . . . I always feel like I have my ancestors with me and I always have, I mean, from being a kid, and I don't know if that's genetic [laughs]. I mean, perhaps. . . . But,

it's always something that I've always . . . I always knew that I had folks watching out for me. And, um, and I think that, um, it started to just kind of click all together and it kinda started to make sense that it was my ancestors. . . . They come in at different times and help me with different problems, you know, and I think that that's all governed by a higher being, you know? . . . by the Creator . . . which is different than the Christian God . . .

Her narrative is replete with references to the influence of ancestors on her lived reality. She even speculates on the role her ancestors may have played in her mother's choice of husbands. Her mother was married to an Apache man prior to her marriage to her father, a member of the Lakota tribe. She finds this to be interesting simply due to logistics alone—there are so few Indian men in the area of the country where her mother grew up, she speculates that there may have been other forces at work influencing her marital choices. Her mother has some distant Delaware heritage, but this is not something her family embraced growing up, and therefore she knows very little about it. According to this reclaimer, the ancestors may have stepped in to make sure her mother met and married Native men, "and so, maybe there's something in her background—some ancestor in her background, you know, one of her Indian ancestors goes, 'Okay . . . it's not gonna end here. We're gonna take it one more level. We're gonna make sure your kids [have an Indian heritage].'"

Another reclaimer speaks similarly of receiving messages telling her that she is "on the right path," although she speaks of it in terms of God's influence rather than being nudged along by ancestors:

A lot of things are falling into place for me now. Um, which is how I know I am on the right path. Um, my visions and things, they stopped after a while because of the fact that I wasn't on the right path. God's not going to reward you for not doing the right thing. He rewards those who do the right thing. I know that I am on the right path because a lot of good things are starting to happen that I couldn't ever explain . . . there are warning signs. Everything is a warning sign. Uh, I wasn't living the right path and God decided to let me know about it . . .

She even directs this message at me explicitly, stating that she hopes I get more out of the interview with her and the project as a whole than simply a dissertation:

I don't talk about myself that much. But, I got a good vibe off ya. And I'm trusting you to do the right thing. . . . I hope you get more, and this may sound really funny, but I'm really hoping you get more than just a dissertation out of this. I'm hoping you're actually listening and absorbing and understanding. And I'm really hoping that your path will become easier because you choose to walk the right path. . . . I guess if I wanted you to learn anything out of this it's that the spiritual side of what the Native Americans are teaching has always been there, for everybody.

Beyond sharing her reclamation process with me, she provides many larger lessons concerning spirituality, the destructiveness of negative emotions such as anger, and the importance of energies that I consider relevant. For instance the following passages from her narrative stuck with me, due to their personal relevance as well as her spiritual intuitiveness:

You can't handle anything sacred if you're angry. Because, and the other thing that most people don't understand, is the sacred is inside. Yes, there are objects that are sacred, very sacred, I don't deny that. But, what makes them so sacred is how you feel inside. If you don't have that inner peace, then any object that is sacred that you pick up is going to pick up on that and its not, it's going to bring discord. Everything you do is not going to work. It's not going to be peaceful. . . . It's all part of an energy . . . there's energy all around you and it's up to you as to what energy you pick up on. You can either pick up on the neg- ative energy, which is common. I mean, everywhere you go there's negative en- ergy. Or you can pick up on what Mother Earth is trying to give you. . . . There are certain people that I will allow in my life and there are certain people that I will not if they send out a lot of negative energy, I don't want to be around that person. It's too stressful. Uh, pushes too much on you . . . and it's more of . . . if you leave a person and just feel totally wiped out, then that person was not good for you to be around. Because somewhere along the line they were just drawing on all of your energy without your permission or acknowledgment, or their body waves were just so fluctuated that it just got you completely stirred up and you were bouncing all the time, and while you may think that you're to- tally relaxed and you leave there and you're totally drained, something was wrong with that encounter. . . . They're [people's energies] a fascinating thing and they can do harm or they can do good.

Another reclaimer speaks similarly about "energy," only she refers to the energy of place more than the energy of people. She describes St. Louis, a city in which she had lived in for a short period of time, as having a

really negative energy. . . . There's certainly something with the two rivers con- verging in the place—in that place that I think really kind of brings that energy into there . . . geographically, I mean. And also, I mean, like, St. Louis is one area but then also is, uh, New Orleans. Actually, the Native people from around those areas did not settle in those areas for certain reasons. . . . [They settled] close but [not in those areas] . . . 'cause St. Louis is where the two rivers con- verge. . . . There's actually a lot of different energy coming into one place . . . makes it conflictual . . . and then also, it's being on all the caves and everything

else which doesn't give a solidity to the land. . . . Yeah, there's a lot of stuff with
St. Louis. . . . You know, if the Native people do not live there, it's probably not
a good place to move.

The reclaimer who mentions that "you're not really wacky" or "psychotic
if you talk to spirits" also emphasizes the significance of dreams when he describes his non-reclaiming brother: "He knows about being Creek, but his hair
is short and he lives in the white world and he's happy there. And I love him.
I respect him. . . . But I think in his dreams people talk to him in another language. I really believe that. . . . And I think the spirits that talk to me in the
waking life talk to him when he's asleep."

Others express their Native spirituality in terms of an emotive state. One
reclaimer says, "The Cherokee have a place called *tawodi*, a place of balance
where everything is as it should be. . . . In finding my own *tawodi*, it helps
me to feel comfortable with who I am." Another young female reclaimer, described earlier as a practicing Catholic who views her Native reclamation and
Catholicism as congruent identities, says this:

> I mean, in a way, it's kind of like, that's my center, like my calm sort of, I guess.
> . . . I also think that Native culture is . . . a lot about balance. I've listened a lot,
> especially since I am also majoring in Religious Studies, Native American reli-
> gion and spirituality really interest me, and uh, the Native spiritual belief in bal-
> ance and keeping everything in balance and that sort of thing. . . . So, it's a lot
> about balance, everything being circular. So, I think that affects my life a lot, I
> think about that a lot. You know, keeping everything in balance. So, there's that
> spirituality aspect of it that I kind of focus on.

A young male reclaimer makes a similar point when he describes what this
newly reclaimed heritage means to him: "For me, it's been more of a search
for inner peace, I guess. A satisfaction with what I am doing . . . like almost
as a religious aspect because whenever I look at Native Americans, they've
always had that kind of peace, that kind of being one with nature, an emphasis on harmony. . . . I guess that's what I try to identify with."

For another reclaimer, what can only be described as a mystical childhood
experience opened the door to her discovery of her Native heritage. She explains,

> When we were little, we'd take the ponies out and ride them. Of course we had
> to ride on the land . . . that mom and dad approved of. We found a way to get
> into the woods with the horses, and there was a clearing and the horses stopped
> dead. They would not go into the clearing at all. . . . None of us paid a lot of at-
> tention to it. . . . So, we went in and gathered up leaves . . . we gathered up leaves
> and we started jumping in the leaves, you know? And I looked up in the trees

and I saw faces in those trees. I got the hell out of that clearing so fast it'd make your head spin. That's when Grandma started talking to me some more. Evidently Grandpa had built her this circle [referring to the design of the clearing] uh, which is a prayer circle, a place where you go to do whatever, meditation, whatever, prayer whatever ceremony you want to do . . . and that's what we found ourselves in . . . and the faces I saw were evidently, um, spiritual. They were the spirits who watched over her prayer circle.

Since she had been so frightened by what she witnessed in the clearing, her grandmother feels compelled to tell her about their Native heritage ,which, she explains, is an incredibly bold thing to admit during that era, since "when she was growing up, any Indian blood in her and she could be arrested and have everything taken away from her and her whole life destroyed." Due to the discrimination of her grandmother's era, she says that her father never knew of his Native ancestry; however, she is granted access to this information simply because her grandmother shares it with her as a way to alleviate her fears.

Another mystical belief a reclaimer I interview associates with her Nativeness pertains to spirits. As she describes, "Native Americans will also put flaws in everything they make. If you spend a lot of time on something and you intend to give it away, do you not feel that a part of you is going with it? . . . So, you put a flaw in it to let that part come back. . . . You don't want part of yourself staying with an object."

The significance of dreams is another common theme among the reclaimers I speak to. One woman called me at home approximately a week after our interview to tell me about a dream that she says she had forgotten to mention during our interview. She explains that at one point, she had quit attending the community Native cultural organization meetings due to a conflict with another individual. She returns to the organization, which for her was a significant vehicle contributing to her reclamation, after she had had a dream that she interprets as encouraging her to reconnect with this aspect of her heritage. In the dream, she explains, she was in a small town, a town she has never actually been to but where her mother had lived as a child. She says she was surrounded by Indian relatives whom she seems to recognize in the dream, although she does not know them in reality. She says they keep saying to her, "Come and search your heritage." She then changes the story a little and says that they didn't actually say anything, but they are instead motioning for her to "come" with or toward them, and she interprets that to mean that that she should return to her pursuit of her Native heritage. She says that she woke up the next morning thinking, "This is it. [This is] God's way or the ancestors way. . . . [I've] gotta get back on the journey."

This story might sound questionable if it were not for the way she relates it. She is embarrassed and giggles as she relays it to me. It seems to me that she fears I will not believe her. And she even explains that she had decided to tell me about the dream, which again she had avoided during our interview, because she had recently been in several conversations with different Native people where the topic of dreams, the importance of dreams, as well as the idea of "genetic memory" came up, and this appears to validate her dream. She again emphasizes that the dream took her by surprise, since she does not usually dream much at all and because it is so vivid that it stuck with her. She says she remembers it all day and keeps asking herself, "Why would I be dreaming this?"

Another female reclaimer speaks a lot about the significance of dreams for her. She describes herself as intuitive because of the power of her dreams, explaining, "In a lot of them [dreams] I can generally direct people away from certain disasters. Or toward certain things. . . . Dreams are a weird thing. Um, you can interpret them, but it doesn't mean you are always interpreting them right. You have to be careful with interpreting dreams." Later she adds, "Dreams are tricky. You've got to know what you're seeing. . . . You always wait to see if it finishes or if it's all you're going to get. . . . Sometimes I'll look at someone I love very much and I'll get flashes, pictures. . . . I think I actually saw my brother's death before . . . [it happened] . . . and that terrified me."

Dreams, spirits, and communication with nature are all aspects of Nativeness that reclaimers embrace and proclaim are spiritual and/or religious in nature. For many, being in tune with the mystical, or spiritual, side of life is both a confirmation of their Native heritage and a way to embrace and practice this ethnicity, as well as being a significant departure from the mainstream. Vine Deloria Jr. explains, "Indian religion required a personal commitment to act. Holy men relied upon revelations experienced during fasting, sacrifices, and visions . . . mystery and reverence . . . surrounded rites and ceremonies, giving them the necessary *mysterium tremendum* by which they were able to influence social behavior" (1988, pp. 102–3).

FOOD AND LANGUAGE

Similar to white ethnics that Waters (1990) studies, food and language are cultural practices engaged in by reclaimers as an affirmation of their ethnic identity. Many reclaimers speak of either embracing their Nativeness through food or recognizing this heritage through the foods they ate in their homes as they were growing up. As Germov and Williams (1999) point out in *A Sociology of Food and Nutrition: The Social Appetite*,

While hunger is a biological drive, there is more to food and eating than the satisfaction of physiological needs. There are also "social drives" that affect how food is produced and consumed. Food is not only essential to survival; it is also one of the great pleasures of life and the focal point around which many social occasions and leisure events are organized. . . . A sociology of food and nutrition concentrates on the myriad sociocultural, political, economic, and philosophical factors that influence the foods we choose, when we eat, how we eat, and why we eat the way we do. (p. 2)

I ask all my interviewees to identify the ways their newly reclaimed racial/ethnic identity influences their daily life. One woman explicitly responds in terms of food, and in particular distinguishes between us along the lines of food implying, I believe, a broader division between us along cultural lines as well:

Well, I know that I tend to eat foods that are a little different from most . . . they're kind of odd. Like, how often do you eat hominy? . . . I've got white hominy that I use like mashed potatoes or rice. I've got whole hominy that I make things with. Um, do you ever use dried sweet corn, for instance? . . . Okay, it's stuff like, I grew up with that. Well, it wasn't until I got to college that I realized, "This is weird." . . . It wasn't until later that I found out, oh, that's Indian food. Um, my mother doesn't acknowledge that either, but she cooks it.

This woman was raised in the middle-class suburbs of a major metropolitan area. She was not raised with any explicit recognition of her Native heritage and even says that her mother still denies their Indian ancestry, despite her reclamation of that heritage. However, despite the fact that her heritage is not overt in her household growing up, she feels that their dietary habits betray their Native ancestry, even as her mother, the one who makes these foods, denies it. Significantly, it is not until this reclaimer goes to college and begins to eat outside of her parents' home that she recognizes how she differs from others along the lines of food consumption. Waters comments, "Often . . . the ethnic foods eaten at home when people were growing up were not seen anywhere else" (1990, p. 120).

A male reclaimer also looks to food as evidence of what was Indian in his household growing up:

Mostly just some of the mannerisms. The way the family interacted. Some of the things they [his family] ate. . . . Some may consider it more of a country style . . . more of a simple way of eating like, oh, corn bread and macaroni and tomatoes and doing things differently than other people might do. . . . Another thing she [his grandmother] did and that Cherokees did a lot was that she'd have fruit trees all over her yard and that's something that the Cherokees were very proud of, their fruit trees, and they would often have a large collection of them . . . just the different way. . . . They probably ate a lot of beans and, like I said, corn bread and fixed things in a different way.

Matson explains, "When historians and archeologists write about Native American food, they often refer to corn, squash, and beans. These three foods were the basis of North and South American Indian diets" (1994, p. 3). He continues, "The main crops of the Osage [a tribe indigenous to Missouri] were corn, squash, and beans. . . . Hominy was made by removing the corn kernel and soaking it in lye made from wood ashes. It was then boiled or dried" (1994, p. 6). Matson's cultural history of food mirrors some of what my reclaimers relate to me in terms of the dietary influence of their Native cultural heritages.

Another reclaimer explains that one does not talk about Cherokee culture; it is instead something that is lived. I ask her to provide me with some examples of the lived Cherokee culture and she turns toward food for her response:

One of the things that, you know how everybody has a "grandma's house smells like . . . ?" My grandmother's house smelled like sassafras and grape dumplings. . . . Grape dumplings are wonderful! Basically, [they are] just dumplings that are boiled in grape juice. So the house smells all grapey. And the sassafras, it's a smell that's just . . . [unexplainable]. So, I make a lot of sassafras. It's kind of interesting because all of my, I have three children and their friends come over and nobody's every heard of sassafras [tea], but they love it and they just drink it by the bucket.

She then jokingly adds that her grandfather says that the only thing worth fighting over is "your family or your food."

While food is certainly one arena where culture is enacted by reclaimers, language is another significant one. Alba points out the significance of language to culture:

Arguably one of the most important aspects of culture has to be language. As with much indigenous culture, languages are rapidly disappearing. . . . [L]anguage represents a major repository of ethnic culture. Culture is embedded in language, thus knowledge of large portions of an ethnic culture is lost to those who do not know the mother tongue. (1990, p. 10)

"Native American culture is multifaceted, with between 250 and 400 language groups among those indigenous to North America" (Ortiz 1999, p. 363). Sociologists have long recognized the importance of language to culture. As O'Brien and Kollock articulate, "Language is a system of symbols that allows humans to communicate and share abstract meaning. Language gives humans the capacity to become social creatures—which is to say, the capacity to comprehend and to participate in culture" (2001, p. 69). As Robert Moore adds, "Language not only *expresses* ideas and concepts but actually *shapes* thought" (2001, p. 171).

Many reclaimers I speak to are of Cherokee heritage, and they often speak of how difficult it is to learn Cherokee. As one woman says, "I know some, but it's real hard. The Cherokee language looks like Yiddish. There's no letter similarity there. It's really interesting. . . . I know a number of songs in the language and I know simple . . . phrases, that type of thing. . . . I can't do the Cherokee syllabary." Many people I speak to express a desire to learn the language but, not surprisingly, find time constraints to actually pursuing it. A reclaimer who says this explains that she wants to learn the Cherokee language and hopes her children will learn it as well, but "I've got books on it and everything for us to do it. It's just [that] right now it's just an extremely busy point in my life." She also feels frustrated with pursuing the language because of the lack of any practical application of it:

If they're [the Native cultural organization she belongs to] going to be able to teach you [the] Cherokee language, you gotta be able to talk it to each other. And most people, even on the reservations, I think, speak English. . . . Well, how could you possibly remember how to speak that unless you use it all the time? You know? I learned Spanish once in school but that doesn't mean I remember any of it 'cause I don't use it. And it's great to learn some of that stuff but unless you're sitting around talking to each other in it it's just not of much use.

There is a tension evident between this reclaimer's two comments. She is not really sure what good it does to teach the language since the lack of practical application of it is problematic, yet she has purchased books and other learning tools so that she and her children can learn the language, which seems to be an acknowledgment that she considers the language a significant aspect of culture to learn.

The individual who teaches the language lessons at the Native cultural meetings is also a reclaimer. He describes the efforts he must take to learn the language: "We don't have anybody left that knows the Cherokee dialect so it's kind of like teaching yourself. So, you get the tapes and get the books. . . . It's very hard." He goes on to explain the difficulties:

It's so alien to English. . . . It's got a syllabary instead of an alphabet. That's right. It's phonetics so what you're saying is the syllables instead of, you know—the English language you . . . don't even pronounce it according to the alphabet in the first place. So, this is more of a speaking phonetics instead of a different word. But, that's really hard because you can't just read it because if it has a different emphasis on a certain syllable it could have a totally different meaning. Like, "um-ah" is salt and water! . . . I'm about 38 years old so I've got a tremendous block now [to learning a new language].

He also adds that there is no one to speak the language to, other than other members of the cultural group, which makes it difficult to learn as well.

A male reclaimer who works as editor of a Native nation newspaper explains that they are working on revitalizing their tribal language by having a special feature each month in the newspaper:

The latest edition of the newspaper, the uh, the language corner, was a, uh, a short, uncomplicated crossword puzzle with the answers to the clues being in the [tribal] language. There is a revitalization effort that's a formal part of our tribal government that we have grants from the federal government to help with that, so there is an effort for people of all ages within the . . . nation to relearn or for those older people—we do have a few [Native] speakers—to teach what they know to younger tribal members. It's—we believe that you not only keep the language alive but a lot of the culture is transmitted within the language. . . . So, if you don't keep the language alive, you're in danger of losing cultural traditions.

A female college student reclaimer that I interview also discusses her efforts at learning the Cherokee language. She also confirms, "It's very difficult. Very difficult. . . . My problem is I have not devoted the time to it that I need to devote to it. You know, college gets in the way [laughs]." She is already bilingual, speaking both Spanish and, of course, English:

As far as [learning] Cherokee, I just started about a year and a half ago and I haven't gotten very far because it is so very hard. . . . I have a computer program and then I also have a tape . . . but it's got sound on it, the computer program does. But, I also borrowed from Mona, who's the Cherokee lady at the Department of Indian Education that I knew in high school, I borrowed her set of tapes and her books. . . . I haven't gotten very far because you've got to learn a whole new alphabet first. You know, with Spanish, you're working with the same alphabet, the same basic sounds . . . Cherokee, totally different! . . . Especially if I want to learn like, Cherokee *Cherokee*, the actual symbols or . . . anymore a lot of people just use the phonetic spelling. . . . So, you don't have to learn the characters anymore but I'd still like to and that's where the program I have starts, is with those characters. I also have a Cherokee-English dictionary that the, uh, Cherokee Nation of Oklahoma publishes. It's got quite a few words in there. . . . It's been pretty fun!

She goes on to explain that a woman she met at a conference and maintains contact with is a fluent speaker of Cherokee, which is an asset to her learning the language. I comment that that must be pretty rare. She responds,

Um, Cherokees probably have more [Native speakers] than most. Um, some of the tribes right now are really pushing their language tapes and getting their language recorded on tape and pushing it to their tribal members to try and preserve the language because the last of the elders that know the language are dying. Um, and also, a lot of those languages aren't written languages, really. Um . . . you know, so at least with Cherokee, it is written and it is, you know around. Then there are a lot, there are a lot of publications with Cherokee language and the Cherokee Nation really tries, like with their Cherokee-English dictionary. . . . So, learning Cherokee is a goal of mine . . .

She explains further that in order to really learn the language, she must be able to speak it, and her friend who is fluent in Cherokee is a long-distance phone call away, which she cannot afford to make on a regular basis:

It's hard to carry on a conversation with yourself . . . so, I'm kind of hoping maybe, you know, if I look at interning or working at the *Cherokee Advocate* for a while, you know, maybe try and get a basic understanding of the language, and then maybe find some speakers there who could help me and kind of get immersed in that culture and language . . . it's pretty complicated. It is kind of an overwhelming task at first.

Waters views the white ethnics she speaks to as, especially in terms of language, exemplifying Gans's notion of symbolic ethnicity because for many, "Once the link with parents or grandparents was broken, respondents had no easy way or little desire to maintain the language in their present situation" (1990, p. 117). This is different for the Native American reclaimers I speak to. They all describe the difficulty involved in embracing their ancestral language, yet most put some effort into doing so, despite the fact that there are some significant constraints to speaking it. This is one way I see Native racial/ethnic reclamation as distinct from the symbolic ethnicity of white ethnics. Waters writes, "The foreign language their immigrant ancestors once spoke survives as bits and pieces, words and phrases that are now cherished because they evoke memories of family" (1990, p. 118). Unlike the white ethnics she is speaking of, Native reclaimers seek to keep their language alive in the face of cultural genocide, rather than merely as a cherished family memory.

The loss of the tribal language is recognized by reclaimers to be a significant blow to cultural perseverance. For many Native reclaimers I speak to, learning their Native language is a desired goal. For the most part they do not pursue this language acquisition in order to put it into daily practice but instead, their objective appears to be more connected to maintaining their tribal heritage. For many, the fact that whites intentionally attempted cultural genocide on Native peoples through BIA boarding schools and their English language requirements is reason enough for them to look to reviving their tribal language.

Nagel writes:

> Research suggests that at the time of European contact, somewhere between 250 and 1,000 languages were spoken by the several million indigenous inhabitants of North America. By 1990 fewer than one third of American Indians spoke a non-English language, and fewer than 3 percent spoke no English at all. This massive linguistic shift toward English language usage resulted mainly from federal Indian education policies. Until the 1960s, in both reservation and off-reservation schools for American Indians, the emphasis was on acculturation and the acquisition of English. . . . The often coercive and zealous imposition of Euro-American culture and English language usage on American Indian students contributed to the decline of Indian languages reflected in the 1980 census. (1997, pp. 115–16)

According to one reclaimer:

> Well, as far as, like, my family, you know, the fact that that's [boarding schools] where a lot of the culture was lost. You know, since the tribes weren't allowed to speak their language, um, you know, a lot of the language was lost. Religious practices, you know, of the tribes, I think a lot of times were lost to boarding schools. Anything that was an Indian act wasn't allowed. So, I think depending upon how long an individual spent in boarding school, if you're not practicing your language, using your language, or practicing your religious customs, then you could forget them easily. . . . So, I think that's where a lot of the culture in my family was lost. . . . I think that's where some of it started to die out.

Tribal languages often inspire childhood memories; certain words, phrases, or lullabies are expressed in their tribal language, yet often are unacknowledged as such. Waters's white ethnics share such experiences: "The experience of most of my sample with their ancestral language consisted of remembering their grandparents speaking it or remembering certain phrases or words that they had been taught as children" (1990, p. 116). According to one woman from my sample of reclaimers, "There were songs [in her home growing up] that weren't in our language, you know, weren't in English, [such as] the lullabies and the things that we sang every night. You know . . . I never knew what language they were until I researched it as an adult [and found that they were in Cherokee]." At the monthly community Native cultural organization meetings I attend, often a language lesson is provided. Simple words and/or phrases are taught, with meaning and proper enunciation emphasized. One reclaimer I speak to attends these meetings, and for her, these language lessons trigger memories of her grandfather and great-uncle speaking in Cherokee. As she says, "I can remember a little of it. And in learning sometimes I hear a word or two where I go, 'Oh yeah, I know what that is.' So, most of it is memory—and some of it is just relearning it."

An Osage reclaimer explains that learning the language of his tribe is important to him because "there's only like ten people—twelve people that speak it really good." As an undergraduate student, he attempts to get university funds to go to Oklahoma and tape-record the language spoken by the remaining speakers. Despite his ambition, the university does not fund his project, but for him it is about expediency. "This isn't something that has much time . . . [it] needs to be done." He later meets an Osage man who informs him that someone has recently done that very project. He is able to connect to the tribal home page and get three volumes of language tapes, explaining, "They're not very long, but they kinda teach you the basics, and anybody who's taken a foreign language, you know, can put things together." He studied German in high school and traveled to Germany so, while not describing himself as fluent, he feels his exposure to a second language helps him learn the Osage language.

Later he explains that there is more at work than personal significance for him to learn the language; it is about keeping the culture alive through practicing the language. Another Osage woman confirms this need: "In our tribe, there are less than twenty Native speakers out of approximately 15,000 adult members. . . . I think it [losing their tribal language] has a lot to do with losing the cultural identity." This reclaimer feels it essential that he and his wife teach their indigenous languages to their daughter. "Like, I'd like for her to not speak a foreign language whatsoever besides English and speak three languages. . . . If she can learn Navajo and Osage, that would be great." He then makes an interesting point. I ask if his wife speaks Navajo, which I assume since she is from the reservation, but he explains that she only speaks a little of the language: "She was too little . . . She understands it real well. She speaks a few words . . . if somebody's talking to her. She can listen and, you know, and respond in English but she couldn't talk back to 'em in Navajo." Native language reclamation, then, is something reclaimers are engaged in, but it is certainly not exclusive to them since so many reservation Indians also speak English as their primary language. He also discusses the broader significance of language to culture:

> Like, my tribe, and a lot of tribes, are dealing with the loss of their language, which is a big cultural thing, actually, I mean, it's like—why I do some of the things I do. It's like, not what makes us Native, but it's what makes us different, I guess. Um, but it's like, if we didn't have our language, if we didn't have our songs, if we didn't have certain things . . . then what would make us different? . . . It's all about your culture.

Native novelist David Treuer illustrates this point poignantly through the words of his main character, Little:

> Still, now, there are words we no longer use, phrases that used to anchor us to our trees and our river that we don't speak anymore. . . . We, Duke, Ellis and me, we were all cut away from our parents, but we were cut away from our words, too. Though we were never boarding-schooled, never mission-educated, we were cut adrift and unmoored from our words, those beautiful, sweet, tricky and twisted words. (1995, p. 59)

Similar to the way spirituality is linked to nature, Treuer emphasizes a link between language and nature and also makes an interesting parallel between being cut off from one's family and being cut off from one's language. In this work, I separate out reclaimer practices of religion/spirituality, language, and food as distinct topics for analytical purposes; however, I want to avoid providing a false portrayal. As many reclaimer quotes throughout this text indicate, aspects of culture are intricately interconnected and cannot be neatly separated.

Another reclaimer explains that his mentor threatens him that he better speak Cherokee when they visit the reservation in Oklahoma: "If you want a drink of water, you better ask for it in Cherokee! . . . You know [he] hollers at me if I don't speak it anymore, but it's kind of tough when I don't have no one to speak it to."

One of my interviewees, a single father of two children, describes a more subtle approach to providing their Native heritage to his children:

> I don't teach culture [explicitly]. I have language tapes laying around the house. I don't speak the language fluently . . . it is Muskogee-Creek. I never say, "You need to learn this. Just because I don't speak it doesn't mean you don't need to." . . . Any question they ask, I'll direct them to it. But, I'm not going to say, you're a Creek kid, you're going to learn this . . . they're going to resent that.

His approach extends beyond language to other life lessons. He explains,

> Every parent wishes for their child to maintain the same set of values. I try to consciously allow freedom there. . . . If they're doing something that I think is culturally wrong, for instance, what I'll do is say something like, "Well, that's not really the way our people perceive that." If they ask me how our people would perceive that, then I'll tell them. If they don't want to hear it, then there's another time for that lesson and they'll ask me sometime. So, I try to teach them the same way my grandfather and grandmother taught me, which is through quiet emulation. . . . When they get stressed out I tell them, do the same thing I do. Go get my medicine bowl, there's some sage in my medicine bag, set it in

your room, burn some sage, pray, and then go to sleep. You'll be fine. And they do that. . . . You teach through lessons, you don't teach by answering questions.

Another Osage reclaimer that I interview speaks of returning every summer to the reservation that his mother grew up on for ceremonies. Every June, there is a big celebration involving drums and songs as a way "to celebrate being Osage and the honor of families. . . . My family has the oldest song, one of the first songs." One of his ancestors wrote the song and it has been in his family for over 100 years. He proudly explains his role in this tradition: "Every year [the] last weekend in June they honor it. And so, like, I get up and I lead. . . . It is an honor to lead first . . . it's all in Osage. . . . It's our responsibility to take care of that song." He explains that his mother "made sure that we took care of it [the family song]. It's important to her and it's been important to me since, you know, I can remember." He says that when he gets married and has children he wants to still go back to the reservation for these ceremonies because "it's just part of who [I am]. . . . I would like to tell them [his future children] who they are and give them a sense of history there, a sense of roots." He later explains, "Our culture is so old. I mean old, and it's losing it fast, I mean, you know, there's like maybe thirty people who speak the language now and a lot of our elders are dying and a lot of our history is dying with [them]." This comment is particularly interesting because there is some sense that cultures are static—that you can lose essential aspects of culture. Yet, at other times, he acknowledges the need for cultural change:

You know, you got to remember who you are and where you came from. I think if you keep that in your memory and in your being, you'll evolve into whatever comes next. Because we all have to evolve. The Osage have to evolve and there will have to be people that will lead the way and if you're Osage and you're grown up, you have a responsibility I think to keep the memories and the tradition alive, but yet, you have to move forward . . . there has to be, uh, assimilation of some kind.

A woman I speak to who is not a reclaimer but instead someone who grew up on the Osage reservation in Oklahoma makes the following comment concerning what Osage elders consider to be their indigenous knowledge:

The one thing the Osages seem to hold on to, they were originally in Missouri, right? [Their] aboriginal land was Missouri, a little bit of Arkansas, Eastern Oklahoma, and the Southern part of Kansas, southeastern Kansas. They were removed from Missouri to a strip at the bottom of Kansas, that was a reservation. Then they were moved to the Osage reservation in Oklahoma. So, most of their history, most of what they concentrate on, is just since they were moved to Oklahoma. In fact, they won't even talk about some of the real old ways, about back in the aboriginal land in Missouri. So, most of what they consider to be their cultural identity is just since they were moved to Oklahoma, which is the very late 1800s, early 1900s. So, they're missing a huge chunk of their culture and heritage. . . . But, what I'm be-ginning to understand is that we have these cultural—this is kind of controversial for me to say this—we have cultural leaders and political leaders. These cultural leaders, if you go and ask them specifically about things in the culture, like "Why do we wear this wedding dress like this?" . . . You know, specific questions, and they don't know. I can understand not knowing specifics, but they're very defen-sive about it. I think it's not that they're guarding information; I think it's that they don't know. . . . I think it's lost and they don't want to admit that, particularly to the younger generation. . . . They absolutely don't know the history.

In this rather detailed reflection, this Osage woman is cognizant of cultural change, noting that the ways the Osage lived and performed their ethnicity while they were in Missouri may have been significantly different from the con-ceptions of "tradition" found in the tribe today. This quote also emphasizes the changing nature of culture, while people too often insist on static portrayals. Simply speaking of "traditional" ways does this; it freezes culture as opposed to recognizing cultural fluidity.

Culture is generally taken for granted and rarely acknowledged. For the re-claimers I speak to, Native reclamation requires that they approach their newly embraced culture with a certain deliberateness. Learning one's tribal language is a commitment to culture that is not seen among white ethnics in past sociologi-cal research (e.g., Alba 1990; Gans 1979; Waters 1990). As Lindsey and Beach argue, "Most people consider language the marker of a distinct culture and iden-tity. . . . If language is a key cultural marker, then learning the language means learning the culture" (2002, p. 65). Yet, there is an obvious tension between wanting to preserve tribal languages as significant aspects of culture and the dif-ficulties involved in learning and using these indigenous languages. The fact that reclaimers intend to learn Native languages is especially significant in light of the fact that even most reservation Indians today speak English. Additionally, the role of food is significant since "food is used to build and maintain relationships in all culture. . . . The consumption of food is a social occasion, there is no cul-ture that promotes solitary eating" (Germov and Williams 1999, p. 151). Beyond language and food, alternative definitions of family are also emphasized and em-braced by reclaimers as distinctly Indian practices.

FAMILY

In addition to religion/spirituality, food, and language, for many interviewees, their sense of Nativeness is expressed in and through their family arrangements as well as their attitudes toward family (both ancestral as well as current family members). One man simply says, "Heritage and family is of absolute importance to Native Americans. Absolute importance. Because you've got to know who you come from to know who you are." Another male reclaimer similarly explains the importance of his Native heritage: "It's the most important thing in my life. It's like—my family, my belief, my religion . . ." Still another says, "In the Cherokee, the old ways, family was everything . . . and to take these children from their families [a practice the boarding schools engaged in] was like the ultimate in desecrating them as a people . . . . Everything you did in life revolved around family. So, to be ripped apart from that is horrendous." Ortiz points out that, despite the great cultural diversity between North American indigenous tribes, "they share some basic universal values—including love and concern for family, community, and their environment—that existed among the Native Americans long before the arrival of Christianity" (1999, p. 363).

While family is described as being of the utmost importance for Natives and Native reclaimers, there is some uneasiness surrounding such a claim. A disproportionate number of my interviewees describe being raised in alternative families for a significant portion of their lives. I use the term *alternative* with some hesitation, hoping to avoid ethnocentric implications. I instead want to emphasize an alternative to the mainstream understanding of families in terms of "nuclear families, consisting of wife, husband, and their dependent children who live apart from other relatives in their own residence" (Lindsey and Beach 2002, p. 379). For the reclaimers I speak to, *family* often has a broader meaning than the mainstream sense of the term. Mary Crow Dog explains that the extended family group is the center of old Sioux society, and that "our people have always been known for their strong family ties, for people within one family group caring for each other, for the 'helpless ones,' the old folks and especially the children, the coming generation" (1990, p. 12).

In several cases, reclaimers or their parents are raised by their grandparents and this family arrangement is something they attribute to their Native heritage. As Bahr explains, they are not mistaken with that assumption: "The expectation that grandparents will play a major role in the physical care and training of their grandchildren is common among most Indian people. In fact, it is one of the notable similarities among the wide diversity of tribes" (2001, p. 503). Bahr looks to cultural patterns for a partial explanation for this pattern: "For some of these women, the memory of having been raised by a grandmother translates into the expectation that they themselves need not be a truly 'responsible' parent until they reach the grandmother stage. At that point, however, they recognize that the responsibility to be 'parent of last resort' is now theirs" (2001, p. 506). Crow Dog also confirms this role of the grandparents to grandchildren: "Grandparents in our tribe always held a special place in caring for the little ones, because they had more time to devote to them" (1990, p. 13).

My interviewees recognize that in many cases, their family arrangements are alternative to that of the mainstream, nuclear-family form. They describe these alternative family patterns in a variety of ways. One explains, "I grew up as a child with my grandparents. . . . Um, um, my parents were alcoholic and abusive and it just worked out better for me to live with my grandparents and so I did." Another female reclaimer I speak to was put in the position of raising her younger siblings, due to her parents "fleeing [their] parental [obligations]." She explains, "Some of the abusive behaviors . . . are kind of passed down in families. I kind of understand where some of that came from now. My grandfather was very abusive and my dad was very abusive with children. . . . I think the Irish-Indian home was a really violent place." Due to such circumstances, she took on the responsibility of raising her two younger siblings.

Another interviewee describes recognizing this deviation from mainstream cultural norms of family in her own family:

> And families are split up quite a bit. So, usually like, I mean, it's not entirely uncommon for two kids out of the same family to have grown up completely separately but yet still be brother and sister. . . . Sometimes, you know, I mean like you just have too many kids and your sister doesn't have as many so she . . . raises one or two of yours. And you know, it's, it's so much more, it's, it's the family unit . . . doesn't necessarily have to be mother, father, children and then that's it. It's sister, brother, cousin, uncle, aunt, grandmother, grandchild, and just, you know, kinda all mixed up. . . . People just take care of each other and that, that's the most important thing. And sometimes you'll have uncles and aunties that aren't, um, that aren't blood, you know? I mean, they, but they are just as important and they are just as strong a part of the family as, as the other person would be. . . . We had family friends that I always knew as uncles and aunts. . . . The only thing that kinda came off as shocking is like, the whole thing of people kind of giving their kids to like their sisters or brothers or whatever. Not giving as if they're possessions but . . . you know, having somebody else raise their children. Um, you know, 'cause in this society, in American society, mainstream society, that would be seen as bad parenting. Um, but actually it's very good parenting to know what your limits are and to say, "You know what? I need some help. And can you please take care of, you know, my three children for a while?"

In this quote, the reclaimer acknowledges a number of things. First, her encounters with her Native relatives on the reservation show that family arrangements are quite different from those of the white, mainstream culture. In this quote alone she acknowledges a number of alternative family arrangements. Second, she acknowledges that this difference, while most likely interpreted negatively ("that would be seen as bad parenting"), is probably beneficial ("to know what your limits are"). Finally, I think it is significant that, despite being raised in the white world but with "Indian ways," she admits to being shocked at the thought of people "giving their kids to like their sisters or brothers or whatever."

This pattern is not generally viewed favorably by members of the dominant culture. As Fuchs Ebaugh points out,

> Almost as stigmatized as transsexuals are the mothers who have given up custody of their children. Our society views these individuals as "weirdos" who are "totally irresponsible," "depraved and immoral," or "crazy." Undoubtedly the most difficult experiences that mothers without custody have to face are the negative social reactions. (2001, p. 334)

She continues,

> The term "mother without custody" has become a label in our society indicating irresponsibility, hard-heartedness, selfishness, and a lack of maternal instincts. The general stereotype of a mother without custody seems to be someone who doesn't care about her children and puts herself before them. (2001, p. 336)

Within some of the reclaimers' quotes, another theme concerning Native families became evident: that of trauma. It is surprising to find the amount of violence, poverty, and family stressors in my small sample of reclaimers. While the reclaimers speak of family resiliency, such as the earlier woman who describes the Native practice of giving away some children due to poverty or some other family stressors that make one unable to adequately care for them, one cannot help but recognize the extreme pressure Native families must currently face, and historically have faced, in order to resort to such practices. These desperate practices are the result of living under oppressive and exploitative conditions. Taylor argues that "social and economic segregation and exclusion from full participation in American life required racially defined minority groups to forge a variety of adaptive strategies to survive and surmount the hardships imposed by the larger society, and these adaptive strategies have produced historical variations in the family life of these groups" (2002, p. 8).

Families bear the brunt of a racist society, and reclaimers provide evidence of this in their narratives. For instance, as many reclaimers emphasize throughout the text, Native Americans face extreme poverty. In order to thrive and provide for one's family, leaving the reservation is often the only choice. And, as reclaimers also emphasize, abandoning culture for material survival is a choice that contains numerous hidden costs. In addition to economic in-security and the stress that places on families, Native Americans, similarly to Black Americans, have faced systematic attempts by the government to de-stroy their family structure. In the case of Native peoples, it took the form of taking children away from their families and placing them in boarding schools to be stripped of their culture. Such practices interfere with a family's ability to function effectively.

In addition to such alternative family forms, many reclaimers, as previous quotes emphasize, recognize non-blood kin as family. One man speaks of why he enjoys attending pow-wows:

> It's friends and family. I mean, there's—there's an extended family. It's like, there's a Ponca man in Kansas City that I kinda consider, um, an elder to me. And like, we're always taught to respect our elders and stuff like that, but I'm kinda different than some people. . . . If they're not in my tribe, then I don't re-ally consider them my elders. I mean, they might be old and I do pay them, pay them, you know, respect . . . like, he's Ponca and since we're related [the Ponca and the Osage are related tribes], I treat him, you know, with respect and like family. He comes over for meals. I go up and work on his truck when it breaks down and stuff. And like ["Chris," another reclaimer], he, without a doubt, is like a brother, both of us to each other.

Pow-wows are cultural events that provide a climate for cultural enactment through ceremony, food, and interaction among families. "Native American families still gather for pow-wows, where traditional dishes made from acorns as well as 'Indian tacos' are enjoyed by an open fire" (Germov and Williams 1999, p. 153). One reclaimer explains her enjoyment of attending pow-wows as follows: "[I go] almost every weekend. At least every other weekend. And you learn a lot from—I like—whenever I go to a pow-wow, I always find the old people and I just visit."

After the first annual campus pow-wow that several reclaimers I interview helped organize, a member of the Native American student organization makes a point at their next meeting of saying that, despite the low turnout for the event, hosting the pow-wow succeeded at showing "Native Americans as families, as extended families, working together, celebrating together, [and] living their culture." Three years later when I interview one reclaimer who helped organize the first campus pow-wow, and several subsequent ones, he provides a story linking the importance pow-wows and family: "She [his mother] always goes to pow-wows with us. She's become one of those old ladies that if I go to a pow-wow, I call it 'makin' the rounds,' I gotta go see all the old people that I know and say 'hi' and everything, and my mom is one of those ladies that just sits there and makes everyone come to her." Pow-wows are not simply cultural events but arenas where Native families are celebrated and embraced.

Another reclaimer similarly recounts how non-blood-related individuals are perceived as family: "He's actually my father's cousin. Um, but we don't have, we don't even have a word in Cherokee for cousin. If they're older than us, they're uncles. If they're our age, they're brothers and sisters. You know, and so, you know, I just call him my Uncle Dick and he calls me his nephew." The following quote supports this comment:

> Another potential problem arises from cultural conceptions of family relationships that differ in meaning from those intended by the Census Bureau. For example, an Indian "grandmother" may actually be a child's aunt or grand-aunt in the Anglo-Saxon use of the term. . . . [T]he term "cousin" also may have a variable meaning, not necessarily based on birth or marriage. (Taylor 2002, p. 228)

One woman describes her favorite Cherokee ceremony, a "Making of Relations" ceremony, in the following way: "Well, white people call it 'blood brothers'—it's the ceremony for making a sibling." The dominant culture has no comparable practice. Instead, family is defined along blood lines, with the exception of adoption. Later, this female reclaimer explains that she views the community of reclaimers and Natives that she interacts with as one of the greatest advantages to reclaiming her Cherokee heritage:

> That community is so much of a family. It's a wonderful group. . . . You know, you meet one person and that connects you with this group and that connects you with that group. There's the . . . Cherokee woman who is our spiritual leader here. She comes and leads our [sweat] lodges and she and I are sisters, you know, adopted.

For many reclaimers, their Nativeness is enacted through their family interactions. One explains to me, "Even if you're removed from the reservation . . . if your family is no longer on the reservation, you still have a parent or parents that have Indian ways and that's how you were raised . . . that's how you learn to associate with people . . . you learn familial patterns from that." She continues, "We grew up urban, but we were raised the Indian way in the respect of the way I treat elders. The way I treat my family. The way we treat human beings. The way we treat the earth." When asked what aspects of her Lakota heritage were most salient in her home growing up, she says,

> Treatment of elders. Respect. We never talked back. I mean, I guess that would be very similar if you had a very strict upbringing. But, the respect for authority figures. The respect for elders. The respect for um, people who, um, would be considered, um, teachers. Those kinds of things. Um, it was really important

never to talk back. . . . I don't even care if you had a good reason. It doesn't matter until you got to be old enough to, uh, stand as a peer, you did not—you did not talk back. . . . Secondly, also was, uh, generosity. Um, our family was very generous even though we didn't have much at all. . . . People are always surprised by my generosity, um, which is always strange to me because it comes very normal for me.

Prior to our interview, I witness evidence of and note her generosity at an organization meeting at which I was conducting observational research. As my notes indicate, she enters the room and presents home-made soup to another member. He unceremoniously accepts the offer of food and begins eating it before the meeting starts. He thanks her and she replies that earlier he had mentioned not getting home to eat, so she had thought to bring this for him. This kind of behavior is certainly not unheard of between friends; it is simply evidence of her generosity.

A male reclaimer makes a similar point: "If you ever run into an Indian who is disrespectful to elders—whether they're white, black, or Indian, doesn't matter, they're still elders—then that person has either forgotten how they were raised or they weren't raised properly." Another woman explains that her Native heritage was salient in her home growing up in the form of

> family cooperativeness, I mean, for at least two or three generations I know that when mothers and fathers weren't able to care for the children, aunts and uncles . . . grandparents, or everyone would always chip in and help out. . . . Especially my great-grandmother, when she was alive, she was always taking in somebody's kids in the family. . . . There was a real sense of cooperative living among those poor folks. I think that's tribal in a sense.

Another reclaimer explains her role of wife as an opportunity to practice her Native heritage:

> Maybe in my role as a wife because I am pretty strong and have to have the equal relationship with my husband at all times and if it's not equal, I speak up and I, there has to be an allowance in one way. . . . I feel that he's not getting the equality that he deserves or I'm not getting the equality that I deserve, I bring it up. I pay attention to it and, and, and I know that a lot of Native American women have had more equal roles in the daily life as far as their responsibilities . . . so, I think in my "wife-dom" I maybe recognize my heritage a little.

There is a recognition that Native people embrace family as the cornerstone of their cultures, and despite the diversity between tribes in terms of family forms, they share a broader definition of family than Anglo-Americans, emphasizing the inclusion of non-blood kin as family. Native peoples, as an adaptive response to societal marginalization, engage in family practices often contradictory to mainstream Anglo-American families that result in reclaimers generating a new understanding of their own families, both ancestral and current, in terms of these racial/ethnic patterns.

CONCLUSION

I think this chapter presents evidence that reclaiming a Native heritage is more than the symbolic ethnicity that Gans (1979) speaks of. Gans feels that white ethnics who seek to embrace their ethnic heritage do not experience conflict because who are merely trying to find "easy and intermittent ways of expressing their identity, for ways that do not conflict with other ways of life" (1979, p. 203). While there is the sense of pride in one's heritage, an embrace of cultural traditions and ethnic foods between the white ethnics Gans theorizes about and the Native reclaimers that I speak to, Native reclaimers appear to not completely adhere to the notion of symbolic ethnicity. While they share an emphasis on cultural traditions and foods, they really stand out when it comes to the time-consuming commitment to learning their tribal language.

Almost every reclaimer in my study is in the preliminary process of learning their tribal language. This is particularly significant in light of the fact that most reservation Indians speak English. Reclaimers' embrace of indigenous languages, then, must be viewed as politically motivated. First, it is evidence of an indigenous reaction against forced assimilation and white attempts at the cultural genocide of Native peoples. Second, it appears particularly significant in an era where the "English First" movement has been working to make English the "official" language in various regions of the country (primarily as a response to rising Latino populations and the bilingual movement). Maintaining indigenous or immigrant languages can certainly be viewed as an explicit rejection of assimilation. And finally, reclaimers see themselves performing their new racial/ethnic identity in their families: how they relate to people, whom they refer to as family, and in their understandings of their particular family arrangements.

In all areas there is evidence of a tension between cultural practices and newly claimed identities, yet this tension is simply evidence that reclaimers are working to make themselves distinct as Native peoples despite being raised in the white, mainstream world. As the quote from Meyerhoff in the beginning of this chapter emphasizes, "Always, self and society are known—to the subjects themselves and to the audience— through enactments . . . enacted beliefs have a capacity for arousing belief that mere statements do not. 'Doing is believing'" (1978, p. 32). Yet, participation in Native cultures is often difficult for reclaimers due to external constraints such as their geographic location versus that of their tribe and the demands of their everyday lives as they "live" in the white, mainstream world and attempt to embrace their Native culture. It is also important to recognize that as reclaimers attempt to practice their new racial/ethnic heritage and in their efforts to demarcate themselves from non-Natives, they actually portray Nativeness as less fluid than it is and as less fluid than traditional, non-reclaiming Natives recognize it to be.

Chapter Four

"If It Looks Like a Duck": Physical Appearance and Reclaimer Identity

As I reflect on race and physical appearance and the significance this appears to hold for the Native reclaimers I have spoken to, I find myself thinking about a particular childhood incident concerning the way race was treated as a biological fact in my life, similar to the way the Native reclaimers I have met treat the concept. While the memory is now over twenty-five years old, I can clearly envision the afternoon. Kenny and I leave our neighborhood park together on a hot summer day after a neighborhood baseball game. I do not remember if any specific incident triggers his comment, but all I remember is he seems disturbed and says, "I don't know why everyone calls me black. I'm tan." As he makes this statement, he reaches out his right arm for emphasis, exposing that he is, indeed, simply "tan." I did not know what to say to *that*! I remember thinking, is he being funny or is he serious? I even felt a little pity for him because he did not seem to know that despite his tan complexion, he was *black*. While there is an obvious absurdity to this discrepancy, and it manages to linger inside me for many years, at the time I wrote it off as his youthful ignorance. He was, after all, younger than me. I was probably eleven years old.

Reflecting on this incident brings up numerous questions for me. How had I so thoroughly internalized the societal one-drop rule? My social worlds were almost completely white (school, sports teams, and the neighborhood, with the exception of Kenny and his family, who were biracial—with an African American father and a white mother of French descent). But, as Roediger points out, "Even in an all-white town, race was never absent" (1991, p. 3). I do not remember explicit racism or racial lessons being taught in my home growing up . . . but they had to be there, because I had thoroughly inculcated the societal racial hierarchy. Where did my assurance of his place

151

in the racial hierarchy, and thus, by default, my place in it, stem from? Davis points out that whites "see less of the spectrum of racial variation in the black community. . . . [W]hites tend to be less aware of the discrepancy between the social-cultural and genetic definitions of who is black in the United States" (1991, p. 173). Indeed.

This chapter is an opportunity to explore the ways the construct "race," the grouping of physically distinct peoples, is alive and well in our social worlds. While Kibria argues that "race operates as an involuntary sign over which the individual has little or no control . . . ethnic options emerge out of the dynamic processes and negotiations that surround this information" (2000, p. 79), Cornell and Hartmann point out that "our [racial/ethnic] identity is also a product of the claims we make" (1998, p. 80). It is important to recognize both the ways race is a process of external ascription and the ways people are active agents in claiming their own racial/ethnic heritage.

In this chapter, I specifically analyze the significant role racial physiognomy, or physical appearance, plays for individuals reclaiming a Native American heritage. To what extent are individuals free to reclaim a racial/ethnic heritage, particularly when this identity is not likely to be reflected back to them? When I began this research, I wondered what dilemmas reclaimers who do not hold phenotypically distinct "Indian" features (dark hair, eyes, and complexion and high cheekbones) might encounter, if any. Despite my initial interest in physical appearance and reclaiming a racial/ethnic identity, when I made my interview questions, I failed to include a question explicitly asking how reclaimers perceive their appearance in terms of their racial/ethnic identity. In hindsight, this oversight possibly implies an assumption of objectivity, that race and physical appearance are obvious and visible. Instead of understanding the subjectivity and subtle yet complex negotiation processes involved in racial assignments, I assumed I would decide which reclaimers "looked" Native and which ones did not. Perhaps not so ironically, I found that most of my reclaimers feel they do not look Native, even when I think they do. Physical appearance turns out to be a significant issue since, despite the fact that I failed to directly ask about it, almost everyone I spoke to brought up the issue, problematizing what I naively assumed to be a straightforward categorization.

"RACE": DECONSTRUCTING AN IDEA

The idea of race, while often treated as an understood, uncontestable, objective and innate category, has not always been with us. As Smedley (1999) points out, there was a time when no structuring of inequality, whether social, moral, intellectual, cultural, or otherwise, was associated with people because of their skin color. . . . When race appeared in human history it brought about a subtle but powerful transformation in the world's perception of human differences. It imposed social meanings on physical variation among human groups that served as the basis for the structuring of the total society. Since that time, many people in the west have continued to link human identity to external physical features. (p. 693)

A basic sociology textbook defines a "race" as "a group of people who (1) are generally considered to be physically distinct in some way, such as skin color, hair texture, or facial features, from other groups and (2) are generally considered by themselves and/or others to be a distinct group (Farley 2000, p. 6). *Webster's New World Dictionary* defines a "race" as "any of the different varieties or populations of human beings distinguished by (a) physical traits such as hair, eyes, skin color, body shape, etc. . . ." (1994, p. 1106). Both definitions clearly link physical appearance to our understanding of race, yet social scientists argue that race is also about much more than physical appearance.

As Farley continues, "Physical characteristics partially define race, *but only in the context of a decision by society to consider those physical characteristics relevant.* . . . Race is a *socially constructed concept*" (2005, pp. 5–6, italics in the original). And as Omi and Winant concur, "How one is categorized is far from a merely academic or even personal matter. . . . The determination of racial categories is thus an intensely political process" (1994, p. 3). Kibria elaborates on the significance of the social and political construction of race: "Race is a system of power, one that draws on physical differences to construct and give meaning to racial boundaries and the hierarchy of which they are a part" (2000, p. 78). While Sollors (1996) states that the term *ethnicity* emerges as an intended substitute for the word *race*, the term and especially *the idea of distinct races*, of groups of people that were phenotypically distinct, as this research emphasizes, are still very much with us today. Cornell and Hartmann argue, "Weber's and Marx's ideas, although very different, had similar implications: Over time, ethnicity and race would decline as significant social forces in the modern world. . . . But the predictions did not come true. It turned out to be an ethnic century after all" (1998, pp. 8–9). And, one might add, a racial one as well.

Most often, for white Americans at least, the notions of race, race relations, and racial oppression conjure up images of Americans of African descent. However, the United States' racial hierarchy is much more complicated than this simple black-white binary categorization portrays. This exaggerated simplicity is part and parcel of the design of the racial hierarchy—it keeps some groups overly visible and others invisible. Whites, for instance, have historically had the privilege of remaining invisible in the racial hierarchy. For Native Americans, however, the invisibility has had much more sinister and destructive results. Native Americans constantly fight the invisibility battle—the perception that they are simply a footnote in U.S. history instead of current members of American society.[1]

While whites have historically had the privilege of invisibility, that is no longer the case. Whiteness is currently being investigated as a racial identity and as a political and social construction (c.f. Haney-Lopez 1996; Roediger 1991; McIntyre 1997; Frankenberg 1993, among others). Frankenberg states, "To speak of whiteness is, I think, to assign everyone a place in the relations of race relations" (1993, p. 6). She continues, "First, whiteness is a location of structural advantage, of race privilege. Second, it is a 'standpoint,' a place from which white people look at ourselves, at others, at society. Third, 'whiteness' refers to a set of cultural practices that are usually unmarked and unnamed" (1993, p. 1). McIntyre proposes, "By whiteness, I refer to a system and ideology of white dominance that marginalizes and oppresses people of color, ensuring existing privileges for white people in this country" (1997, p. 3). In effect, both Frankenberg and McIntyre see whiteness as a practice, privilege, and unmarked identity.

Haney-Lopez analyzes the emergence of whiteness or white identity in law. He is interested in how "law ascribes racialized meanings to physical features" (1996, p. 14). Haney-Lopez states:

> Laws and legal decisions define which physical and ancestral traits code as Black or White, and so on. Appearances and origins are not white or non-white in any natural or pre-social way. . . . [T]hey [the courts] defined the racial semiotics of morphology and ancestry. It is upon this seed of racial physicality that the courts imposed the flesh of normative racial meanings, established the social significance of the very categories they were themselves constructing. (1996, pp. 16–17)

Courts decide who is white and do so partially on common knowledge, saying this person and persons like him do not "look" white (Haney-Lopez 1996, p. 17). A participant in Dalmage's study of multiracial families describes the constructed nature of race in the following way: "'I like the terms *black* and *white* because they are both equally impossible. Just as there are no coal-black people, there are no snow-white people either. And so you can see they've been constructed to mean what they mean'" (2000, p. 27, italics in the original).

This increasing emphasis on whiteness, white identity, and white privilege is a powerful challenge to the existing racial hierarchy because it exposes it as just that—a socially, politically, and legally constructed hierarchy: "The idea of a White country, given ideological and *physical* effect by law, has provided the basis for contemporary claims regarding the European nature of the United States. . . . Whites do not exist as a natural group, but only as a social and legal creation" (Haney-Lopez 1996, p. 18, italics in the original). Those who actively seek to reclaim a Native heritage also challenge the existing racial hierarchy and the invisibility of indigenous peoples. Reclaiming a heritage previously denigrated acts as an explicit challenge to the hegemonic racial structure, as Dei and James point out: "To *claim* an identity, rather than passively accept one, is a political act" (1998, p. 94, italics in the original).

In the social scientific literature, with rare exceptions, constructions of race are actively and continuously being destabilized. The question remains, however, to what extent are traditional understandings of race still alive and well in the mainstream? According to Cornell and Hartmann, "The fact that Americans so often believe race to be a given indicates how successful the construction project has been" (1998, p. 93). Do reclaimers see themselves as challenging the *racial* hierarchy through their reclamation? One way to see the active role race plays in the day-to-day lives of Native reclaimers is to look at the role of appearance in racial/ethnic identity construction. Do people rely on physical appearance as a marker of their "Indianness"? To what extent does the emphasis on physical appearance among reclaimers reify the racial hierarchy and to what extent does reclaiming challenge the racial hierarchy? Subordinate groups have never simply passively accepted dominant group ideologies. For instance, Sturm (2002) argues that in the case of the Cherokee, in time, they embraced the European race system, yet altered it:

> By the late eighteenth century, in response to these various maneuvers on the part of European colonists, Cherokees had internalized an understanding of racial differences and racial prejudice that articulated with Western views. At the same time, Cherokees manipulated the existing racial hierarchy, aggressively placing themselves at the top. (p. 50)

In this example there is evidence of the power of the dominant group, in that a racial classification system introduced by colonizers was incorporated into Cherokee culture, and agency among subordinate groups, in that the Cherokee refuse to accept the dominant groups' racial hierarchy and instead establish their own racial hierarchy.

CONSTRUCTING A RACIAL/ETHNIC IDENTITY: THE ROLE OF APPEARANCE

Research on racial and ethnic identity construction exposes a connection between appearance, race, and identity. Waters's (1990) research on ethnic identity among white ethnics argues that "this leads to the logical presumption, often true in practice, that members of the same ethnic group will resemble a certain physical type. . . . Individuals are nonetheless aware of their own physical appearances and of how closely they resemble stereotypes of their ethnic group" (p. 74). Pierre van den Berghe (1985) argues that people tend to walk around with an image or mental picture of what a model group member looks like, that these models are accepted by both insiders and outsiders, and that such images are often used to judge instantaneously whether a person is a member of your own ethnic group (Waters 1990, p. 75). Physical appearance, he argues, is used to gauge whether a person belongs to a particular ethnic group or not, and it is both insiders and outsiders who are involved in this assessment. Nagel (1996) agrees, stating that ethnic identity "lies at the intersection of individual ethnic self-definition (who I am) and collective ethnic attribution (who they say I am). Ethnic identity is, then, a dialectic between internal identification and external ascription" (p. 21). Waters argues that physical appearance constrains or enables a person's ethnic identity choice, stating that if one believes one is "marked" as Italian as opposed to Irish, one tends to identify with Italians (1990, p. 75). She continues, "Those I interviewed were aware of how others used their physical appearances to estimate their ethnicity or ancestry. To a very great extent, they carried around mental images of what various ethnic groups look like" (1990, p. 76). Cornell and Hartmann concur: "The world around us may 'tell' us we are racially distinct, or our experiences at the hands of circumstances may 'tell' us that we constitute a group, but our identity is also a product of the claims we make" (1998, p. 80).

Waters's ideas, as well as those of Cornell and Hartmann, on ethnic identity choice resonate with me. Why do I claim my Irish heritage, yet downplay my Polish heritage (and the multiple other minor influences)? There are many factors at work, including the fact that my surname is obviously Irish, my grandparents are Irish immigrants, and Irishness was the heritage emphasized in our home growing up. However, physical appearance is also a big part of it. I look Irish. What does that mean? It means that people have always commented on my often-sunburned, freckled complexion: "You must be Irish." Irishness is the ethnicity I wear most visibly and the one that is reflected back to me most often.

While Waters looks at white ethnics, others focus on racial identity construction among racial minorities. According to Cornell and Hartmann, "All cultures and collective identities are constructions of some sort or another; they are changed and reformulated—continually reconstructed—over time" (1998, p. 92). Rockquemore and Brunsma's (2002) research on biracial identity explores the significance of the appearance, race, and identity link. As they argue, "Cognitive understandings of differing racial categories interact with significant symbols to influence that way in which people understand themselves and their relationship to others. The most salient symbol representing group membership is a person's appearance" (2002, p. 76). Appearance plays a significant role in identity construction simply because it presents our identity to others in social interaction. Rockquemore and Brunsma state, "Unlike the case with ethnic options, appearance plays a counterintuitive role in the way biracial people choose their racial identity" (2002, p. 77). These two scholars operate from a symbolic interactionist perspective, emphasizing "color as both a personal and a social characteristic; that is, people perceive their skin color, but they also interpret their appearance through the eyes of others within any given interactional sphere" (2002, p. 80). They continue, "Appearance simultaneously presents a person's identity and serves as the source of identity. . . . Through appearance, the self presents an identity" (Rockquemore and Brunsma 2002, p. 82).

For a few of my interviewees, the fact that they look Native is something they see as a privilege. But for many others the opposite is true; their physical appearance is incongruent with the racial/ethnic identity they are actively seeking. For individuals whose physical appearance is incongruent with their sense of self, there are constant messages from others challenging their newly reclaimed racial/ethnic identity. "People's appearance helps define their identity and allows them an embodied means to express their self-identification. It is in this process that identities are negotiated and either validated or contested" (Rockquemore and Brunsma 2002, p. 56). From a symbolic interactionist perspective, individuals gain an identity and a sense of self through social interaction. "Identity cannot be defined in isolation. Identities are relational. Individual and group cultural identities intersect. To *claim* an identity, rather than passively accept one, is a political act which involves one's self and others" (Dei and James 1998, p. 94). We engage in self-presentation, and others either accept or challenge that presentation:

> Identity is really a process; who we are is an ongoing development. . . . [O]ur identities matter in what we do; they matter in what we try to communicate to others; they matter to others. . . . [A]t the heart of identity is social interaction, for it is through social interaction that identities are formed, maintained, changed. It is important to understand identity formation as a negotiation process that unfolds as we interact. (Charon 2001, p. 160)

Charon continues, "The work of Goffman reminds us that creating identity is an active negotiation process between who others tell us we are and our continuous attempts to present who we think we are to others" (2001, p. 165). For individuals whose physical appearance contradicts widespread stereotypes of what Indians look like, more "identity challenges" are experienced. According to social psychologists, "Social interaction is a perilous undertaking, for it is easily disrupted by challenges to identity" (Michener and Delamater 2001, p. 229). In fact, such suspicion on the part of others can make one's self-presentation appear more tactical, where we are perceived as working to establish a public image of ourselves that is consistent with what others want us to be, when in fact it is authentic, when we are working to create an image of ourselves in the eyes of others that is consistent with the way we view ourselves (Michener and Delamater 1999, p. 215). One of my objectives here is to analyze this identity dilemma and how it affects a physically unrecognizable Native reclaimer's sense of self and racial/ethnic identity.

It is also important to acknowledge the role of structure in such interactions. Although too often portrayed as such, it is not merely the interaction of individuals that influences an individual's identity construction, but the interaction between dominant and subordinate groups. As Rockquemore and Brunsma point out, "A person's physical body is, in social psychological terms, a collection of cultural meanings that supply basic information and interpretations to others. . . . [R]ace, as a universal category of identity, is subtly important to most social interactions because of its link to the distribution of power and status in society" (2002, pp. 84–85). Race functions as a master status in our society. One way these asymmetrical power relations play themselves out is in terms of racial/ethnic identity assessment: the power certain groups have over others to define group membership. "The simple fact is that in much of the world's history, Whites have been more likely than others to have the power to make racial assignments, to organize social life in racial terms, and to define and value the categories as they saw fit" (Cornell and Hartmann 1998, p. 29).

Historically, in the case of African Americans particularly, we see the imposition of the one-drop rule, or hypo-descent, "meaning that racially mixed persons are assigned the status of the subordinate group" (Davis 1991, p. 5). For Native peoples, this manifests itself in the opposite direction, with the federal government insisting on significant blood quantum for determining whether one was a member of a particular Native American tribe, a practice that manages to exclude many people of Native heritage from officially being recognized as such. Sturm elaborates on the motivations for such actions:

> Quantification of Indian blood was as much a disaster for Native Americans as a boon for Euroamericans. Because the federal government had imposed a strict new definition of Indianness based not only on blood but on a particular blood quantum, there were not enough Native Americans who met this criteria to absorb all of the existing reservation acreage. The remaining land was immediately made

available for non-Indian use, an important factor in the massive reduction of tribally held lands, not to mention tribal power generally. . . . What motivated the federal government to introduce a more restrictive definition of Indianness based on
blood quantum? . . . Because of its historic treaty-based obligations to provide ongoing economic assistance to Native Americans in exchange for land, the federal
government had to find a way to minimize or avoid paying these payments altogether while appearing to honor its commitments. (2002, pp. 78–79)

As one of my interviewees points out, "As far as I know, we're the only minority that has to legally prove who we are." This individual perceptively acknowledges the role the dominant group plays in individual identity construction for minority group members. Whites, as the dominant racial group,
play a significant role through legal and political maneuvering in determining
who is and who is not Native in much the same way they determine who is
and who is not black (see chapter five). Charon points out that while symbolic
interactionists focus on identity as a negotiation process, power does indeed
matter: "Power—based on intelligence, wealth, control of employment,
grades, and so on—will play a role in whose definition wins in the long run"
(2001, p. 162). This negotiation process is carried out in everyday interactions
between Native reclaimers and whites as well. This is significant in understanding identity construction as well—the role of the dominant group in influencing the ethnic identity choices of non-whites needs to be understood, as
well as the agency of subordinate group members in defining themselves.
Cornell and Hartmann point out, "Ethnicity and race are not simply labels
forced upon people; they are also identities that people accept, resist, choose,
specify, invent, redefine, reject, actively defend, and so forth" (1998, p. 77).

"SEEING RACE": THE IMPORTANCE OF APPEARANCE
FOR NATIVE RECLAIMERS

There are some clear similarities here between the Native American reclaimers I speak to and Waters's interviewees with white ethnics. For instance, my interviewees encounter individuals, both Native and non-Native
(although many reclaimers felt it was non-Natives that seemed to more explicitly "police" this) who seem to hold stereotypical views of what Indians
look like, and it is due to their perceptions of what Indians should look like
that cause them to challenge the racial/ethnic identity claims my interviewees
make. Interestingly, Native reclaimers themselves are no exception to this.
Many of them struggle with their own mental images of what Indians look
like and compare these to their own phenotypical features. Waters argues that
physical appearance works to help white ethnics choose which ethnicity to

emphasize, implying that they often choose an ethnicity that is at least to a certain extent congruent with their own physical appearance: "And they often use these images and their understanding of their own physical appearances to choose which branch of their family or which of their possible identities they could use to self identify" (1990, p. 76). In many cases, the Native reclaimers I encounter are choosing a racial/ethnic identity that is incongruent with their physical appearance. As Mihesuah confirms, "Not all individuals claiming to be Indian 'look Indian'" (1998, p. 193). In this way, many of my interviewees differ from the white ethnics of Waters's research. Most of my interviewees deal with identity struggles surrounding claiming a racial/ethnic identity that is incongruent with their appearance.

Snipp's analysis of the 1980 census shows that the majority of persons who claim Indian ancestry do not claim to be of the Indian race. In later work, he differentiates between describing Native Americans in terms of race or ethnicity. He says, "Using racial characteristics to define the boundaries of the Native American population presupposes that the concept of race is itself well known and clearly defined. On the contrary, few concepts are as misunderstood as race" (1989, p. 28). He continues,

> By any definition or set of criteria one might choose, there can be little doubt that American Indians are a bona fide ethnic group. The authenticity of American Indian ethnicity is widely recognized by social scientists . . . [however] there are a number of reasons why it is reasonable to think about American Indians and Alaska Natives as a multi-ethnic population. (1989, p. 39)

During my interviews with Native reclaimers, I ask each individual if they prefer the term *race* or *ethnicity* for describing Native Americans. I got varied responses to that question. While there appears to be little doubt in the minds of social scientists such as Snipp (1989) as to whether Native Americans are an ethnic group, no such assuredness is found among the reclaimers I encounter. While most do not place any significance on such terminology, others provide elaborate explanations as to why they prefer the term *race* or *ethnicity*, and one even provides a rather impressive understanding of the social construction of race (despite sociological efforts, this does not appear to be an idea that has achieved much common understanding). One woman, for instance, simply replies, "It doesn't matter to me," and moves on. Another woman says,

> Either term works . . . neither term bothers me. They both mean the same thing. Um, I guess when I hear *race*, that means something more specific to me, um, I think race means Caucasian, Negro, and Mongol. There's three races. And that's what I learned when I was in school, there's three races. And if they've changed the definition, I never heard about it.

A male middle-aged interviewee answers, "I probably don't use [the term] *ethnicity* ever." I ask, "So, you use *race*?" He replies, "Uh-huh." A graduate student reclaimer in her mid-twenties answers, "I mean, it's really interesting . . . but, uh, I practice my race." And I ask her if she prefers the term *race* or *ethnicity*, to which she replies, "Um, well, I don't necessarily prefer the term *race*. It's just . . . when we're talking about . . . Lakota that is—that is one thing, and that is a particular race." An undergraduate male interviewee provides the following answer:

> It's sad that we should even have terms like this, terms like *race* and *multicultural-ism*. . . . I think *ethnicity* is probably more accurate. . . . In that Peace Studies class . . . he [the instructor] brought up an interesting point that offended a lot of people. . . . He said something to the effect that there really should be no such thing as race because genetically we're all the same. . . . Differences are based on personal perceptions and cultural differences, not biological or genetic differences. So, I tend to follow that line of thought—race is something that we've created for ourselves.

This interviewee accepts the social construction of race argument introduced to him in a college course. While this is a perspective I share, I cannot help but wonder why he is the only one making a constructionist argument when answering the "*race* or *ethnicity*" question. Considering the educational level and programs of study many of my reclaimers are engaged in, it seems unlikely that he is the only one to have encountered it in his course of study.

I speculate that for the reclaimers I interview, particularly those who have dark complexions, hair, and eyes, their lived experience makes race too real to accept a social constructionist argument, despite the fact this argument insists on the significance of the societal definitions of race and the meanings attached to such. While they may not always be recognized as Indians, dark-skinned reclaimers are constantly questioned as to their racial/ethnic heritage; they are obviously "something," something other than white. Again, we can turn to Sturm:

> Both race-thinking and the scientific buttressing of race as a biological category continue to this day with profound effects on social reality. It is in this context that race is both a falsehood and a fact, being false in its biological, scientific sense and factual in its very real effects on lived experience. (2002, p. 15)

However, there could be more to reclaimers' embrace of the notion of race; for instance, they could perceive a racial essentialist argument as advantageous to them in some way. Despite the fact that biracial people are evidence of the social construction of race, clear distinctions between groups may be necessary for those individuals in ambiguous racial categories, for those not fitting neatly into a dichotomous system.

Another male interviewee replies that he would probably prefer the term *ethnicity*. When asked why, he responds,

> Because I think ethnicity takes in culture as opposed to just genetic. Uh, and I think it's more inclusive. When you talk about race, well, there are a lot of people I know who are racially Indians, but ethnically they're not Indians. There are a lot of people who are racially white, but ethnically they're Indian. So, in thinking in terms of ethnicity, it's more inclusive. If you're talking about social structure, then you need to talk about ethnicity.

According to this reclaimer, being Indian is about culture and a way of living, being in this world, not about physical appearance. For Cornell and Hartmann, "Once established, an ethnic or racial identity becomes a lens through which people interpret and make sense of the world around them" (1998, p. 94). They continue, "In acting on the basis of those identities, people reproduce them" (1998, p. 100).

A male interviewee in his mid-twenties gave a rather interesting response to the question:

> I think race and ethnicity are different. I mean, I think that—'cause to me somebody who's, like, Hispanic is European. I mean, to me, that's what they are. They're European. . . . So, it's like when I think of Indian, I don't always think of just North American. I think of South America . . . 'cause those are just political lines that get drawn. . . . Some of the Indian people are like, "Oh, he's Mexican." I was like, "Well, that doesn't make him not Indian."

In this quote, he recognizes that Indians span both North and South America with the arrival of Europeans, again exposing the socially constructed nature of race by challenging the supposedly distinct categories of "Hispanic" and "Indian." Later he adds a rather sophisticated understanding of the political and social construction of "white": "Like, throughout history the term *white* has been used not so much as a, well, in the mainstream it's—it's race, but in the Indian sense, it's a way of doing things. It's a political aspect mostly. Um, government, when they talk about white, they usually mean government and stuff like that." This comment reveals the political nature of the concept of race rather than as a reference to physiognomy. Additionally, his comment "in the Indian sense" implies that there is an understanding among Indians that "white" is not about skin color; it is instead a reference to the white, Euro-American government with which Natives have historically interacted, which is a powerful cooptation of the Euro-American concept of race.

Even when individuals appear to answer this question with assuredness, there are still contradictions embedded within their narratives that expose the ambiguousness of the concept of race. A middle-aged female reclaimer answers the "*race* or *ethnicity*" question emphatically:

Race. It's not something that you can choose to be or not to be. Like you can't choose to be black or not to be black, you can't decide, "I don't want to be black anymore." You know? How a black person behaves and what sort of religion they practice doesn't have anything to do with the race. You know they are what they are. And I feel the same way about Indians. You know you got the skin, you're wearing the skin, it doesn't matter what your religious practices are. It's a race.

While this woman answers with assurance, claiming "It's a race," there are a lot of contradictions embedded in her narrative. I ask her if she can visibly pick out Natives, to which she replies, "Oh, most of the time." I then follow by asking her if she thinks she looks Native, to which she replies "Yeah. . . . Well, I've been told all my life. That's been a problem for me all my life, you know? As a little kid, even, people would say, 'You're Indian, aren't ya?'" Yet, earlier in the conversation she says that her siblings do not completely embrace their Native heritage. She explains,

It's kind of interesting. They want all the information I accumulate and they want all the benefits. They want their children to get funding for schooling and things like that, but they don't want to claim any of the responsibilities of being a minority. . . . They don't publicly say that they're Native American. They pass for white. . . . Our Chief in the band that we have says you only get to claim you are Indian if you've had at least one day in your life you wish you weren't.

Mihesuah similarly discusses the potential dilemma of "being part Indian and not really looking it affords a form of status among some Caucasian groups" (1998, p. 204). This parallels the experiences of light-skinned African Americans, where their skin color provides them status among whites but can be problematic in the black community. There "has been . . . divisiveness in the black community over color differences among blacks. The lightest mulattoes feel pressure to prove their blackness" (Davis 1991, p. 169). Davis explains,

Greater educational and economic opportunities have meant upward mobility and increased effectiveness for many [light-skinned blacks], and the black community resents the potential loss of its more talented leaders through total integration into white institutions, and certainly through passing or intermarriage with whites. (1991, p. 138)

While the previous reclaimer argues that being Native is not something one can choose, and therefore it should be referred to as a race, she acknowledges that her own siblings do not embrace this heritage. Instead, they assimilate into the mainstream, white culture, explicitly challenging her claim that "it's a race" and one can't simply choose to be or not to be Indian.

Clearly, there is a certain amount of racial/ethnic identity choice for reclaimers, particularly those who do not look Native.

Many Indians, reclaimers and non-reclaimers alike, don't have phenotypically distinct features partially due to the high rates of exogamy among Native Americans. As Taylor states, "American Indians have extraordinarily high rates of exogamy compared with blacks and whites. Among married American Indian men and women, only about 47 percent are married to other Indians . . . . In contrast, marital endogamy is close to 99 percent among whites and nearly 98 percent for blacks" (2002, p. 235). However, my objective is not to disregard the reclaimer's point by emphasizing the contradictions embedded within her narrative. My hope, instead, is to emphasize the subjectivity of race and ethnicity rather than overemphasizing these as objective categories. Why does *she* feel that being Indian is not a choice, when her siblings feel it is something they can distance themselves from? There are bound to be multiple answers to such a question and some may pertain to appearance. She acknowledges that she looks Indian and that this is what has been reflected back to her since she was a child. Maybe her siblings do not have "the look." Maybe her pull toward her Indianness is due to something more intangible than her appearance. At the end of our interview, she says that reclaiming this heritage is hard for her, but that "I feel like it's what I have to be, you know. I can't pretend I'm something I'm not. I'm not going to go through this life denying what I am and pretending I'm something else because it is safe. That is not a valuable life." Maybe such contradictions can be summed up simply with her comment about her tribe, the Cherokee: "It's not a racially pure tribe at all."

Another reclaimer I interview emphasizes the relative and subjective nature of race in terms of location, explaining that when he lived in California, he did not get the "what are you?" question, because "you were kind of . . . [California is a place] where minorities are a majority, uh, you know, you just learned not to think about it anymore." However, upon returning to his hometown in the Midwest, he explains, "When I come back here . . . where it's white and suddenly I'm aware of everybody staring at me. Why are they staring at me? Oh, yeah. I forgot. I'm a minority." I ask him, "So, anybody with a tan is stared at here?" He answers,

Yeah. Exactly, that's it. I get Samoan a lot. Italian. Hawaiian. . . . So, I, you know, I deal with it on a case-by-case basis. . . . I would change the subject just so that people wouldn't focus on it and maybe piss me off and I'd have to deal with that rage issue again. . . . It used to get to me, but I wouldn't let it show . . . . I would just let it roll up into a big ball of pain. Uh, I always pointed it inwards. . . . A lot of people stare at me and I know why they're staring at me— 'cause I'm a freak. At least here I am.

As someone with dark skin, this reclaimer experiences the lived reality and the pain of racism. He struggles to come to terms with the meaning and distinction between race and culture:

> If you go to our reservation [the Osage], the only thing that differentiates us from, like, the other part of town is skin color. I mean, we all have microwaves and clocks . . . [but] because my skin is a different color and I have a shared ancestry with another group of people, that would make me part of that culture. However, I'm also out here in the mainstream doing mainstream things. . . . I have cable TV, and I pay taxes and insurance and I play video games and Nintendo and ride my bike and play basketball and eat McDonald's.

Feagin and McKinney (2003) speak of the costs of racism, including the psychological costs, in their aptly titled book, *The Many Costs of Racism*. Speaking in terms of black reactions to white racism, they argue, "For most whites, it is likely hard to imagine living with this constant sense of justified rage. For many, if not most, African Americans, this is a recurring reality. . . . Systemic racism has dealt African Americans a very hard hand to play" (2003, pp. 43–44). Certainly the same can be said of Native Americans and reclaimers, like this young man, who are marked, visible representations of their group. African American author bell hooks uses similar language to describe the manifestations of dominant group control of black representations:

> It rends us. It rips and tears at the seams of our efforts to construct self and identity. Often it leaves us ravaged by repressed rage, feeling weary, dispirited, and sometimes just plain old broken-hearted. These are the gaps in our psyche that are the spaces where mindless complicity, self-destructive rage, hatred, and paralyzing despair enter. (1992, p. 4)

Obviously, there is great disparity in the responses reclaimers give to the "*race* or *ethnicity*" question. But what I find most significant is that, regardless of their response to the "*race* or *ethnicity*" question, all the interviewees repeatedly discuss the importance of physical appearance. Whether or not they have, for instance, what are stereotypically viewed to be Native American features is significant to them. Snipp articulates this discrepancy well:

> A basic source of ambiguity about who is American Indian stems from the popular stereotypes of American Indians that attribute to them physical characteristics such as well-defined cheekbones, reddish-brown complexions, straight black hair, almond shaped eyes, and very little male facial hair. It is true that many American Indians have one or more of these characteristics. It also true that some American Indians have none of these features, and in any event characteristics

such as straight black hair and high cheekbones are not found exclusively in the American Indian population. Obviously, physical appearance is a wholly inappropriate criterion for deciding who is and is not an American Indian or Alaska Native. (1989, p. 26)

Yet, it happens repeatedly: physical appearance is used as a criterion for group membership. The significance of the appearance-race-identity link is obvious in its recurring presence throughout my interviewees narratives. To paraphrase Cornel West (1993), it appears that race, the idea of physically distinct groups of people, does indeed matter. Even in Mary Crow Dog's popular autobiography *Lakota Woman* (1990), we find such evidence as she laments the fact that she feels her appearance isn't quite Indian enough:

> I have white blood in me. Often I have wished to be able to purge it out of me. . . . My face is very Indian, and so are my eyes and my hair, but my skin is very light. Always I waited for the summer, for the prairie sun, the Badlands sun, to tan me and make me into a real skin. The Crow Dogs, the members of my husband's family, have no such problem of identity. They don't need the sun to tan them, they are full-bloods — the Sioux of the Sioux. (p. 9)

Despite this passage, later in the book Crow Dog argues, "I should make clear that being a full-blood or breed is not a matter of bloodline, or how Indian you look, or how black your hair is. The general rule is whoever thinks, sings, acts and speaks Indian is a skin, a full-blood, and whoever acts and thinks like a white man is a half-blood or breed, no matter how Indian he looks" (1990, p. 49).

A reclaimer I met makes the following distinction:

> A lot of my family and friends say that there are Natives and then there are what they call apples, people who are red on the outside but white on the inside. They really want to be white because they want to do well and succeed in all the material things. So, they look Indian, but they are white on the inside.

Interestingly, among the Native reclaimers I interview, gender appears to influence their sense of the congruency of their appearance with their racial/ethnic identity. While not exclusively so, it is more likely for a female interviewee to speak of her physical appearance positively and as representing her ethnic identity accurately. As one woman explains, "It makes me proud that I have it [the "look"] because there are many more people who have more [blood quantum] than me and don't look it. So, I've always known I am blessed to have the skin I do." Another young woman explains that she cannot prove her Native heritage, that it is just part of family lore, but adds as evidence, "First of all, you can't deny that my great-grandmother and my grandmother and my great-, great-grandmother all look that. You know, I mean, 'the look.'" She later adds, "People have always recognized me: 'You're Indian, aren't you?' It's in my features enough and now in my dress enough, that people recognize it right away."

Bowles's research shows a gender interaction at work with appearance and racial identity. Her research, however, finds the opposite phenomena with black/white biracial women than I find with Native reclaimers: "that women had a more difficult time accepting their black physical features than men" (Rockquemore and Brunsma 2002, p. 79). This can be attributed to the negative representations of black women in our culture and the relative invisibility of Native women. The way black women are portrayed in film, music, literature, and television "determines how blackness and black people are seen and how other groups will respond to us. . . . The deeply ideological nature of imagery determines not only how other people think about us but how we think about ourselves" (hooks 1992, p. 5). Native American women are more likely to be invisible in popular culture, and therefore, dominant group imagery does not manifest itself in the same way as it does for black people.

When asked what benefits she finds to being Native, or to reconnecting with this heritage, one female reclaimer immediately replies, "My looks, looking Native American has benefited me. Um, people have raved about how beautiful my look is, the high cheekbones and the dark hair, the long hair and my, my body structure. In that way, I have had a lot of compliments." Another woman talks about how her looks have won her some approval and validation from an older Native man she met through a local Indian organization. She says, "He's nice. He just—he thinks I'm a beautiful Cherokee woman. I get that from him and a couple of guys there 'cause they think I look that way." Reflecting on this, she makes an interesting reevaluation of some of her high school experiences:

> I remember my dad in high school. I couldn't understand why I couldn't have any boyfriends when he's telling me I'm beautiful all the time. . . . Now I think back, did I look different to these people back then? You know, when I was in school, maybe I looked different and they didn't approach me for those reasons. . . . But I never thought about it until recently. It [reclaiming her Native heritage] has made me think about things I've never thought about and made me see myself a little differently.

This process is what Strauss refers to as biographical relocating, which is when we reinterpret meanings into a reinterpreted biographical context (1993, p. 124). This woman, now actively claiming her Cherokee heritage after being raised without an explicit recognition/celebration of it, exemplifies the process of biographical relocating through her reevaluation of her high school experiences. As a genealogy buff, she talks a lot about her research and her findings and points out to me what she describes as an interesting pattern she found in her research: "usually the white men marrying the Indian women." To this she confidently adds, "Who could blame them, though, they're beautiful!"[2]

Other women are more ambiguous about their appearance, but not necessarily because their appearance is more ambiguous, per se. One explains that she has not personally experienced discrimination due to her Native heritage because "I don't think I look extremely visibly Cherokee, [so] it wouldn't be hard for me to fit in as a regular American person." I point out to her that as I sat awaiting her arrival for the interview, I saw a woman coming toward me whom, as my notes indicate, I thought "could be" her. She has long dark hair, a tan complexion, wears jeans, and it immediately registers that she looks more Indian than anyone else on that sparsely populated sidewalk that afternoon. She responds,

> That's an interesting thing, too. . . . To other people, I guess, you know, I have met Native people or people with the knowledge of Indian history, culture, that have been able to look at me and go, "Oh, you're Cherokee, aren't you?" . . . I think sometimes if you know I'm Cherokee, it might make it easier to begin with. I haven't had too many just average Caucasian people, you know, know that I was Cherokee from the beginning. Right now I'm a little tan. . . . I think that I look Native. Um, you know, the cheekbones, the eyes. . . . [I'm] pretty dark right now.

Her comments intrigue me. She starts off denying that she looks "visibly" Cherokee, then shifts to how those "in the know" can tell she is Indian, then plainly states that she thinks she looks Native. Why doesn't she admit to that immediately? Why does she first deny her racial/ethnic phenotype? It makes me wonder if it was my presence as a white interviewer that results in her initial denial. Maybe she is not denying her perception of her physical appearance so much as attempting to interpret her appearance through the eyes of her white interviewer. Several other interviewees explain that while other Natives do not question their heritage, even when their appearance is incongruent with the stereotypical perception of what an Indian should look like, they find themselves constantly questioned by whites. Does she think I will challenge her Indianness and her claim to a Native identity?

This interaction exposes several important aspects concerning the appearance-identity link. The first, which is well documented in the symbolic interactionist literature, is that we at least partially develop a sense of self in interaction with others. Others, both Natives and non-Natives, clearly have an influence, through reinforcement or challenges, on how reclaimers view themselves. Symbolic interactionists focus on how identity is constructed in social interaction; however, we less often acknowledge the research site itself as a potentially influential interactional sphere. Researchers, who we are, our locatedness, may influence how individuals see themselves. Interview situations can be thought of in terms of asymmetric power relations, and additionally it needs to be recognized that the interview is embedded in larger, influential, asymmetric relationships. In this situation, for instance, my concern is, are societal race relations, the historical and current intersection of race and power, influencing the interaction?

Another female interviewee explains how her appearance leads to others questioning her sense of self, and how this provides her with an identity dilemma before she learns to value her own role in defining who she is:

> It's so difficult in this society to be something when you don't take on an appearance that says you're this thing. . . . And it's so difficult because then if you're a person who's still trying to find your identity and you have people telling you, "Well, you don't look . . ." or what I would typically get, "You look Hispanic," "You look Italian." I even got Lebanese! . . . And it took me doing a lot of searching to come to that and realizing that it was up to me to decide what I am. Not what you think. Not what she thinks. Not what the press tells me I'm supposed to look like . . . but rather, what I know that I am inside. And I am Native. And I am . . . Lakota.

This woman's comment supports Charon's assertion that despite power differentials in the identity negotiation process, "we are not helpless in social interactions. . . . We are active participants in our identity formation" (2001, p. 164).

Struggling to find one's identity in the face of such challenges can be overwhelming. As mentioned previously, many challenges come from dominant group members. One middle-aged female reclaimer with light skin and blue eyes says, "Oddly enough, full-bloods don't do that [challenge her claims to a Native identity] to me. . . . Whereas the little white boy at work looks at me and goes, "No you're not [Indian].'" When I ask her why she thinks that happens, that her authenticity is challenged more by whites than Natives, she really does not want to answer the question, finally providing me with an exasperated, "*I really don't know.* . . . He doesn't want to accept that. It's different and, and he just couldn't accept it. I didn't meet his stereotype of what I should look like is all I can figure it is."

While other interviewees say that it is primarily non-Natives who challenge their Indianness, another woman I interview says she finds a lot of challenges from other Indians at pow-wows. As she explains,

> Where I see a lot of the rustling of the feathers, which is what I call it, you know, when they're like, "Oh, I'm more Indian than you . . ." It happens at pow-wows.

It's really strange. . . . Like, well, you know, kind of having to prove your authenticity . . . Indian-ness. . . . And so then, it's a—it's a sort of an idea like,
"Well, I'm gonna prove who I am by this appearance and so I'm gonna make
sure that you're who you are."

Mihesuah's (1998) research affirms such dilemmas surrounding appearance and identity for Native Americans:

Another limiting factor in choosing identity is the most obvious aspect of one's
racial heritage: appearance. The color of one's hair, eyes, and skin are the
barometer used to measure how "Indian" one is and either limits or broadens
one's choice of ethnicity. If an individual doesn't "look Indian" she is often suspect for claiming Indian identity regardless of her cultural knowledge. (pp.
212–13)

Despite the fact that challenges come from Natives and non-Natives, I
feel there are significant differences between them. For instance, when Natives challenge the racial/ethnic identity of a reclaimer, it may reflect historical colonization patterns and past and present discrimination. Mihesuah
continues,

The idea that a Caucasian appearance is "better" serves as a point of contention
among many people of color. As among Blacks, darker-skinned Indians often
distrust lighter-skinned ones, arguing that their non-Indian blood takes them out
of touch with the realities of Indian life. Because it is assumed that light-skinned
Indians have a choice as to which world they inhabit, their dedication to fighting the various social, political, religious, and economic oppressions faced by
"real" Indians is questioned. A person who looks Caucasian, was raised in white
society, and has little, if any, connection to his tribe but still claims an Indian
identity will be looked at with suspicion. . . . Why call oneself a "person of
color" if one looks white? (1998, p. 212)

As Dei and James emphasize, "Race and difference are subjective lived experiences" (1998, p. 92). Reclaimers who do not "look Native" can go
through life, intentionally or unintentionally, with white privilege. Privilege
is often hard to recognize since it is, as McIntosh describes, "an invisible
package of unearned assets that I can count on cashing in each day, but about
which I was 'meant' to remain oblivious" (2001, p. 30). Ethnic studies professor Patricia Penn Hilden, a Native, actively tries to avoid remaining oblivious about her light-skin privilege when, as she writes, she does not claim her
Native heritage when applying for positions because "she looks phenotypically white and was fearful that people might mistake her for a wanna-be"
(Mihesuah 1998, p. 212).

On the other hand, when dominant group members are dictating group membership, it is about power. "Thus, race and power, historically and today, have been tightly intertwined" (Cornell and Harmann 1998, p. 28). One reclaimer elaborates on how she sees this connection operating:

You know, there's been attempts for many years to dilute and eliminate the race [Native Americans]. The government occasionally declares that a tribe no longer exists, whether they do or not, and takes federal recognition away. So, you know, if you're a [Native] . . . person . . . and the government says [your particular tribe] no longer exist[s], you no longer exist. . . . Yeah, now you're white! And that's what they've been doing to tribes forever and ever and people are bitter and very angry.

As Dei and James point out,

Race may be defined as a social-relational category, determined by socially selected physical characteristics. . . . Race . . . is socially constructed and politically produced. . . . [I]t emerges out of a construction of race differences. These differences can only be understood in the context of power and domination. (1998, p. 95)

None of my male interviewees are comfortable in their appearance as Native. One young man in his mid-twenties, with black hair, brown eyes, and a dark complexion says, "If somebody asks me, like, 'Are you a full-blood?' I'm like, 'No. Look at me. Do I look like it?'" One woman does not think she looks Native either, explaining her genealogical search for her heritage in this way: "I don't have black hair and brown eyes, you know, [or] very dark skin. So, people look at me and go, 'Oh no, you're not.' And, but, uh, oddly enough, full-bloods don't do that to me."

Another male reclaimer expresses how it feels to not be recognized as Native:

My grandmother used to tell us how proud she was of her Cherokee and her dark, copper-colored skin and the dark, black eyes and all that. . . . You know, I grew up in the schools around here, in the community, and I didn't—nobody knew that I had Cherokee background because I didn't look like Sitting Bull and, uh, I don't wear feathers in my hair and all that stuff and uh . . . now that I am out there telling people who I am and getting involved . . . it is hard for people to swallow. These are people in my everyday life—it's hard for them to accept. You just don't fit the mold, you know, you're not like the guy on the Indian head, you're not like the guy in the movies, you know. So, you're too much like us, you know, in your everyday life. . . . You can't really be legitimate and so they make fun of me a lot. It's all part of the joke on the job.

He adds that sometimes he does not mind joking around like that with the guys on the job, but sometimes "it hurts quite a bit for them to be that way." I ask him if he would feel different if he "looked like Sitting Bull," to which he replies, laughing, "Yeah, that would really help a lot." Later in the interview, I ask him how he is made aware of his race and ethnicity in his daily life, a question that tends to draw a diverse range of responses, and he again turns to appearance for his response: "Well, because I don't have those features and I have light skin . . . I just pass off as white." While the previous comments expose his subjective experience of invisibility as a Native person, he also recognizes that it is more than simply his individual experience. He also recognizes that there is a collective invisibility of Natives in his region of the country, especially for those who do not hold stereotypical Native America features. The following comment exposes his recognition of this:

> You can go around [his county] here, these people, they're nailing shingles on the roof, they're working the cash register, they're serving, you know, they're serving you at the restaurants. Sometimes you can tell, a lot of times you can tell just by the way, the features on their faces or their mannerisms.

One of my first interviewees is a male college student, who does not by any standard "look Native"; instead, he has reddish-blonde hair and a light complexion. He always seems very concerned about the fact that he does not have "the look." In our interview, he speaks about his brother who is also seeking to connect with his Native heritage, and he says, "Oh, he's got dark hair and his skin is darker. . . . I'm the only one in the family with hair this color. . . . I don't look anything like the rest of the family." I find this to be a rather odd statement since I had met his mother a few years prior at a campus event and there is a clear family resemblance between the two of them. As a Cherokee reclaimer, the fact that his Native heritage is through his father rather than his mother is somewhat limiting for him, since the Cherokee are matrilineal and clan names, for instance, are passed on through the mother's line. Despite not being Native herself, his mother has been highly supportive of his reclamation process. So, I find it rather odd that he disregards, in a sense, her influence on his appearance. If he is disregarding her influence, is he doing this because she is not Native and therefore if he looks like her he is clearly not going to "look Native"?

This young man was instrumental in getting a campus pow-wow organized and at the event there were pamphlets intended to educate non-Natives in attendance. On this pamphlet, there was this quote: "Leave your stereotypes at home! (Yes, there are some blonde tribally enrolled Indians)." I remember thinking at the time that this is a quote directly from him since I find him to be greatly concerned with his appearance and overall Indian authenticity (see chapter five for more on authenticity). His situation seems to be illuminated by something that Mihesuah describes: "A stumbling block to identifying with only one group is if the person's self-perception differs from how others perceive them" (1998, p. 210). This reclaimer views himself as Native, but this racial/ethnic heritage is rarely reflected back to him by others. In fact, his appearance, more often than not, results in challenges to his racial/ethnic identity claims. This appears to result in him relying on more outward cues in terms of impression management: he wears long hair, silver and turquoise jewelry, has tattoos of Native significance, and often wears t-shirts which explicitly declare his connection to Native peoples. This reclaimer relies on more outward cues of his ethnicity than any of the others that I spoke to, and I could not help but wonder if this is due to his white appearance.

DENYING RACE

While the reclaimers I speak to certainly "see" race in that they are concerned with their physical appearance and the fact that they are, too often in their own eyes, not visibly Indian, their narratives also expose a reluctance to extend any credibility to the notion of a race. Again, structure must be kept in mind here. Many of the reclaimers I met acknowledge that racial physiognomy is not an appropriate measure of one's Indianness and that race is, at some level, a political construction. One woman explains,

> You know, the Cherokee were notoriously open to anybody . . . intermarriage . . . anybody is welcome to be part of their tribe and to call themselves Cherokee. And many of the people who are descendants were white or black. A lot of slaves, you know, escaped plantations and were taken in by the Cherokee and hidden and became a part of the tribe. It's not a racially pure tribe at all. And there were blue-eyed, blonde Cherokee when the first English settlers arrived here from the Vikings.

Another woman describes the ambiguousness of using appearance as an identity marker in this way:

> One of my closest friends, you know, has got blonde hair and you know, Caucasian features, but he's just as much Indian as anybody I know. So, it's not up to me to decide and it's certainly not because of physical features that people are. And what I have to remember, too, is that in America, um, the Native people are

stretched across two continents, you know? I mean, so you're gonna be all kinds of different colors and all kinds of different shapes and everything else. And, um, my people are from the very far north . . . and so, I mean, so of course we're gonna be lighter skinned . . . I mean, we're not in Arizona.

The woman who makes this comment has black hair, brown eyes, and a tan complexion, so I say to her, "You're not light skinned to me." She responds to this with the following:

Um, I think in comparison to someone who is, you know, maybe who is Apache or who is Pueblo, yeah. Oh yeah. I mean, I'm substantially shades lighter. But, if you put me compared to someone who's . . . Irish, you know [laughter], then it's gonna be a little different. Yeah . . . but people, people don't realize or recognize that in this society because of media and because of old westerns and this idea of what Indians are supposed to look like. . . . Yeah . . . it gets to be really difficult.

One young female reclaimer emphasizes her understanding of the range of appearances among Native Americans, but she still reflects on the fact that she does not have the stereotypical Native appearance. She explains that when she looks at her friend's fiancée, who is full-blooded Navajo, she thinks, "I don't look anything like her." However, she follows this comment with a logical explanation for these differences in their appearances:

I mean, you have so many different colorings of people . . . and there [are] just different colorings with each tribe. Like I have a lot more reddish tint than my friend . . . who is Kiowa. Like, when I tan, it is more of a red than she is. . . . The Cherokees and the Navajo don't look anything alike.

There appears to be a tension in her narrative between her appearance and what she thinks Natives look like, while at the same time she knows that Native peoples range in skin colorings.

A male reclaimer comments,

You know, I study Cherokee faces of different people through history . . . such a wide range, such a wide variety of what they did look like. I even met a, I met a pure-blood Cherokee man that was white as snow. And he had snow-white hair. There's something wrong with this picture! But . . . some of them, or part of them, they called them white Indians—they were very white skinned and they had more European features and stuff.

This is the man who spoke of not looking like "Sitting Bull" and of how the men he works with often tease him about being Indian, despite looking white. Does meeting a full-blood Cherokee who is "white as snow" validate his racial/ethnic sense of self? As he has become more familiar with the Cherokee culture he is reclaiming, he is beginning to recognize the range of skin colors and facial features among them, and this possibly provides some validation for his own reclamation despite his white appearance.

Another male reclaimer, when asked if he feels there are any enduring stereotypes about Native Americans, replies,

> Uh, well . . . you got the dark skin. Our tribe is, like, light-skinned and, like, always [in other words, they are light skinned all year around]. . . . And a lot of Eastern tribes were, too, because you're not out in the sun. . . . If you look at the tribes that are really dark, it's like, out west . . . and southwest. . . . It's like evolution and things like that where you adapt to your environment and stuff. And you didn't need that dark pigment [in the north]. . . . There's that whole thing, the dark skin, the dark hair. You know, we all have black hair, whatever.

This is a pattern that I find intriguing. Reclaimers repeatedly bemoan the fact that they lack stereotypical Native features and therefore are not recognizably Native, yet they logically explain how ridiculous and irrelevant such stereotypes are concerning Native appearance. To me, this is evidence of the symbolic interactionist understanding of the development of self as a product of social interaction. Due to the persistence of racial imagery in this culture, race is alive and well, and therefore individuals seeking to reconnect with a racial/ethnic heritage who lack the stereotypical physical features of their race face ongoing identity challenges.

PERFORMING IDENTITY

Obviously, appearance is more than the genetic code dictating how dark our skin, hair, and eyes are. Symbolic interactionists look at appearance in terms of

> everything about a person that others can observe. This includes clothes, grooming . . . choice and arrangement of personal possessions, verbal communication . . . and nonverbal communications. Through the appearances we present, we show others the kind of persons we are and the lines of action we intend to pursue. (Michener and Dalamater 1999, p. 220)

Anselm Strauss views appearance in terms of performances, by which he means "carrying out an act. This may be done for oneself as well as for, before, with, or through others" (1993, p. 120). He continues,

> It is also well to add that actors present themselves, deliberately managing their appearances. . . . These *presentations* of self (Goffman 1959) involve the body . . . either self-consciously or simply as part of the action. . . . These serve to

enhance, promote, denigrate, destroy, maintain, or alter performances, appearances, or presentations. Hence it is through these processes that much of the shaping of interactions, selves, identities, biographies, and body features occurs. (1993, p. 1221)

Strauss insists that we remember the following:

> In a general sense, "the" body is a necessary condition for all of our actions and interactions. It is the medium through which each person takes in and gives out knowledge about the world, objects, self, others, and even about his or her own body. . . . [C]ommunication also occurs through the body. Communication entails cooperative activity with others and is the basis of shared significant symbols, giving meaning to what one feels, sees, hears, smells, and touches. (1993, p. 109)

Charon adds:

> Our appearance is a substitute for our past and present action, and it tells others what to expect from us. Clothing tells others our proposals in the situation . . . it even goes further than our actions: Our friends, cars, religious objects, neighbors, clothes, and hair tell others what we want them to know about us, the identity we wish them to see. . . . The work of Goffman reminds us that creating identity is an active negotiation process between who others tell us we are and our continuous attempts to present who we think we are to others. (2001, p. 165)

Many of my interviewees describe this racial/ethnic identity performance explicitly. For half of the men I interview and all the woman, for instance, wearing long hair acts as a symbolic gesture, a racial/ethnic identity code of sorts. One man says he is made aware of his Native ethnicity in his daily life by reactions to his long hair. He simply states, "Like, I have longer hair than probably 90 percent of the female faculty there [the college campus where he teaches] and certainly than most of the male faculty." But for another young man, this ethnic code is not entirely unproblematic. He works at a grocery store where there are issues with him wearing his hair long. In response, he brings in a pamphlet explaining religious freedom in order to guarantee his right to wear long hair despite company policy. He explains to his supervisor as he drops off the pamphlet, "Here's the stuff. You can talk it over with your lawyer if you want. . . . I've highlighted some sections in here you might want to read. . . . Most of it has to do with prisoners who have less rights than normal people do, so you can imagine how things are going to go with this."

After he describes this confrontation to me, I ask him what long hair means to him, assuming it carries significance due to his attachment to it. Oddly enough, he has some difficulty answering the question. First, he responds,

"We're, we're taught, like, we're not supposed to cut it unless someone dies. When your hair's short it's—it's a sign of mourning." I ask if that is true for his tribe, the Osage, or overall, and he replies, "I don't know. But, that's just what I was taught. . . . And nowadays they don't even do that so much anymore but somebody might, like, cut a lock of their hair off and then put it with someone, or do something like that." He then adds, rather vaguely, "It's part of our—our—like our ethnic, you know, identity, I guess. We have long hair." I find his answer interesting. While there are cultural reasons for Native men to wear long hair, and for some tribes short hair is apparently indicative of mourning, it is clear he has not explicitly thought about why. He views long hair as part of performing a Native identity, yet to what extent does this reify stereotypical portrayals of Nativeness? Later he addresses this very issue when he talks about how wearing long hair can be problematic because it reinforces stereotypes surrounding Indians. As he says, "You struggle between what you wanna do, but at the same time it's like, I like to have my hair in braids, you know, and I think it'd be cool, blah, blah, blah. At the same time, it's like, 'Oh, Indians wear . . . have to wear braids and if they don't, they're not Indian.' You're battling that kind of, like, a stereotype." Yet, his reasons for wearing his hair long, aside from personal preference, do not appear to be at the level of discursive consciousness.

For many racial/ethnic groups, hair is an important symbolic statement. For African Americans, for instance, race relations are, to some extent, played out in daily discourse concerning hair (notions of "good hair," etc.). As Mercer (1997) states, "Although dominant ideologies of race (and the way they dominate) have changed, the legacy of this biologizing and totalizing racism is traced as a presence in everyday comments made about hair. . . . [R]acism first politicized our hair by burdening it with a range of negative social and psychological meanings" (p. 421). For Native Americans, reclaimers and non-reclaimers alike, wearing long hair is a statement of their Nativeness. Many reclaimers, although certainly not all, embrace long hair as a way to embrace their Native selves and as an outward message to others as to their racial/ethnic identity. Again, Mercer states,

> Hair is never a straightforward biological fact, because it is almost always groomed, prepared, cut, concealed and generally worked upon by human hands. . . . In this way hair is merely raw material, constantly processed by cultural practices which thus invest it with meanings and value. (1997, p. 420)

A female reclaimer tells a story about discrimination her Native grandmother experienced as a child. She says that her family never really denied their Native heritage but that it was not taught to them either due to "the discrimination that the earlier members of my family had paid when they were growing up, and it was obvious by the way that they looked that they were different from other people." I ask her if she knows any specific stories about discrimination her relatives have faced, and she provides one example:

> My grandmother told me this: she went to school one day and she had, she has really dark, dark hair. It was long and in a braid. . . . So, this is her first day of school, I believe in first or second grade or one of those, somewhere around there. . . . Some kids ganged up on her and were stoning her. . . . And one of the kids cut off one of her braids in class. . . . They used to call her half-breed and that kind of stuff.

This story exemplifies the significance of long hair for Natives. In her grandmother's era, that was one sign you were Native, and one way to harass you for that would be to cut off the braid. While long hair today, particularly for men, certainly is not unheard of, it is still unconventional and in certain environments, considered unacceptable.

Wearing long hair is not simply an ethnic code for others, however. One female reclaimer spoke of her six-year-old son's desire to wear braids to school. She worries about this because she feels it is dangerous to send her son to school with braids in his hair because, as she describes, "My little boy wants to wear braids. I can't send him to 'Bubbaland' with braids in his hair. You know? He'll be tormented to the ends of the earth. . . . All his favorite people have braids and pony tails, the men in his life, you know, and he can't do that because it wouldn't be accepted here." Would a boy today really be "tormented" if he wore long hair? Or is this reclaimer fearful due to her own experiences with discrimination (she was the one who grew up in communities where she saw "No dogs or Indians allowed" signs)? One can't know for sure. However, it is significant that she has such fears. Clearly, she does not feel our culture is completely open and tolerant of Nativeness. While the adult males I spoke to wear long hair, in braids and ponytails, their reasons for doing so are aesthetic as well as political.

One cannot assume political motivations behind a six-year-old child wanting to wear braids, but children do learn where they fit in the world at an early age and they also subtly learn their place in the racial hierarchy:

> In addition to home values, the child is influenced by teacher, television, radio, books, sports mascots, and people on the street and their reaction to the child. Seemingly positive comments directed towards the mixed race child may cause him to realize that he is different. To illustrate, at around the age of three, children become aware of skin, hair, and eye color. . . . Appearance may be one of the first catalysts for exploring identity possibilities. (Mihesuah 1998, p. 202)

Studies have shown that children learn to make judgments about themselves in relation to the world by the third or fourth grade. "James Comer, M.D., a professor of child psychiatry at Yale University, says that at this age children begin to understand where they stand in the American hierarchy" (Prothrow-Stith 1991, p. 166).

As a Native parent, the previously mentioned reclaimer finds herself in a quandary because she feels her son will be "tormented to the ends of the earth" if she lets him wear braids to school as he wishes, but she also recognizes that teaching him to hide who he is provides him with a subtle lesson on the racial hierarchy and his place in it. These are the kinds of dilemmas she talks a lot about in terms of parenting and reclaiming her Native heritage. For example, she says, reclaiming has been rather uncomfortable for her because

> of things like . . . my children coming home with a poster about Columbus being a hero. In their geography lessons they learn about Mount Rushmore and what a beautiful thing that is—that's a sacred Indian site that was desecrated! . . . Every face on that mountain is an Indian killer . . . and they come home with this lesson on what a wonderful sculpture it is. And what do I do with that, you know? How much conflict do I create for my children? How many lies do I let them believe so that they can get by? It is an uncomfortable place to be. . . . I want them to know the truth and I want them to grow up knowing their heritage and being proud of it. But, how much risk is there in that?

Again, one can look to black families in America for similar experiences. A young black live-away father whom Hamer (2001) interviews for her research describes this dilemma: upon experiencing discrimination in a store while he is with his son, he says he feels

> himself "icing up" and trying to control all emotion. At one level he wanted to let his son know that "this is the way it is for us black men," but simultaneously he did not want his child to see the ugliness or pervasiveness of the prejudice directed toward African Americans. "It's my job to protect him," he said, "but I know I got to prepare him, too." (p. 29)

Another female Native reclaimer with whom I speak feels she looks Native and has heard comments throughout her life to support that self-assessment, talks about reclaiming resulting in an even stronger impression in terms of her appearance. When I ask her how she maintains her ethnicity on a daily basis, she replies, "I try, when, when I can afford it, I try to purchase clothes or things that will make me look more my heritage . . . jewelry. . . . It makes me feel more 'in it.' More a part of it. . . . It's a symbol, a symbol of how I feel inside, you know. And I'm real aware of myself and connected with myself." And later she adds, "People have always recognized me: 'You're Indian, aren't you?' . . . It's, it's in my features enough and now in my dress enough that people recognize it right away." This reclaimer is conscious of her performance, conscious of ways she is recognizably Indian and that this helps her feel more Native, presumably because her racial/ethnic sense of self is being reflected back to her.

While many reclaimers do not explicitly speak about it the way the previous reclaimer does, almost everyone I speak to wears something on their person that would make one think they might be Indian. For instance, all the women I met wear their hair long, parted down the middle, in the stereotypical Native look. Many reclaimers I met wear numerous pieces of silver and turquoise southwestern Native American jewelry. This is, of course, interesting since many of them are wearing southwestern Native jewelry, yet belong to eastern tribes. It is possible that turquoise and silver jewelry has attained symbolic meaning beyond its southwestern tribal origins; maybe it has become part of the emerging pan-Indianism (Cornell 1988).

I met with a campus Native American student organization as part of this research, and my notes of the first meeting I attended exemplify the role of appearance:

> I arrived a little early. . . . I was nervous and wondered how I would recognize them [after people began arriving]. It wasn't too hard to tell they were members of a Native American group because they wore their cultural identity on their sleeves; they were wearing plenty of silver/turquoise traditional Native American jewelry. Although such jewelry is quite fashionable, the members, both male, were wearing more than most college [aged] males do (i.e., two long, dangly earrings, necklaces, rings).

In another set of observation notes from a couple weeks later, I write:

> While discussing the weekend antics, one of the members directs the conversation at me and describes an incident at [local breakfast place]. He said that a table full of frat boys were giving them shit. . . . When I asked why, he said, "Well, because we're Indian." . . . I asked how the frat boys would know such a thing (after all, the reclaimer who is relating the story looks as Native American as I do). He seemed uncomfortable [with the question] and commented that they just knew, people just know. . . . Then he goes on to discuss how aware he is when he's wearing his jewelry (he wears two long earrings, necklaces, turquoise rings . . .) and particular t-shirts in certain areas of the country.

These notes initially make me wonder if people who do not to hold stereotypical Native features more consciously wear their ethnicity in other ways. Do physically unrecognizable reclaimers wear extra jewelry as a conscious celebration of their ethnicity for their own purposes and sense of self, or is it a message for others, as exemplified in this case, for the table full of frat boys? Many reclaimers wear provocative t-shirts or buttons on their backpacks that express their allegiance with Indian country. One reclaimer proclaims,

> We do have some fun t-shirts. I don't have any of them, but [a friend] has some fun ones that are, like, very powerful statements. . . . [Another friend] has the "Custer had it coming" bumper sticker and [another friend] has one that has like Sitting Bull and Crazy Horse and it's . . . there are like four pictures of like Indian leaders and it's a black shirt and in red it says, "Our heroes, your enemies." I like that one. That is one of my favorite ones.

Clearly, reclaimers engage in impression management in order to project their authentic self, their Native identity, outward to others. Many reclaimers do not have stereotypical Native features and are therefore rarely recognized as Native American, due to both intermarriage rates among American Indians as well as to tribal diversity. Thus, they all must engage "outward cues [to] indicate to others inward identity and help others place the individual" (Fuchs Ebaugh 2001, p. 330).

WHITENESS AS NON-IDENTITY

For some reclaimers that I speak to, connecting with their Native heritage provides them with a cultural identity. One reclaimer addresses her incongruent physical appearance and racial/ethnic identity with the following response: "If somebody wants to know what my ethnic background is, I am a white Native American woman." Prior to reclaiming, one man described himself as simply a white guy, "white bread," with no heritage. Another says, "I was a mongrel white guy. I think there's some Irish and English . . . other than that, the Indian heritage, a typical American." He continues with what reclaiming his Indian heritage means to him:

> [It] gives me something that is ethnic to celebrate. To be attached would be a better way to describe it. Um, almost everybody here in America is just a typical American. We're all products of uh, inter-marriage between cultures, or a good portion of us are, and a lot of us don't have a certain ethnic background to point to, and I didn't . . . and then knowing all along that I have the Indian, that's the part that's sort of exotic and interesting and then making the connection [to this heritage] later in life . . . at age forty, uh, gave me something that, there is culture there. There is a distinct heritage there.

This interesting issue, the idea that being white is cultureless, is explored by Frankenberg (1993) in her research on the social construction of whiteness.

Hooks argues that white commodification of black culture similarly spices up "the dull dish that is mainstream white culture" (1992, p. 14). Frankenberg (1993) describes whiteness as an "unmarked" category, "for a significant number of young white women, being white felt like being cultureless. . . . Whiteness as a cultural space . . . [is] amorphous and indescribable" (p. 196).

One reclaimer I meet says that her boyfriend is envious of her culture because he, as a typical American, does not have such a cultural connection. Another reclaimer interestingly links her previous, non-reclaiming self with whiteness in a political/economic way. As she explains,

> When I first started reading about my Native heritage, um, I was very white. Very into working too hard, spending a lot of time at a job, and I think my kids saw, uh, a very big, obvious difference. 'Cause when I began to realize that what I wanted to be was what my grandfather and grandmother had taught me, it made a difference in life choices.

As a child, she says, her white features gave her some pride, yet she no longer views her whiteness in the same way:

> I think my skin is too white [laughs]. I have Native relatives who look much more Native than I. They all have these [she points to her own high cheekbones] but have very dark complexions. . . . My grandmother said that my, because all of my relatives are very, very dark, my dad was, and my brothers, I am the only white person among all these dark people. My grandmother said that I looked like a little porcelain doll because my skin was so white and my hair was so dark. Um, so I liked being white until I realized what all that meant . . . because my grandmother, because I felt so different, my grandmother sort of told me how special that was . . . and that was okay until I learned what being white was all about.

Her description is interesting in that once she understood *whiteness* to be about more than skin color, the descriptor no longer appealed to her. When it is a term used to describe her special skin color in the context of her family, it is considered a compliment. However, once she begins to see whiteness in it terms of its political connotation, she no longer considers it a compliment. This is evidence of the social construction of race, yet reclaimers are not accepting the dominant group's definition of race as associated with phenotype and genetics. Instead, the connotation associated with whiteness refers to a state of being, an outlook, a political position, and it is not a complimentary term.

CONCLUSION

This chapter explores how the concept of race informs Native American reclaimers' sense of self and their racial/ethnic identity construction. Reclaimers, as lifetime members of the dominant, white culture, at some level hold stereotypical images of what Indians look like, and these are used to gauge their own Nativeness, despite the fact that most fall short on such measures. On the other hand, they are all aware of the social and political construction of race and/or the diversity of physical appearances within Native America. Their narratives exemplify explicit identity struggles surrounding external racial ascriptions and internal identification with a particular racial/ethnic group. Symbolic interactionists ask,

> To what extent is the experience of self and subjectivity a matter of performance, development, or constitutional endowment? . . . How does the self exist both on the surface of the skin as well as in the eye of the audience? . . . Recognition of the socially constructed nature of race has led to the view that race, like gender, is always a matter of performance rather than a matter of disposition. (Leary 1999, pp. 86–87)

As Davis argues,

> Physical features are so important as indicators of ethnic identity that they are often accentuated. When racial differences between two ethnic groups are small or nonexistent, it is common for physical differences to be exaggerated or even created by hairstyles, dress, jewelry, scars, or other bodily decoration. . . . Perceptions of and beliefs about the physical differences, whether the traits are natural or created, are affected by cultural differences and experiences with the groups concerned. (Davis 1991, p. 160)

Many reclaimers use impression management, paying particular attention to our personal fronts, which consist of "the expressive resources we consciously or unconsciously draw on in our everyday interactions and performances" (Sandstrom, Martin, and Fine 2003, p. 110). One key resource reclaimers rely on is physical appearance, including clothing and hairstyles.

While one can look at reclaimers' embrace of racialized discourses as troublesome and as a reification of the European social construction of "race," it is also possible to recognize that reclaimers are not passively accepting dominant group definitions of race. For instance, several reclaimers describe "white" and "whiteness" as having meaning beyond skin color and instead being a political construction. They are actively deconstructing dominant group privilege through their challenge to the racial hierarchy. Sturm adds,

> *Indian* originally was an external label of colonial oppression that incorporated diverse indigenous nations into a system of racial and social classification. "Racing" Native Americans rationalized their oppression. Race, then, was an overt discourse, the ideology of a dominant white, colonial class that helped maintain and obscure power relations. But racial ideologies often double back

on themselves, and when they become a habit and are no longer in the realm of discursive struggle, they slip to a tacit level and are hegemonic once more. In this instance, people began to take "Indianness" for granted, and over time it became an "unquestionably" racial category. (2002, p. 24)

As Sturm implies, dominant groups may establish racial ideologies and impose them on subordinate groups; however, subordinate groups interact with dominant ideologies, adapting them to their own needs. Sturm emphasizes the former notion of race as a dominant ideology obscuring power relations that has now taken on a very different meaning among the Cherokee. Indians now embrace the notion of Indianness as an "'unquestionably' racial category." Subordinate groups' embrace of racial catogories means something fundamentally different than the imposition of racial categories by dominant groups on subordinate groups. This is evidence of a shift in power relations.

Physical appearance is only one aspect involved in gauging someone's authentic Nativeness. The next chapter examines authenticity battles that reclaimers face and actively engage in. Throughout the chapter there is evidence of reclaimers embracing Nativeness as a distinct racial identity, and challenging white racial hegemony in the process.

NOTES

1. Interestingly, while I was writing this chapter, a message came across our department listserv. A professor in the department wanted to inform us of a public website that contained attitudinal data about race. I quickly went to the site and found an updated version of a book, *Racial Attitudes in America: Trends and Interpretations* (Schumer et al. 1997). This book draws on data on racial attitudes between 1940 and 1997. While the book focused on the racial attitudes of blacks and whites, the website acknowledged that the picture is more complex and even social scientific research was beginning to reflect this—therefore, the current site contained data concerning Hispanics and Asians as well as whites and blacks. The racial attitudes of Native Americans or racial attitudes toward Native Americans are apparently not part of Schumer et al.'s study—unfortunately contributing to the invisibility of this population.

2. While it certainly may be true that many white men married Native women because they "are beautiful" as this reclaimer implies, we cannot discount the role of structure completely. She is correct that many European men married Native women. Weatherford in *Native Roots* (1991) discusses the propensity for European men, especially the French and the Scottish, to marry Indian women, particularly in areas of the country where there was a shortage of white women. One of my other interviewees explained that many white men married Indian women simply in order to acquire their land.

Chapter Five

"Wanna-bes" and "Indian Police": The Battle over Authenticity

The previous chapter explored the role appearance plays in a Native reclaimer's sense of self and racial/ethnic identity reclamation. One interesting point emerging out of that analysis is how not appearing Native, not resembling what people hold to be the stereotypical Native features of dark hair, skin, and eyes, and high cheekbones, presents a reclaimer with powerful challenges to his or her racial/ethnic identity claims. Such challenges are ultimately questions of authenticity, the act of questioning whether someone is "Indian enough." Among reclaimers, such authenticity challenges or claims to authentic Indianness are pervasive, including and going beyond issues of appearance.

There are several levels at which reclaimers face authenticity challenges. The most common challenges are at the individual level, where individual reclaimers are deemed inauthentic, with authenticity being either subjectively or objectively defined. However, there are also collective-level challenges, where tribes are accused of being inauthentic. There are also subjective and objective dimensions to this level as well. At the subjective, individual level, for instance, many reclaimers face family members who deny their Indianness. This, then, presents a challenge to their identity claims. Another authenticity challenge I find among the Native reclaimers pertains to the issue of blood quantum. Questions surrounding amount of Indian blood, proof of that amount, whether it should even matter, and its significance for legal categorization are commonplace "objective" challenges. Again, subjective challenges take the form of reclaimers facing suspicion from non-reclaiming Indians for being "wanna-bes" primarily due to current trends, for instance, where "Indian chic" is the fashion. What this means for them is their sincerity is often questioned and they are all too often perceived as "wanna-bes." Beyond the individual level, there are authenticity challenges at the collective level as well, with state-recognized tribes struggling to gain federal recognition and the authenticity dilemmas they face. Authenticity challenges come not just from the dominant culture but often are found between Natives, between reclaimers, and between non-reclaiming Natives and reclaimers, as well.

Individuals reared in the white, Anglo, mainstream world often face the accusation they are "wanna-bes" which Brayboy (2000) defines as "a person who claims to have cultural [Native] ties that do not really exist." Reclaimers are perceived as preying upon the current trendiness of Nativeness as well as perhaps embracing this heritage for economic, or perceived economic, gain (Brayboy 2000):

> As the popularity of American Indians has increased in recent decades, more and more people seem to be "getting in touch" with the "side" of them that is "Native American" (Nagel 1997). Most often, these individuals say they have a grandparent or great-grandparent who was American Indian. Among the indigenous people I know, this is commonly referred to as the "Cherokee Grandmother Syndrome." The argument that many individuals in this position make is that, because they have an ancestor who was American Indian, they also have some type of repressed cultural gene which is waiting to emerge if they read books or endeavor to reclaim "part of who they are." (Brayboy 2000)

An academic of Native heritage, Brayboy expresses concerns he feels Native people have with wanna-bes.

Embedded within Brayboy's preceding passage is the accusation that a genetic link is not enough to make someone Native and that to "read books" as part of a reclaiming process will not make someone authentically Indian; reading cannot replace lived experience, from his perspective. Reclaimers have not had the privilege of living this aspect of their heritage their entire lives; therefore, reading books, engaging in web-based research, and talking to other Natives are their avenues of cultural exploration. Because the reclaimers I speak to are from the American mainstream, without a conscious celebration of their Native heritage, they feel they have to take an aggressive approach to acquiring such knowledge. Yet, according to a few of my interviewees, reservation Indians, and people like Brayboy, are often critical of this approach. One of my interviewees, a history major with plans on pursuing Indian studies at the graduate level, speaks of this conflict explicitly; stating that he finds himself marginalized from the dominant society for pursuing his Native heritage, but at the same time, he is criticized for pursuing his Indian heritage in academia. He claims that tribal members tell him he should be with the tribe learning the language, ceremonies, and culture.

FAMILY MATTERS

Many reclaimers are searching to reconnect with a heritage that had been either explicitly denied in their family or sometimes simply subtly suppressed. Since ethnicity is based upon heritage, if one's family denies this aspect of one's heritage, it presents a reclaimer with an authenticity challenge. Ethnicity is defined by sociologists as shared cultural characteristics such as nationality, language, and religion (Farley 2005)—all things we are generally first taught in our homes. The role of the family in perpetuating ethnicity cannot be denied: "Ethnicity is largely determined by the ethnicity (or ethnicities) of one's parents" (Farley 2005, p. 7). What this implies, of course, is that families can choose to embrace and celebrate particular heritages, or they can neglect aspects of their ethnic heritage that are considered problematic. One woman in particular jokes, "My mother, to this day, says I am the only Indian in the family. I am not sure how that works genetically [laughs]." Another reclaimer I speak to often conflates her Nativeness with her paganism and views her family's Christianity as an obstacle to their embrace of their Native heritage. Therefore, her reclamation is challenged within her own family because, as she explains, her mother does not want her Christian friends to know she has Native heritage. Another woman, who adamantly pursues genealogical research, shares a similar story: "My dad thinks he does not have any Indian in him. . . . I think I will prove him wrong."

How does the denial of Native ancestry by family members affect someone reclaiming a racial/ethnic heritage? Several members make comments to me concerning the significance of family for Natives. One in particular says, "to Indians, family is of the utmost importance." For two of the three women quoted earlier, they respond to the challenge of family members by seeking to find "proof" through genealogical investigation. Such genealogical evidence is viewed as objective and incapable of being refuted, even by one's parent:

> Since tribal rolls were established, blood quantum has usually been determined by tracing genealogical histories back to these early records. Traditionally, tribal rolls have served as a basic reference point for most administrative definitions of American Indians. (Snipp 1989, p. 334)

For people pursuing genealogical evidence of their Native ancestry, their expectation is that proof of a genetic link will be enough to dispel claims that they are not authentically Indian, especially from family members. It is also all they have, since they lack the lived experience of Nativeness. My research finds, however, that such genealogical evidence is not quite as objective and "cut and dry" as my reclaimers hope.

POLICING INDIAN AUTHENTICITY:
OBJECTIVE MEASURES

The idea of proving one's Nativeness through establishing a genetic link has a long history. As Snipp explains:

> Historically, "blood quantum" has been a central concept in administrative definitions of Native Americans. In the nineteenth century scientists believed that blood was the carrier of genetic material and cultural traits. The mixing of racial characteristics was equivalent to mixing blood types. . . . Cultural differences, no less than physical differences, were the result of different blood types. (1989, p. 32)

Such nineteenth-century scientific knowledge would certainly be contested today, and most people currently would not argue for the existence of the link between cultural difference, physical differences, and blood type. Yet, within the Native community, the language of full-blood, half-breed, and so on is still very much present, albeit not without controversy. The idea of using blood quantum emerges in the nineteenth century among scientists and became a central tenet of the eugenics movement (Snipp 1989, p. 32). Basically, blood quantum designations "led to the belief that the amount of blood that a person possessed from a particular race governed the degree to which that individual would resemble and behave like other persons of similar racial background" (Snipp 1989, p. 32). Despite challenges to the accuracy of blood quantum to reliably determine Nativeness, it is still a significant issue because both the federal government and tribes base Indian status on blood quantum. Snipp points out this importance:

> The BIA, for example, uses 1/4 blood quantum as a minimum requirement for entitlement to certain government services. . . . Furthermore, a large number of tribal governments use blood quantum criteria ranging from 1/16 to 1/2 for determining tribal membership. American Indians are the only group in American society for whom pedigree bloodlines have the same economic importance as they do for show animals and race horses. . . . Nevertheless, there is little justification for believing that someone who is 15/64 blood quantum is decidedly "less Indian" than someone who is 1/4 blood quantum. (1989, p. 34)

There is quite a bit of tension surrounding the idea of blood quantum and authentic Indianness in general. Therefore, the reliance among many reclaimers on genealogy and the pursuit of a genetic link is not unfounded. Blood quantum is viewed by reclaimers as a significant criterion of authenticity, often treated as a literal measure of one's Indianness, despite the ambivalence surrounding the issue. As one woman explains in an exasperated tone,

Well, according to the records, my grandmother . . . is a pure-bred, which I find offensive anyway. It's like the American Indian Kennel Club. Have you ever asked a black person how much black blood they have? . . . Have you ever asked an Asian man? . . . It's really offensive. It's like asking . . . pedigree, like I'm a breeding dog. . . . And you hear them [those terms like *half-breed, full-blood, pure-bred*] from Indians more than anybody else. There's a lot of that . . . talking about whether they're actually Cherokee or not, you know?

This quote exemplifies numerous authenticity issues. First, blood quantum is often used as a gauge, despite numerous problems associated with using such a measure, of authentic Indianness. Second, she emphasizes how blood quantum is used to determine who is Indian, yet other racial/ethnic groups do not face such membership criteria. Third, this is an authenticity criterion that is used by Indians among themselves as well as by dominant group members.

Almost every reclaimer I meet expresses resentment at being asked, "How much Indian are you?" The woman quoted previously says simply, "I don't think I've ever said I'm Native American to anybody that didn't say, 'Oh, how much?'" Similarly to the earlier quote, a male reclaimer I speak to expresses his irritation at the question:

It's rude to ask somebody, like, how much Native they are because a lot of people are just like, you are or you aren't. You are not part of something. I mean, people don't say, "Well, are you—are you part German?" You know? You don't find that. Or "Are you part Irish?" . . . To me, you're like either Native or you're not.

This reclaimer's point warrants interrogation, however. Many white ethnics do define themselves in this very way—describing themselves as half-Irish and half-German, for instance. And, many reclaimers I speak to also describe their non-Indian ancestry in this way (as half-this, or some-that). There may be a number of explanations for such a discrepancy. It is possible that we simply do not have adequate language to describe ancestry in any other way; therefore, reclaimers use the terminology of half, a quarter, and so forth, to explain their various ancestral influences. Another possible explanation could be that reclaimers are more sensitive to the question of "How much?" since they are already dealing with authenticity challenges. An additional explanation could pertain to their awareness that blood quantum distinctions are relatively arbitrary (with tribes differing from each other, to the federal government definitions contrasting with those of tribal definitions of acceptable blood quantum) and are social and political constructions. It is obvious to several of the reclaimers I speak to that the United States federal government has an economic incentive to define many individuals with Native ancestry as "not Indian enough."

One interviewee expresses the following concern:

> Um, and then there's that whole question, too, with the whole blood quantum thing, you know, which can be really gross. . . . "Well, what part are you?" . . . You know, you wouldn't, wouldn't ask that of an African American person. You wouldn't ask that of a Hispanic person. . . so, it kind of makes you feel discounted . . . you know?

Interestingly, as the quote from Brayboy exposes, it is not just white people who use blood quantum as a gauge of someone's Indianness; this is also a practice among Indians themselves. As one interviewee explains,

> There are a kind of Indian police . . . the Native people who are of higher quantities of blood and think that you ought to have a certain quantity of blood or you ought to know this many facts about your tribe before you can really be classified as an Indian, you know? . . . So, there have been those people in the Native community that have questioned whether or not I have enough Native blood to call myself an Indian. And that gets a little annoying at times.

As this quote exemplifies, there are considerable questions surrounding authentic Indianness, some of which rely on blood quantum and others of which rely on cultural knowledge: "You ought to know this many facts about your tribe before you can really be classified as an Indian."

If blood quantum is a social and political construction of the dominant group, why do Native people use it to determine each other's authenticity? Sturm writes, "The racial logic behind this [the use of blood quantum] lies at a much deeper hegemonic level" (Sturm 2002, p. 80). In other words, Native use of blood quantum as a challenge to authentic Indianness may simply be a result of white racial hegemony. On the other hand, subordinate groups often appropriate terms and ideologies of the dominant group, yet alter them in ways that are empowering for them. Non-reclaiming Natives engaging in authenticity challenges through blood quantum may be doing so as a way to maintain their distinct cultures in the face of historical and current threats of assimilation.

Whatever the reason, many reclaimers whom I spoke to emphasized being challenged by other Natives on their authenticity. One reclaimer explains that the worst discrimination she has experienced has been intertribal: "The angst over who's a real Indian—there's a lot of really angry Indians in this world and with good reason." While she fails to elaborate on her point, she seems to be implying that Indians are angry due to centuries of oppression and discrimination and that this manifests in hostility toward reclaimers like herself. Another male interviewee says, "There are people out there who are just like, 'Oh, if you're not full-blood, I don't want nothing to do with you.'"

Another reclaimer provides a detailed explanation as to when she experiences such identity challenges:

> . . . where I see a lot of the rustling of the feathers, which is what I call it, you know, they're like, "Oh, I'm more Indian than you." . . . It happens at pow-wows. It's really strange. I mean, there's a lot of questions that come out—the attack almost. And it's very much like an attack. Like, you know, having to prove your authenticity . . . Indianness. 'Cause a lot of people are, um, very intolerant, um, now of people who come in and say, "Oh, my great-great-great-great-great-great grandfather was one-two-hundred and twenty-fifth Cherokee."

In this quote, the reclaimer interestingly criticizes the authenticity challenge reclaimers face from non-reclaimers, yet at the same time, her comment about people who "come in and say, 'Oh, my great-great-great-great-great-great-grandfather was one-two-hundred-and-twenty-fifth Cherokee'" betrays her own bias that there is room for doubt as to who is really an Indian and that blood quantum must count for something.

Yet the idea of blood quantum, with its semblance of objectivity and reliance on such biologically based criteria, is problematic. As Snipp argues, "American Indians of pure genotype probably disappeared sometime after the beginning of the sixteenth century" (1989, p. 31). One of my interviewees explicitly makes this point: "You're not going to find a lot of full-blooded Cherokee. . . . There's a full spectrum of people who are Cherokee." And another reclaimer comments, "There's so many multicultural people, it's really kind of ridiculous to be bigoted against anybody. I don't think there's anybody anymore that can call themselves pure-bred anything." Embedded in discussions over blood quantum are "notions of racial or ethnic purity, which, given the reality of intergroup contact throughout history, are impossible to achieve. Within the indigenous community there has been a great deal of intermarriage among different tribal groups as well as with non-Indigenous people" (Brayboy 2000).

Another interviewee explains what she views as a problem with relying on blood quantum as a determinant of one's Indian heritage: "I can't judge somebody else's family history and what they know about their family and . . . the whole thing is based on such chaos. I don't know how anybody can have really accurate records. Everybody's not documented. They can't be; there's no possible way."

Another interviewee describes a discrepancy between the family lore concerning her blood quantum and the official estimate:

> It's kind of odd. Officially, like according to the Bureau of Indian Affairs I am 1/16 Cherokee. Um, family history and like, the way I had always learned the

lineage of the Cherokee side of my family, I am 1/8 degree of blood. So, my grandfather, officially, is 1/4. I grew up always thinking and knowing he was 1/2 Cherokee. . . . So, I guess I'm technically 1/16.

I ask her why she thinks there is a discrepancy between the official records and family lore. She replies,

I don't really know. It must have just been that my mom had always said that her grandmother was a full-blooded Cherokee, when in fact her grandmother was 1/2. And I guess, you know, with Indian people, a lot of times it's hard to tell. You know, you can have someone of one tribe that is only 1/4 that looks like they could be completely full-blood. So, it's sometimes hard to tell. If you look at the pictures of my great-grandmother, she looks like she could easily pass for full-blood. So, I think that was part of it. We didn't really know the quantities until my mother went through the process of getting us on the tribal rolls and registering us.

I ask her if this discrepancy is significant for her, assuming that it must be since she goes into such detail to explain this to me and especially since I feel her choice of terminology betrays the significance in the former quote when she says she grew up "thinking and knowing" her grandfather's blood quantum. She surprises me by stating that she has no reason to doubt the official estimate of 1/16 and that "it really doesn't matter to me too much." I feel her elaborate explanation belies a different message, however. And if she does doubt "official" records, there is plenty of cause for her to do so. As Snipp points out in his discussion of the history of blood quantum, "the blood quantum information haphazardly collected in the early rolls is at best unsystematic, if not altogether unreliable" (1989, p. 34).

What does seem to bother the previously quoted woman is being discounted due to her degree of Indian blood. She says she finds this type of authenticity challenge from both whites and other Natives: "You know, people saying, 'You're barely, you're just 1/16 . . . does that really count?' . . . 'You can't really call yourself an Indian, you don't have enough blood.'" She replies that being Native is not simply a matter of degree of blood: "It's not about what degree of blood I have, you know, we all bleed the same color, whatever, you know. What matters is what's in my heart and what I identify with." Many other reclaimers express themselves similarly: "They have cards and documented . . . what percentage of their blood is Indian, which I think is funny. Either you're Indian or you're not, and if Indian blood flows through your veins, you're Indian, not whether you know [how much]." And later this same reclaimer adds, "I was taught that being Indian, it didn't matter what percentage of blood [you had]; it's what's in your heart . . . [that determines] whether you are Indian. If your heart tells you you're 100 percent Indian, you are 100 percent."

Another woman acknowledges an encounter with such "Indian police," as my reclaimers refer to them. She is at a pow-wow and she describes a man who manages to insult "everyone in the place" when he says "he was so proud of his drum group that they were all full-bloods, there were no half-breeds, wanna-bes . . . it caused quite a stir. But, then, it's a small group and I suppose there are bigots in every culture." Another woman describes a bad experience she has at a pow-wow: "I did not enjoy the one in [city], though, because unfortunately between the Indians there are feelings between the full-blooded and us, 'wanna-bes' they call us." When I ask her what that means, she explains, "Wanna-bes, yeah. People who don't have full heritage, who aren't 100 percent Cherokee." Her definition of a wanna-be is interesting in that it differs from what Brayboy (2000) defines as a wanna-be. To Brayboy (2000), a wanna-be has no legitimate claim to Native culture but pretends to. As a reclaimer, this woman feels other Indians challenge her because she is not full-blood Cherokee, so she is therefore labeled a "wanna-be."

Another interviewee explains how blood quantum does not really describe her, or her father's, Indianness very well at all. Her father is from the Lakota reservation and I ask, "Is he full-blood? Is that a term people use?" Her response supports Snipp's point that one is unlikely to find any Indians of pure genotype anymore:

> Yeah. I mean . . . if you went by blood quantum, no. But he is because he was from the reservation, his parents were from the reservation, their parents from the reservation. . . . My last name . . . goes back seven generations from me. So, seven generations back we have some French-Irish [ancestry], but by the time it made it down to me, there's not a whole lot left [of her French-Irish ancestry]. . . . So, by standards he wouldn't be considered full because there's some, like, little trace amount of French-Irish in his background, but that's it.

She later talks about how degree of blood has been used to challenge her claims to Indianness:

> . . . and this whole idea in America which makes me so angry . . . without being a full-blood, without being a pure-blood, then I really couldn't be [Indian], you know? All of a sudden to know, "Well, you're diluted so you're not really anything." You know what? . . . That's total bunk . . . that's so damaging to the personality—and you can see that with anybody who is multicultural.

Her comment exposes the hegemony of race, as the earlier quote by Sturm emphasizes: "Blood quantum was widely embraced by nineteenth-century scientific thought as a rational measure of racial identity and racial 'purity.' Thus, the racial logic behind this lies at a much deeper hegemonic level" (2002, p. 80). This reclaimer's comment emphasizes our cultural insensitivity to multicultural people, as our history betrays through, for instance, the use of the one-drop rule for African Americans and the recent controversy over the addition of a multiracial category on the 2000 census, both of which are evidence of the operation of racial logic and notions of racial purity.[1]

Another interviewee explains that another problem with relying on historical documents such as the tribal rolls for determining who is Indian is that, especially among the Cherokees, name changing is a common practice. As one goes through life, one takes different names that are more reflective of that particular life stage. Additionally, she explains that "many of them also didn't know how to read or write, as with my second great-grandfather. He didn't know how to read and write, so his last name is spelled four different ways." Another reclaimer adds, "What's interesting is, that sometimes they're on the census and sometimes they're not. A lot of it depends on how well they got along with the census taker." These inconsistencies obviously can cause a future genealogist trouble.

One woman discusses some interesting legal ramifications of the use of tribal rolls and reliance on blood quantum for tribal membership in the Choctaw tribe:

> The Choctaw side of my family, um, my mom's cousin's kids . . . she wanted to get her kids on the rolls of the Choctaw tribe and she know, knew my mom had gotten us on the [Cherokee] rolls. Well, they can't because the tribal members of my Choctaw relatives have been disqualified from the Choctaw tribe. Because of the 1910 census, there was so much discrimination going on that a lot of Natives checked white if they could pass for white, that's what they said. You know, they disowned their heritage. But, you know, at the time, with so much discrimination, if they could pass for white and that would save them from persecution, you know, that was a choice they made. Um . . . I wasn't in those circumstances, so I don't know . . . you know, I don't really blame them. Who's to say I wouldn't have done the same thing? . . . My Choctaw ancestors said they were white because they could pass for white, they didn't want to suffer discrimination anymore, and what the Choctaw tribe did was, any of their tribal members who didn't mark Native American on the census [of 1910], they kicked them out of the tribe. They were disqualified by their roll numbers—no longer valid! . . . The Supreme Court even told them, you know, you can't disqualify their tribal members. . . . Their [the Choctaw tribe's] response was, you know what? We are a sovereign nation and we don't have to listen to the Supreme Court. . . . And so, yeah, the Choctaw tribe isn't backing down.

This is an interesting legal prescription in terms of who is Choctaw. While many tribes are looking to increase membership, this is an example of a tribe that restricts membership.

Another reclaimer I met has multiple strains of Native ancestry that create interesting dilemmas for her as a reclaimer. She explains,

> I'm Cherokee. I'm proud of being Cherokee. There's also Sioux and Apache in there. . . . Apaches, unfortunately, never kept records, so they are impossible to track. They don't have a web, anything that you can actually check. . . . Cherokees are actually the best bunch to track. Sioux, unless you are half, you can forget pretty well anything along those lines. . . . [Why? I asked] It is very hip to be Native American [sighs] . . . and there were a lot of false groups going up and I cannot blame the Sioux or Cherokee or the Apache or any of the others for saying, "Wait a minute. Don't claim this if you ain't this."

Sturm (2002) cites her own struggle with conflicting tribal membership designations:

> I investigated whether or not I was eligible for tribal enrollment through my grandmother. I was surprised to find that the Choctaw Nation in Oklahoma had no minimum blood quantum requirement and only asked for proof that my great-grandmother had moved to Oklahoma and was listed on an earlier tribal roll. However, my grandmother had been born in Mississippi, the original homeland of the Choctaw people, and had never moved west. Moreover, even with proper records, I failed to meet the Mississippi Choctaw Nation's minimum racial standard of one-half Choctaw blood or more. Had my grandmother moved to Oklahoma, I would have been in, but because she had stayed in Mississippi where the racial definitions were stricter, I was out. This frustrating experience is a common one for Native Americans whose identities are administered and verified through what are often rather haphazard paper trails leading to racially quantified ancestors. (p. 6)

The idea of blood quantum, particularly in its use by the federal government, is obviously wed to the notion that Native Americans are a distinct race, not simply a collection of ethnic groups, which might explain the lasting significance and use of this otherwise outdated scientific concept.

Why does blood quantum still exist as a determination of Indianness? Whose interest does it serve? It appears that what began as a system of identification that works in favor of the federal government, as reclaimers allude to, now is being reinforced through its embrace by tribes and individuals. Tribes are compelled to embrace this faulty authentication procedure because land allotments are tied to tribal enrollments (Sturm 2002). Reclaimers and even non-reclaiming Indians embrace the concept because it is presumed to be an objective measure of Indianness and provides them with a genetic claim to their Native heritage, particularly when cultural heritage and/or appearance are lacking.

The previously mentioned reclaimer, whose father is from the Lakota reservation, speculates on the political motivations of having such strict categorization criteria:

> . . . that ties into, again, economic reasons. And there were reasons the U.S. government wanted people to be defined as black . . . because if you were black there were certain things that were kept from you . . . because you didn't have certain rights. And so that was good for the U.S. government. And then on the Indian side, if we [the United States Government] could lead you out, then that was good for us because we wouldn't have to pay . . . or have to meet treaty rights.

She also recognizes that such government policies and practices have a detrimental effect on Native Americans by creating an environment where people are pitted against each other: "Then it's internalized and it becomes almost a standard, um, in the culture and it's unfortunate but that does happen. . . . There's some of that on the reservations . . . there's the question of authenticity." She provides a minor example of authenticity challenges she faces on reservations: "I've been to different reservations—there's always some standard questions that you have to answer. . . . You know, 'Who are you? What Nation are you?' And then they kinda look you over. You have to explain some crap . . . and then usually there's the door that opens up, you know?" She feels that this is especially harmful to individuals whose Native heritage is more distant than hers, recognizing that her last name gives her an "in" on the reservation " . . . where someone else who, maybe [their] grandparents left or great-grandparents left [the reservation] . . . that makes it a lot harder for them . . . it makes it a lot harder for them to make a connection."

Another individual I spoke with criticizes the government and use of tribal rolls to determine tribal membership. He describes it in terms of issues of equity and recognition, however:

> It's the most wealthy country on earth, but, um, they do not want to accept anybody that wasn't on the . . . roll in the past. They had a cut-off time, a cut-off date. You had to fit into that category. You had to live in Oklahoma. You could not be a Cherokee and you just kind of vaporized—you turned invisible after that, so . . . I guess one of my biggest frustrations is that, uh . . . not being included in the history of so many different things.

His ancestors are not on the rolls because they escaped the Trail of Tears, and he is critical of the fact that due to their ability to avoid forced relocation, they are no longer officially recognized by the federal government as Indians. Interestingly, he is critical of the government's use of the rolls, but he does not criticize tribal use of the rolls for determining tribal enrollment. He, for instance, cannot claim membership in the Cherokee Nation of Oklahoma due to his ancestors not moving west, so he therefore is seeking membership in a Cherokee tribe that is state recognized but not federally recognized.

Another woman similarly complains, "They weren't part of the removal. They were Indians, but they couldn't go to Oklahoma and they weren't allowed to stay here and so they really got caught in a pinch. . . . That's the difficult thing, searching for people who are hiding." Yet another woman lays the foundation of tribal animosity at the feet of the federal government:

> There's lots of animosity between tribes. Everybody says "an Indian's an Indian" and that's not [true]—there's over 600 tribes in this country, 600 different languages, 600 different traditions. . . . [In] the Cherokee Nation alone, there's the Northern, the Eastern, and the Southern, and the Western, and in each one of those groups there's difficulty about who should be in, who shouldn't be in, who should be leaders, who shouldn't be leaders. There's all this dysfunction that was brought in by whites, governmental practices [that have] demolished the community system.

Despite the problems with proving blood quantum, many reclaimers I met are avid genealogists and work diligently to prove their genetic claim to a Native American tribe. One woman simply describes her search in this way: "I have to prove it. . . . You know, I have to—I know I got it, I want to know [how much]." One person I spoke with feels that being tribally enrolled is the most important thing he could do. As he explains,

> I'd known since at least first or second grade, uh, maybe even earlier than that, I was some Creek. My mother taught me how to count to ten in Creek and a couple of other Creek words ,which I no longer remember. So, you know, I told people all along, but it really was not a part of my life and I did not feel very connected. Um, this was a way to officially, sort of, seal that situation, that bond, and a way to, uh, I guess, mainly that would be the major thing. To signify to myself something concrete, some action that I had now gone from just saying if it came up in conversation, uh, hey, I am Indian or I have some Indian heritage or I have ancestors who were enough Indian so that they had to register on tribal rolls nearly a century ago. It went from that stage to taking a step that formalized it for me . . . that probably is a more important step to me than if I were to be adopted [by his tribe], were to get an Indian name, or something like that.

In this reclaimer's narrative, the significance of proving his lineage, to making it formal, makes it more than a topic of conversation and instead makes it something that informs his sense of self. Another blue-eyed, light-skinned female reclaimer explains that she pursues genealogy as a way to authenticate her Indianness in spite of not appearing so: "I knew enough to know that it was there [her Native heritage] and I was interested in it, so I dug it up to prove it. Because, um, you kind of, I mean, I don't have black hair and brown eyes, you know, [or] very dark skin." Again, a symbolic interactionist understanding of the development of self is evident by her comment. As a woman who does not hold stereotypical Native features, she does not get her reclaimed racial/ethnic self reflected back to her from others. She therefore is searching for more, presumably, objective evidence of this heritage.

Another reclaimer, also a genealogy buff, explains how to go about authenticating one's Cherokee heritage:

> When you go to do Indian genealogy, the only way to track your ancestors are by the rolls that people took . . . some kind of lawsuit in 1909 saying that if you have an ancestor that has Indian blood in them or you are full-blooded, you could sign up for this. . . . But, you had to prove that you had enough in you for that and if you want to join a tribe today you have to find an ancestor on that [the rolls]. But, the problem is that most people wanted to keep it hidden in 1909, so there are a lot of people in Missouri who can't even prove from that.

While this reclaimer is working to prove her Indianness according to official records, she also recognizes the limitations of overreliance on such documentation.

What is interesting about this process of relying on genealogical histories for evidence of one's Native heritage is that the process itself keeps alive nineteenth-century definitions of race through the underlying assumption that racial designations are static, objective, and reliable. This is in complete contrast to current notions of race as a social, political, and legal construction. Other groups, for instance Irish Americans, have been able to "become white" (Ignatiev 1995) over the course of time. Yet for Native Americans, as long as they are forced to rely on historical records to prove their heritage, they will never be able to escape their racialized status, and their subordinate position in the racial hierarchy will remain constant.

Giroux explains that authors such as Ignatiev (1995), Roediger (1991), and Frankenberg (1993), among others, have been effective at

> challenging both what it means to be White and the experience of whiteness as an often unstable, shifting process of inclusion and exclusion. . . . [They] attempt to arbitrarily categorize, position, and contain the "other" within racially ordered hierarchies. Dislodged from a self-legitimating discourse grounded in a set of fixed transcendental racial categories. (1999, p. 228)

To what extent, then, is reclaiming a Native heritage a challenge to the racial hierarchy and to what extent does it reify that very hierarchy? At some level, reclaimers challenge the notion of race as a fixed category because they are white and Native, yet they are actively working on changing their racial status, on becoming non-white. Clearly, that is evidence of the fluidity of race rather than the perception of racial categories as fixed. However, if "unbecoming white" for Native reclaimers requires proving blood quantum, wouldn't that very process maintain white dominance? Of course, for the most part indigenous peoples do not want to "become white" and in fact have fought against assimilationist policies and practices such as BIA boarding schools, which attempted to create "white red men." But, while assimilation has been the encouraged route out of a denigrated racial status for individual Native Americans (not to mention numerous other ethnic minorities), the racial category "Indian" and its subordinate place in the racial hierarchy has yet to be challenged. Continued reliance on blood quantum helps ensure the maintenance of white racial hegemony.

The reclaimer quoted earlier, who recognizes the limitation of official documentation, has ordered a copy of the Geon Miller rolls, which list the "documented" Cherokees, in order to assist her in her search for empirical evidence of her Cherokee status. She explains to me that in the back of the book are lists of people who failed to get accepted into the tribe because they "couldn't prove enough . . . [some] didn't have enough blood to prove it." I interpret her comment as well as the practice of listing those who fail to prove their blood quantum sufficiently and therefore are not able to tribally enroll, as authenticity claims. The practice of listing those who do not gain tribal membership status is evidence that this is a "real" tribe, with legitimate standards, and that not just any New Age person who feels connected to Native culture can become a member of the tribe. This is explicit boundary maintenance being performed. For someone searching for her heritage, this practice appears to validate the legitimacy of the tribe in her eyes. She makes a comment previously in her narrative about a person she finds in her genealogical research that qualifies for enrollment in some unspecified tribe. She hopes that this will be her tribal connection, but when she orders her materials, she says, "I see no connection at all. Very vague. I don't know why this tribe let her in, but I heard it was a shady tribe anyway. . . . They allowed things that shouldn't be allowed. Just let anybody in and stuff like that." So, while she still has work ahead of her in terms of proving her ancestry, she takes comfort in the fact that she will not be a member of a "shady" tribe.

Proving genetic ancestry is important to most reclaimers I meet. Out of my seventeen formal interviews, ten are tribally enrolled, three have completed the paperwork and are waiting to hear if they have been accepted into the tribe, and four are not currently enrolled and are not in the process of getting tribally enrolled. Of these last four, two describe themselves as simply lazy and they could get tribal enrollment status if they sought it; one never mentions her enrollment status; and only one person I meet explicitly says it does not matter to her—her knowledge of her Native ancestry through family lore is all the legitimation she needs.

What I find additionally interesting about the idea of blood quantum is that despite reclaimers' expressed disdain for the terms *half-breed*, *full-blood*, and other such designations, my interview transcripts are full of such references. For instance, one reclaimer I meet is talking about his wife and I say, "Is she Native?" He replies, "Yeah . . . she's full-blooded Navajo." This comment is made within minutes of his lambasting people for asking the "How much [Indian] are you?" question.

Reclaimers repeatedly use such terminology, yet they consider it an identity challenge if they are asked about their own blood quantum. One could write off such contradictory positions as simply hypocritical, but I think there is more meaning behind the tensions surrounding the issue. First, it can be viewed simply as evidence that people's beliefs and behaviors are often contradictory. The previous chapter emphasized, for instance, how attention to appearance among reclaimers reinforces the idea that Native Americans are a distinct race, yet not everyone agrees that Indians are a distinct race; many prefer the term *ethnic group*, and most of them did not think they "looked Indian" and certainly disagree with use of appearance as a criteria for Nativeness. Second, there is a clear tension around the idea of blood quantum among reclaimers because many may not be able to prove theirs. Again, after being raised without this cultural heritage, these are people who feel constantly called on to authenticate their Indianness. So, questions such as "How much are you?" are often interpreted as identity challenges. Yet, at the same time, these are terms that are used among Indians throughout the United States; therefore, one could look at reclaimers' appropriation of such terms as part of their embrace of Native culture.

Brayboy examines his own habit of gauging authentic Indianness in others and resolves,

> Knowing that I have these biases of who counts as "real" and being critical of myself, and others who hold similar ones, does not preclude me from engaging in the very behavior to which I am opposed. Again, there is a real contradiction and tension surrounding what we believe (our theories as it were) and what we do (our practices). (2000, p. 424)

POLICING INDIAN AUTHENTICITY:
SUBJECTIVE CONCERNS

Reclaimers find that even when they meet blood quantum requirements, they are still often considered "wanna-bes." Brayboy speaks of a certain amount of cultural capital (Bourdieu 1977; Bourdieu and Passeron 1990) one must have in order to be considered a real Indian and to avoid the stigma of being considered a wanna-be. He is interestingly vague on what this cultural capital is, arguing, "These individuals also needed to be concerned about certain political issues. . . . [A]ccording to this classification, indigenous people live their lives with particular values. These values include a strong belief in 'Native American' ideas . . . that cannot be explicitly defined." In his research on Native Americans in academia, he describes how he feels about one subject he encounters, describing her as culturally bankrupt, adding, "I wondered, 'How can she identify herself as Native American when she doesn't even know the rules?' . . . Clearly, I was taken aback by someone whom I believed was 'posing' as a Native American because she thought it might benefit her in some way" (Brayboy 2000).

One of my interviewees says reclaiming has been difficult and uncomfortable for her, often due to the presence of such "Indian police," enforcing such "rules":

> Rules about what I have to do to be an Indian. . . . There are traditionalists who say if you don't practice the ways and if you don't do this, this, and this, that you're not an Indian, you know? If you can't dance and play basketball, you're not black? [laughs] You know, I'm sorry, that isn't the criteria. It's kind of the same thing, if you don't do sweats every week and if you don't, you know, do the pipe and women can't do this and they can't do that. [Additionally] there's a lot of adopted sexism.

Another reclaimer finds herself constantly frustrated by the authenticity challenges she receives from another reclaimer who is a member of the same Cherokee organization that she belongs to. She explains, with pride, how she goes about learning her Cherokee heritage, and yet, someone else is always correcting her knowledge:

> Well, I'm a take-charge kind of person, so when I want to learn something, I look at books and videos. To me, there's an unlimited amount of information out in the world. It's just a matter of getting a hold of it because I felt frustrated with the people. This one lady in this particular group—she would be a "Miss Know-It-All"—and it would really aggravate me . . . if you brought something like leather hair tyings. . . . I brought those in and the fringe wasn't cut just perfect.

"No, no, no, that won't do." It's got to be precisely this or that. And she is just this person, I guess she didn't grow up with it. . . . But anyway, I went to the Cherokee gift shop and I looked to see what videos they had. . . . I went to the library, you know . . . you know, I want to have a little bit of knowledge when I go there [to a pow-wow].

She goes on to enthusiastically talk about a shawl she had learned to make through a video, and she adds that she was criticized for this. "The way I made my shawl and the way I folded it was not the proper way for her [laughs]." In order to settle this authenticity dispute in her mind, she simply says,

Well, when I made my shawl, I made it like the one off this video and I'm folding it that way and that's the way I like it. . . . According to this video, that's how you do it! But you get these people with their mind-sets. How the fringe should hang! On the video, it's a personal preference. If you want the fringe on the outside, you can do it. If you want it on this side, you can do it. Well, she says it shouldn't be on the outside. It should only be on the inside. And I wanted to say, "Hello! I've got this full-blooded Cherokee woman from over there in Oklahoma who does this all the time telling us how to do it [on video]."

The woman quoted here is a reclaimer who is relatively new to the process, and she is having a difficult time reconciling what are correct cultural practices and which ones are not and who is in a position to know this. She resolves this contradiction by discrediting a fellow reclaimer and instead places her trust in someone who is both full-blooded and from Oklahoma—two significant criteria of Indianness, from her perspective.

Those without proof of blood quantum, or those simply not wanting to overemphasize the importance of blood quantum, tend not to emphasize the importance of such evidence. For instance, one interviewee who adamantly polices others' attempts to reclaim their Native heritage, explains to me that he does not have his federally issued BIA card (Bureau of Indian Affairs or CDIB—Certificate of Degree of Indian Blood card) or his tribal enrollment card. He says he does not really care about the BIA documentation, but someday he might enroll in his tribe:

I just don't get around to it. . . . Someday, when I can get the information I need, then that's fine. My aunt's Mormon, I think I could just go in and get the stuff because they have all those great genealogy records . . . and I'm just lazy and busy . . . I don't do it. Like [another reclaimer I spoke to] is the same way. He can go tomorrow if he wanted to and get signed up but he just hasn't done it yet.

For this young man, the issue is, or should be, "What is it really about?" Instead of focusing on proving his Native ancestry through genealogical research, he instead argues,

> It's like, a big thing with like, Native identity, is that you're dealing with like — like we talked about — when we were talking about if somebody's Indian, it's not like, it's not always — not always their blood quantity. And I know people that are full-blooded that don't know jackshit about nothin'. . . . There's people that are like, you know, like us that know a lot of stuff, but we're not full-blooded but, man, we know, you know? . . . The big question is like, *what is it really about?*"

In this quote he acknowledges the dilemma reclaimers, especially those who have not proven their blood quantum, face. Their knowledge is questioned based upon their lack of genetic proof. His argument to this is, what does blood matter anyway?

A young female reclaimer agrees, stating that when she began her reclaiming process, she was shy and did not speak up much because she was unsure of her tribal and Native knowledge after having been raised in the white, mainstream world. But, after several years into the process of reclaiming, she says, "I don't have to qualify that anymore, that I didn't grow up in the environment so I don't know a lot of things." She believes that blood quantum is a pointless measure because "what matters is what's in my heart and what I identify with." In other words, her years in college, interacting with a Native American student organization, reading, and searching, have provided her with knowledge that she considers sufficient to allow her some sense of comfort in her cultural knowledge as well as in her racial/ethnic identity claims.

Another reclaimer expresses a similar sentiment: "When you talk about race, well, there are a lot of people I know who are racially Indians, but ethnically, they're not Indians. There are a lot of people who are racially white, but ethnically, they're Indians." This comment reflects that genetic endowment does not imply cultural knowledge, and that one without the other is insufficient (a complete contradiction of the notion of blood quantum, interestingly). This begs the question, however, is he comfortable with someone with no Indian blood claiming an Indian identity?

Crow Dog similarly discounts blood quantum as a criterion for Indianness: "I should make clear that being a full-blood or breed is not a matter of bloodline, or how Indian you look, or how black your hair is. The general rule is, whoever thinks, sings, acts, and speaks Indian is a skin, a full-blood, and whoever acts and thinks like a white man is a half-blood or breed, no matter how Indian he looks" (1990, p. 49). Left unanswered are the questions, what does it mean to think like an Indian? Act like an Indian? Sing like an Indian?

Is it even possible to establish a set of criteria for each of those on which all Indians of all tribes would agree? It seems unlikely, yet on the other hand, there also seems to be, at least potentially, an essential Indianness that many reclaimers refer to, even if abstractly.

Many reclaimers I meet, for instance, feel that reconnecting with this aspect of themselves makes them feel whole, makes them feel like, in the words of one man, "You're not really wacky!" It explains many thoughts, emotions, and likes and dislikes they had their entire lives that always made them feel different, like an outsider, an "Other." For instance, many speak of not fitting in with other children growing up, or feeling a tremendous connection with nature, and a sense of spirituality. A reclaimer who has no interest in discovering her blood quantum explains to me:

> It's not important to me to have papers saying that. I feel it. I know, you know, and I've grown up with the stories. . . . Getting back to nature and doing what I do now is the closest that I've come and I've just related with it and fit right in and it works for me. So, that's more important to me than the paper.

One Osage woman I interview, who is not part of my sample of reclaimers but instead is from the Osage reservation in Oklahoma, explains that her people believe that no one can completely walk away from their Indianness, that a connectedness will always be there. As Brayboy says,

> Intellectually we understand that there are not essential traits commonly held by all members of a group and that members of a group may be defined in multiple ways. In real life, however, many in our groups—including ourselves at times—may use essentialized notions to define membership. Reconciling this tension is a difficult process. (2000, p. 420)

Another reclaimer I interview, who has not proven his genetic heritage but claims to have Cherokee on his father's side of the family, often speaks very emotionally about what being Cherokee means to him. At one point he even says, "You know, even though everything about me is Cherokee, I can also see white, too," which seems odd since he looks white, his mother is white, and he was raised in the white world, one would think that "seeing white" would not be difficult. Yet what he is really doing with this comment is making an authenticity claim—emphatically pointing out his Indianness. He is interesting in that he mentions multiple times during our interview his size, the fact that he is a big guy, with comments to the effect of "and I'm a big guy" or "here's this big guy" in relation to getting very emotional over some issue related to his Nativeness. For instance, he describes an incident at a pow-wow at which he intended to dance in the contest, something he enjoys doing. When he goes to dance, he drops one of his feathers. He explains to me that when you drop a feather, you're disqualified and an elder man has to be brought in to bring the spirit back into the feather, and the person who drops the feather then gives them away because they are not considered theirs anymore. In his words, "I mean, I was this big dude and I was bawling my eyes out. I was upset. I went outside and sat down and cried." Another time he tells me about some conflicts he has had with administrators on his college campus over a repatriation issue:

> I went outside and sat down and cried, you know, just pissed, it's so frustrating . . . that one instance I snapped, I went outside crying and saying I was going to cut my hair and pretend I'm white but I couldn't live with myself because, you know, I am a Cherokee person, you know? I guess it means everything to me.

Clearly in these passages he is trying to get me to understand the depth of what being Cherokee means to him. I think his emphasis on his size and the fact that he wants to show he is not afraid to cry over issues concerning Nativeness are specific legitimacy claims—the message that being Cherokee carries more weight than even his masculinity.

This young man initially encountered Native culture and began exploring his own Nativeness in the context of pow-wows. When he began to reconnect with his Cherokee heritage he was in high school, and his mother would go with him to pow-wows in the metropolitan area in which they lived. He eventually acquired regalia and began to dance and sing at pow-wows. Later, he organized the first pow-wow held on the college campus he attends (one which became an annual event). By the time we met in 2001, he had reached a point where he was disgusted with the direction pow-wows have taken. As he explains, "I'm just fed up with people that only dance when it's for contest and when it's for money and I'm fed up with it." His best friend, also a reclaimer I met, expresses similar sentiments: "A lot of things . . . are changing. Like, especially around the pow-wow arena that, that to me, aren't right. . . . They're kinda getting lax on some things." When asked to elaborate on what has changed or gotten lax about pow-wows, they both tell a similar story. As elaborated on earlier, the story has to do with preparing to dance in a contest and then dropping a feather. When the reclaimer dropped the feather, he voluntarily pulled himself out of the contest. As he explains to me, "When you're in a contest, if you drop an article of your outfit—a feather, anything—you pull yourself out of contest. I'm getting pissed because I see people not do that as much anymore. If I'm the judge, I disqualify them on the spot, that's the way it goes." He continues with his explanation that a dropped feather is not considered yours anymore, and when this happened to him, he gave his feather to an older man at the pow-wow. What disturbs him most about this incident is that this older gentleman

. . . [was] just shocked, this old guy, and he was shocked that I gave it to him. And I was kinda pissed. I'm like, uh-uh, this is the way it goes. This is tradition. I'm supposed to give it to you. But they were shocked that I actually did it. And I just, I got pissed because everybody has strayed so much from tradition, I'm like, there's almost no honor in dancing and I haven't danced since.

His friend adds, "It's switching for more of a good time and uh, a good event and a celebration and like, sometimes [instead of] giving thanks and dancing and healing it has become all about prize money and stuff. I mean . . . I'm like, 'Yeah, I wanna win' . . . but that's not why I am out there." His implication with this last point, of course, is that the lure of prize money, while not his incentive to participate, is why too many others dance at pow-wows. They both feel that pow-wows bring out the "weekend Indian," which they find offensive.

There are a lot of authenticity claims embedded in their discussion of pow-wows. One continues, "When I learned how to dance [at pow-wows], I learned a lot the old ways, you know, just little bits of detail. And when I'm a judge, you know, at pow-wows that have a contest, you know, I stick to that stuff. I mean I'm strict and I'll stay strict. . . . I'm like, if you're gonna dance for money, you're dancing for the wrong reasons." According to this interpretation, pow-wows are traditional ceremonies. There are clear rules that govern pow-wows, and somehow, in the last three to five years, the standards have gotten lower, primarily due to "weekend Indians," who participate for the wrong reasons.

My interviewees' comments are part of the "policing" of behaviors that goes on among Indians—reclaimers as well as non-reclaimers. One can question just how traditional pow-wows even are. As Stephen Cornell points out, they emerged in the late nineteenth and early twentieth centuries, what he refers to as "the reservation years," as "intertribal social gatherings and festivals. . . . [S]ponsored by a particular tribe, they drew Indians from other reservations, some quite distant, for several days of ceremony, socializing, and dancing" (1988, p. 111). Another dilemma pertains to these two reclaimers' perceptions of the "old ways." Their quotes imply, of course, that there are traditional, accepted rules governing pow-wow practices that have their basis in history—the fact that it is how it has always been done. This view is problematic because it treats culture as static and unchanging. The fact that pow-wows even exist shows that Native cultures are continuously changing, since pow-wows are a celebration of pan-Indianness, which is a relatively new phenomenon in itself. My interviewees' view is also problematic because treating Native cultures as static, as existing in the past rather than in the present, is a perception Indians are often struggling against. As one woman I spoke to puts it,

I think there's also another stereotype that, uh, that maybe people are still living in the past, um, but we're not. You know, like to be a Native person in this society, uh, just doesn't make sense for people. You know, it's like, you know, if you're not dressed up in buckskins and wearing . . . beads and stuff . . . then we're not really Indian.

The idea that the twenty-six-year-old man I spoke with is a practitioner of the "old ways" is striking. Who is to say what qualifies for "old"? One woman I met, who is not part of my sample but provides me with some understanding of the lived experiences of someone raised on the Osage reservation, made an interesting comment. As mentioned previously, she finds that many Osage elders will not speak of the old, old ways. She claims they refuse to discuss the era prior to the Trail of Tears when they were located in Missouri. She emphasizes how sad this is because she feels their refusal to speak of it implies that this cultural history is gone, it has been lost. Her comments challenge us to recognize the fluidity of culture, and how cultural change is ongoing. This is not something I see my reclaimers doing. Instead, they treat Native cultures as static, where they learn "traditional" ways, which provide them with a greater claim to Native authenticity. Maybe being a "real Indian" actually requires the ability to recognize an imposter.

My interviewees also seem to imply that pow-wows mean the same thing for everyone, which is not an assumption one can make about any aspect of culture. Hall and Neitz argue, "Everything humanly created or thought has its cultural aspect. But not all of that culture is 'in use' at any given moment, and the culture that *is* being used may be accorded various kinds of significance by different users. . . . Even culture that is in active use does not always have a uniform significance for everyone" (1993, p. 15). For example, another interviewee's perception of pow-wows is very different than what these young men see them as, and she is therefore less critical of what happens at them:

Pow-wows . . . a lot of people mistake them for ceremony. A pow-wow is just show day, you know, it's like a family reunion. You all get together and have a potluck dinner. We sell our feathers and our beads to all those white people, sing and dance and show off. It's like Prairie Days at the local fair where you all dress up in suspenders and square hats. We don't dress like that anymore, you know. People think that's what we do all day . . . it's called regalia, it's called pow-wow, and it's production, not ceremonial.

The fact that a pow-wow is even held in this location, mid-Missouri, is criticized by one reclaimer. In his critique, he expresses what pow-wows mean to him:

The reason you have a pow-wow is 'cause there's a whole bunch of people who want to get together and dance and dance for money. And you're going to draw a big crowd to make money. This guy just threw it just to . . . 'cause there's no real interest here for it. . . . You know, to me, it was just for show. He was just showing that he was Indian and he can do this and great. . . . I guess I didn't think he put it on for the right reason. . . . You know, I'm not, I've never been comfortable with the whole showing us off as a parade thing.

While the male reclaimers quoted previously bemoan the lower standards of pow-wow participation, one also recognizes that they are a pan-Indian phenomenon. He says he prefers to concentrate on learning and practicing his tribal culture:

But, uh, I've decided, you know, pow-wows are kind of a pan-Indian-type deal and I'm just like, you know, yeah, a lot of Cherokees' pow-wow, you know, it's a Cherokee national holiday—which is Labor Day weekend every year—you know, has a big pow-wow and all. Yeah, pow-wow is not my tradition of dancing of anything—stomp dancing is.

His friend takes a similar position, saying that instead he chooses to participate in an Osage dance, which he describes in this way: "In our tribe, it's a serious tradition."

The tension between a static culture, represented by "traditional ways," and the fluidity of culture is evidenced in other areas as well. For instance, the friend describes the different perspectives on sweats:

It does mean different things to different people. Like, some people being traditional, you're in the sweat lodge and it's men and women. But the way I was taught, like in the old days, women didn't sweat, um, and they definitely didn't sweat with men either. So, that's, like, that's my tradition is that you don't sweat with—at all—men do the sweating and stuff like that. And the girls have their moon lodges and, and, time to be away and things like that.

In this quote he acknowledges that people approach this ritual with different beliefs that inform their practice, yet he tends to privilege his practice by assigning it the value of tradition.

Another woman I met refers to this type of attitude as "adopted sexism" rather than traditionalism. This tension comes up again as the previously mentioned male reclaimer discusses how he and his wife plan to raise their daughter. He says they want to make sure she is raised correctly, in the Native tradition. But which Native tradition is he referring to? He is reclaiming his Osage heritage, his wife is a full-blooded Navajo, raised in Arizona on a reservation but currently living far away from her tribe. The Osage and the Navajo have very different cultures. Which one is the "right" way to raise their child? When asked, he simply says, "I'm very big on making sure that our daughter is raised up right." He fails to elaborate, thus discounting, in his mind, any ambiguities in his belief system concerning what Nativeness means and what traditionalism stands for.

The tension between presumed "traditional" ways and more modern adaptations of Native cultures was evident in the first campus pow-wow as well. My notes from that weekend describe an elder woman taking over the microphone after being asked by one of the pow-wow sponsors to provide some feedback, criticism, and so on, on their first event. My notes indicate the following:

> She went on to scathe everyone for slighting an elder. . . . Apparently during a dance, people had passed up an elder man who was moving slowly. This resulted in him not completing his circle. She mentioned that traditionally, everyone would be aware of this and go slowly behind him out of respect. . . . She went on and on about how important it is to complete the circle, and therefore how offensive this was. . . . She apologized for offending anyone in the crowd, but argued that this was sometimes the only way to learn.

Then, the master of ceremonies took the microphone and reiterated the same theme, stating, "Lots of things done in this . . . metropolitan area are done incorrectly . . . [due to] being so far from Indian country. . . . They're far away from where the culture is traditionally practiced and, therefore, there are bound to be mistakes." It is certainly true that in the city where this pow-wow occurred there is very little visible Indian presence. However, despite the Midwestern location, there are pow-wows in the vicinity every weekend of the summer according to other reclaimers I speak to. Therefore, the accusation that lack of proximity to Indian country results in the alteration of cultural practices, any more than enacting any cultural practices exposes them to alteration, does not really apply. Additionally, it is interesting to hear Indians refer to the West as Indian country. I would think that, despite Native invisibility in the dominant, mainstream culture, current tribal members would be aware of the Indian presence, both historically and *currently*, throughout this nation. Lack of this awareness represents white racial hegemony—Indians appear to exist *even to other Indians* only in the areas designated as Indian country (i.e., reservations) by the federal government.

The pow-wow program had as part of its etiquette section the following statement:

> Do not touch anyone's dance regalia without permission. These clothes are not "costumes" and yes, we use modern things like safety pins and such because we are a "living"culture, and our regalia is subject to change. Leave your stereotypes at home! (Yes, there are some blonde tribally enrolled Indians). (Nov. 9–10, 1996)

My notes from the afternoon indicate that all of the drummers were elder males. It is explained to me that it is an honor to be asked to drum and that women are not allowed to touch the drums, although no one is able to explain the significance of this tradition. I cannot help but think that for a "living culture," as is stated in the program, it is funny what traditions are adapted without challenge and which ones remain as invariable aspects of "tradition." Ironically, this pow-wow breaks with tradition on another issue. They have high-school-aged people as head dancers, which is apparently unusual, but they do this because it is a pow-wow that is supposed to raise money for a college scholarship fund and it therefore seems appropriate to have young people involved at that level. This is apparently viewed by these individuals as an acceptable break with tradition, whereas allowing women to drum is not an acceptable break with tradition.

Pow-wows, then, are arenas of authenticity contestation. While pow-wows are celebrations of Nativeness amid the Anglo-dominated society, they are also arenas of conflict for Native peoples (reclaimers and non-reclaimers alike). Many reclaimers I met use these celebrations as their introduction to, and for some their sole exposure to, Native culture, and they attach considerable significance to these events. It is no surprise that some reclaimers are critical of pow-wows because they bring out the "weekend Indian." They know this to be true, because many of them have been "weekend Indians" at some point in their lives, marginally participating in Native cultures, primarily through pow-wows. Reclaiming a Native heritage is a process, one where individuals involved become increasingly immersed in Native culture and particularly their tribal cultures, and slowly accumulate cultural knowledge. Maybe people present who have less familiarity with Native traditions reflect back to the reclaimers their old selves, who they were prior to their reclamation.

On rare occasions, I hear wanna-bes challenging reservation Indians. While I do not see these as necessarily authenticity challenges, they are a challenge to how Indians are expected to live in the modern world. One middle-class, suburban woman who had been reclaiming only for a few years expresses some prejudice she recognizes she holds toward reservation Indians:

But, even as I am watching . . . and beginning my journey on my heritage, I had so many thoughts, you know. Why can't they [reservation Indians] come out of that? Why are they that way? On the reservations and in poverty and everything like that, but, there is still a lot of, I don't know why it is, but I do know that many people have told me they're called rez's and it's like another world. . . . But, it still saddens me, I mean, I guess if I went and visited one it would help me understand it more, but so many of them still stay in poverty and I have trouble understanding why they don't want to come out of that. But, it's probably, it's how they were brought up. It's their culture and they're not going to find it in the white world, it's a different culture. You know what I'm saying?

Another man similarly expresses his perception of disproportionate Native poverty:

If you can do well in school, you can get a scholarship or you can do something and you can move on. It's gonna take a whole lot of hard work, it's gonna suck, yes, it's the accident of birth, you know? If you want to do better, you're going to have to do it. You can wait around for it and that's what a lot of people do, I think, on reservations is wait around for it . . . and they don't do anything else and it perpetuates the cycle.

Both of these quotes are really not shocking explanations of poverty coming from middle-class Americans, raised in the dominant, mainstream world, despite their newly reclaimed racial/ethnic identity. Cultural "blame the victim" explanations for poverty are constantly espoused in our society, and therefore, many people accept them at face value without acknowledging the role of structure and power in understanding who is impoverished. However, I also see these quotes as a type of authenticity challenge—they are, in effect, saying, "I don't have to be poor and on a reservation to be Indian." They are working to find a comfortable place between their existence as newly reclaiming Native people and middle-class Americans. For a lot of reclaimers I speak to, these are very incongruent goals. For these two, adopting a "blame the victim" attitude is one way they resolve any ambiguities within themselves over issues of social class.

"REAL WANNA-BE INDIANS"

While the reclaimers I speak to are constantly fending off accusations, both real and perceived, that they are mere "wanna-bes," they acknowledge where such skepticism comes from. Many discuss the popularity of Native culture and how this is detrimental to Native cultures. One man in particular sees appropriation of Native cultures as threatening the very existence of such cultures. During our interview, he mentions that some things he speaks of should not be written down and therefore need to be edited out of my transcript. I agree to edit them out of the transcript, and I ask him why certain aspects of Cherokee rituals and ceremonies should not be written down. He explains,

I think the main reason is, is because like, Lakota spirituality, man, you can read that in a dozen books over at our library, you can read everything [about it]. You can read about every ceremony and because of such it has gotten bastardized really badly. And, I mean, it's gotten bad. I mean, you can go almost anywhere and pay a hundred bucks to take part in a sweat lodge. . . . Which is another argument I make with people in this town, you know, pay money to be involved in a sun dance. . . . And you know, a lot of New Age fruits are takin' that stuff out of the books and bastardized it. I'm like . . . you've taken enough of that shit, leave the religion to us. That ain't for you.

Despite his claim that being able to read about Native cultures and traditions contributes to white expropriation of it, he, and many reclaimers I meet, use books as reclamation tools in their journey. To what extent do published accounts of Native practices preserve cultural tradition rather than contribute to cultural demise? Is he operating under the assumption that the oral transmission of culture is superior to written cultural traditions? Don't cultures transmitted orally run the risk of alteration over time, simply due to communication and interpretation problems?

The previous reclaimer took college classes in Native American spirituality and describes his colleagues in those classes as "those type of people that I say bastardized Lakota religion." Another reclaimer explains the dilemma this way:

There are a lot of white people who, this New Age thing going on, that want to be Indians. We call them wanna-bes. You know, they go to the reservations and they get into ceremonies and they build sweat lodges and they think they're being Indians, you know, and they think that's very cool. . . . You know, it's tokenism, it's really kind of disconcerting. They don't want to get to know you because they think you're an interesting person, it's because "Oh, you're Indian, I want to collect you," like they collect beanie babies [laughs]. You know? Which is kind of a bizarre feeling.

When I ask her where she encounters this type of treatment most, she replies,

A lot of academics. You know? The woman I told you about [previously] . . . is an academic and a relatively intelligent woman and she's just, I don't know, she's living in this fantasy world, she's pretending to be something she's not . . . it's really disturbing to me. She's set herself up to be an expert and as being Indian, and she's white. She doesn't have a drop of Indian blood in her. Where is she getting the expertise? You know, until somebody's spit on you and told you "no dogs or Indians allowed" you don't get to say you're Indian. How can someone who hasn't had that experience relate to what it's like to be an Indian? . . . Oh yeah, she uses all the skin dyes, you know, and the hair dyes and dresses in all the stuff, you know. . . . She even does programs about Indians. She goes into school systems and presents programs about Native heritage and I just find it really disturbing. . . . And you know, the school systems around here are aware of all the Indians that are here, you know. There are so many First Nations people right here in this community that could do that if they wanted somebody to do it. You know? Why are they calling this white woman? . . . 'Cause she's non-threatening. She won't correct their history lessons.

Another woman is concerned with the appropriation of Native cultures by wanna-bes, in Brayboy's (2000) sense of individuals with no true connection to Nativeness that try to pass as Native:

I think that there's been a, um, movement in this country for the last twenty years of people trying to figure out their spirituality, and some people have latched onto Native spirituality and then feel, um, a connection to Native people. . . . I think that sometimes it . . . can kind of cross over and people then start to feel like they're part of the community—part of the race and ethnicity, which is not the case. And I think that that makes—causes a lot of hurt feelings, but then, you know, the Native people, too, also don't want to be told how to be Native.

She talks about how she sees a lot of wanna-bes at pow-wows,

Because people come out in their costumes and, uh, you know and—and I'm not calling the dancers in their costumes. I'm talking about the people who come in trying to kinda claim this Native thing . . . and so they put on their beads and they put on their, you know, buckskins or whatever and—and those are costumes. . . . And for those people . . . who are legitimately within the culture, within the family, whatever, um, then I think those people are probably just a little tired of the people who are dressed up in costume. . . . And it's very frustrating, I think, for a lot of people.

This quote again exemplifies how pow-wows are sites of challenge to authentic Natives by wanna-bes.

Later this woman talks about difficulties reclaimers have, especially if they do not have tribal connections as she does, because

the visibility of Native American people in this country is still very low, and so for people who do wanna come back to their culture—let's say they've assimilated or their parents have assimilated, so they're trying to come back. Um, it's sometimes hard to find those resources and it's even harder sometimes to feel like you're accepted into those resources, too, 'cause, um—and then, unfortunately, we've got people running around calling themselves shamans and this, that, and the other . . . who are not, and those people [reclaimers] get lead astray.

This woman even claims that she does not trust books as a source of information for her reclamation process because she questions the legitimacy of the authors.

This woman is obviously aware of authenticity issues and legitimacy claims pertaining to Indianness, yet despite her ability to articulate the issues, she has trouble with questions of legitimacy. She abruptly stopped our interview at one point, saying,

> . . . um, there's—there's one thing, though, I wanna say because—'cause it's really important. It's not up to me to decide who's Indian and who's not. That's up to them to decide. . . . It's totally not up to me to decide, so I hate the idea of the blood card and, I mean, tribal enrollment I can understand, that makes sense to me. . . . You know, you're removed [from the tribe] but you can probably trace it back and figure it out, okay good. But the blood card? It's kinda gross. . . . So, I don't like that . . . so, I will never say to anybody, "You're not this and you're . . ." Excuse me? When did I become God? When did I decide I could tell people what they are and what they aren't?

In this statement, she declares her desire not to participate in the policing of Indian authenticity, but she also seems critical of the role of the federal government in determining Indianness through the BIA blood quantum criteria for obtaining one's "blood card," the Certificate of Degree of Indian Blood. Yet, after saying this, she later adds,

> I know quite a few Native people who are pretty non-Native [laughter]. At least in their customs . . . but, I wouldn't call them any less Native than I am. It's just their way of being. And they have to—and again, it goes back to who they have to answer to . . . it's not for me to decide what they should or shouldn't be, so.

There is ambiguousness in this comment—is there an essential Nativeness or not? Could someone who does not have such characteristics be Native? It seems that the tension surrounding authentic Indianness pertains to the idea that one should not judge others and their path, yet that, on the other hand, a "real Indian" knows a "real Indian." Brayboy's quote, elicited earlier, again applies: "There is a real contradiction and tension surrounding what we believe (our theories as it were) and what we do (our practices)" (2000, p. 424).

A young man I spoke to is very critical of the appropriation of Native cultures by non-Natives, and he even places a relative of his in this category. I ask him what his family thinks of his reclaiming, especially his grandmother, who taught him little things about this aspect of his heritage when he was a child. He answers that his grandmother is not really aware of it because she has Alzheimer's, but that his aunt is, explaining,

> My aunt is pretty into it . . . but, see, that's another thing I have a problem with, she's into the "New Age" aspect of it and that's another big problem I see . . .

the idea that it is kind of "hip" to like Native American stuff and to be into it and not really understand what it's about really. . . . It's just like going to Colorado and driving around and everyone's got a dream catcher hanging from their mirror, but no one knows what it's about.

He later qualifies this statement, saying, "I don't really feel like I'm in a position to criticize anybody for what they do, even though I think it's kind of silly sometimes." Later he talks about other peoples' reclaiming process in this way: "I don't want to make generalizations, it does sound silly. But, I guess to do anything like that [judge the authenticity of others] you'd have to study people, what they think about, psychologically . . . but, yeah, I often feel it's contrived." I hear this over and over from interviewees: their own search for their racial/ethnic heritage is completely authentic and legitimate, yet they are critical of other's approach or connection.

The two reclaimers I talk with who are best friends explain to me that when they met at the Native American student organization meeting on campus and found out they were both from the same metropolitan area, they were each suspicious of the other since they had never run across each other in the Native community in their home city. As one explained, "Some people just make up lies." The point is that there are so many "wanna-be" Indians out there that they did not even trust each other initially. They are also critical of what they refer to as "weekend Indians": "You know, they're only Indian on the weekend, like when they're out dancing and stuff and other— after that they don't care." His response to people like this who challenge his blood quantum is, "Well, what do you do during the week?" In other words, while his blood quantum often results in him being discounted, he responds with his claim to living the Native life daily (at least since he began reclaiming this heritage). When confronted with biology, he responds with culture. Yet, in the same breath, he judges the authenticity of others' Indianness.

BEYOND INDIVIDUAL AUTHENTICITY CHALLENGES: CHALLENGING TRIBAL LEGITIMACY

Another type of challenge to authentic Indianness is interesting because it is a challenge at the collective or tribal level and not necessarily a challenge to individuals (although challenging the authenticity of someone's tribe can sometimes be used to discount an individual). As one interviewee says, there is a lot of "angst over who is a real Indian," but embedded within reclaimers' narratives is also an angst over which tribes qualify as real Indian tribes as well. Brayboy (2000) outlines the criteria for establishing the hierarchical status of tribes:

> Among Indigenous people throughout the USA, much attention is paid to the perceived status of an individual's tribe. There is a hierarchy (depending on who you talk to and when) of status of what counts as "real" or not. For American Indians, this status is loosely based on a number of factors influencing tribal status including: what form of recognition is given to a tribe (Federal recognition is better); the locale of the tribe (west of the Mississippi is good); what one looks like (this is variable, but the closer one appears to have walked out of the set of "Dances with Wolves" or "Geronimo" the better); if one speaks his or her language; if one sings, dances, makes pots or any other form of "culturally recognized art"; and how one chooses to live his or her life (that is, is it "Indian" enough?). (2000, p. 423)

In my research location, the conflict between federal versus state tribal recognition is alive and well. I spoke with many people from a state recognized tribe that is working on gaining federal recognition, and numerous tribal authenticity claims are found embedded within their narratives. Other reclaimers that I talked to, living in the same community, yet not participating in this tribe, are overtly critical of them and actively work to delegitimize the tribe as a whole. For example, one reclaimer refers to them in this way: "We call them, and a lot of people call them, wanna-be tribes because they want to be Indian." He also mentions an issue that divided the local Indian community and in his description he says, "We went down and the room was split. You could see the legitimate Indians on one side of the room . . . then you could see these . . . [members of the state recognized tribe] you know, on the other side of the room."

For some people I met, members of the state recognized tribe lack authenticity because there originally was not a tribe by this name. One reclaimer speculates on why they would form their own tribe:

> Well, they pretty much do it because either one, they can't prove they're Indian. And I'm not saying that they're not, but they're not . . . that's my big thing. I'm not, I don't play Indian police. If somebody says they're Native, then I'll go along with it until they can—until I'm proved or think otherwise. And, and I mean, I've been wrong before . . . it happens. But, it's like, they're either Eastern or they could be the Western band, but they're definitely not a different tribe.

It seems that he is uncomfortable "playing Indian police" with individuals, but he seems sure of policing the boundaries at a collective level. His comment is intriguing, and it appears to pertain to whether one adheres to a traditional and static view of culture or an understanding of culture as fluid and contested. Another reclaimer who is hostile toward the idea of this state recognized tribe being legitimate outlines his own Cherokee heritage to me, explaining:

> There's still real Cherokee tribes—try and look it up and there are about a thousand of them. You know, a lot of them are what people call state recognized or wanna-bes or whatever. But, you know, there's the Cherokee Nation of Oklahoma . . . and then there's the Eastern Band of Cherokee Indians in, uh, Cherokee, North Carolina. Those are the only . . . real, so-called tribes of Cherokees.

This reclaimer does not address how there ended up being two tribes of Cherokees to begin with—have there *always* been an Eastern and a Western band? Or is that a result of an earlier conflict and split? Pertaining to the latter quote, I ask him what he means: "Official according to Native peoples, you mean?" He replies, "Official according to Native people and according to the federal government. . . . Those are what are called federally recognized . . . . In other words, they're the only legitimate ones." This final point is especially intriguing because so many Indians distrust the federal government—with good reason after so many years of betrayal—and therefore relying on federal recognition of tribes is interesting because it places a lot of power in the hands of the federal government, a situation most Indians would like to avoid. My interviewee continues, discrediting the state recognized tribe by stating,

> Even the Cherokees don't recognize them. . . . 'Cause they're not. I mean, what these people stem from is a bunch of people who are, I mean, I'd say they probably do have some Indian blood in them, whether it's Cherokee or not remains to be seen, so instead of trying to join their own tribe, they go off and form another one because they can't prove that they're really Indian.

When I ask a member of this state recognized tribe to explain to me who exactly is considered a member of this tribe, he explains,

> Anybody that wasn't on the . . . rolls that moved west pretty much is a . . . Cherokee Indian. . . . They're old settlers and they came before the Trail of Tears. Some of them are ones that actually escaped the Trail of Tears, but anybody that stayed east is not one of those. Or anyone who was an official member of the Cherokee Nation of Oklahoma . . . they're not members of our group. But, historically, all the rest of them that are west of the Mississippi are.

They refer to themselves as the "lost Cherokees" because they have been "officially" lost—not counted among the Cherokees in Oklahoma and not counted among the Eastern Cherokees. They end up in the Midwest one of two ways: either they ventured here ahead of the Trail of Tears, because they could see the writing on the wall and wanted to control their own destiny, or they were part of the Trail of Tears and escaped prior to entering Oklahoma.

A reclaimer I met who considers herself a member of this tribe relates the following narrative, which appears to authenticate the story of the lost Cherokees to herself and to me at the same time: "I think about these people living out there, because it is so remote. I mean, and this, you know, is back in the 1800s. Of course, they could exist and have their own group of people there and nobody would ever know it." She also relates a story she heard from another woman that seems to validate her own Native identity claims and the story of how the lost Cherokees came about:

> She was saying how her grandfather had come off the Trail of Tears and that's what happened with a lot of them. They didn't want to go and they hid in the hills. But, I think the case with my family is, they were here before the Trail of Tears because ten years prior to the Trail of Tears these people knew—President Jackson was already talkin' about this stuff and they knew it was coming and they came before. But there were Indians, Cherokee Indians, in Missouri in 1791.

One of the male reclaimers who is highly critical of this theory argues,

> They don't know what they're talking about. They, you know, they preach, "Oh, we're the lost Cherokees . . . the ones that strayed from the Trail of Tears in Missouri," which people didn't just stray from when they had armed guards watching. You know, they didn't just decide to stop here. But, yeah, honestly, they don't know what they're talking about.

His argument is full of contradictions, however. For one, he recognizes the Eastern Cherokees, yet their existence, according to Bonvillain (2001), is due to remarkably similar conditions as this state recognized tribe. Bonvillain explains the origins of the Eastern Cherokees in this way: "Cherokees who were able to elude the U.S. Army sent to remove them from their homeland to Oklahoma eventually settled in the Great Smokey Mountains of North Carolina" (2001, p. 139). Additionally, it is not unheard of for people to have escaped the Trail of Tears, despite the intentions and weaponry of the U.S. Army. Similar things have happened before—with runaway slaves, for instance. There is a black community in Livingston, Guatemala, which originally began as a settlement of runaway slaves. People, individuals and groups, are able to hide in extremely remote areas of the country in order to escape persecution and, in the case of Indians, relocation. So one is unable to discount the credibility of a tribe on such information alone.

I find a constant tension in the narratives over the role of the U.S. federal government in terms of establishing Indian identity and legitimacy. For instance, I ask one young man how he feels about the latest (2000) census, which allows him to include his particular tribal affiliation. He replies,

> I thought it was pretty good and I thought it was kind of empowering, too . . . [but] I don't need anybody in Washington, D.C., to tell me whether I'm Indian or not. . . . It also kinda poses a problem, too, 'cause you got these people like these [members of the state recognized tribe], uh, people here in town that are kinda like, "Well, we're [Indian]," but the—the tribe never existed.

He perceives this group, and especially their ability to fill in a government document (the census) with their tribal affiliation, as somewhat of a threat. I ask him why he thinks they perceive themselves as distinct tribe and why he feels that is problematic. He answers,

> Well, they're trying to get, like, state recognition and federal recognition so they can get money. . . . And a lot of 'em, it's just like wanted to be—that—that's like a big thing and it's like . . . I mean pretty much since *Dances with Wolves* came out and like Indian people weren't like the people that just killed cowboys. . . . And after that, it's like, that was a big thing, man, everybody's poppin' up, "I'm Indian, I'm Indian." But, it's good because one, it provides money, federal money to people . . . but like, Indian people, for them to go and sign up, it's great because it just increased our population.

Clearly, this passage exemplifies his perception of members of this tribal Nation as "wanna-be" Indians. While the presence of "wanna-bes" in general is viewed as problematic, he sees their census enumeration as valuable to Indians as a whole because it increases federal funds to federally recognized tribes, of which they are not one.

Pertaining to his former comment, that he does not need the federal government telling him whether or not he is Indian, he ironically uses federal standards to *define out* others. He relies on the federal government's power for defining the existence of tribes, but then claims they have no power to define an individual's Native heritage.

Why do these young men expend so much effort trying to delegitimize state-recognized tribes? One went so far as to explain that there really is no such thing as a state recognized Indian tribe, anyway: "They wanted the state to declare them a tribe. And they'll say the state has, but the state never has. There are no state recognized tribes in Missouri." He even went on to claim that a local state representative told him that he sent the tribe a letter of recognition, which is virtually meaningless, paraphrasing the state representative this way: "'If I wanted to honor you for your birthday, I could write you one.'"

This is all part of the "angst over who is a real Indian." I believe that much of it stems from threats to individual reclaimers' authenticity. The man quoted earlier affirms that by saying, "It's ironic how most of them would turn around and accuse me of being the 'wanna-be' who didn't know anything. You know . . . I had this tribal chairman e-mail them saying, you know, you don't want to mess with this guy because he's legitimate and you're not." This reclaimer's Nativeness is established through the confirmation of some unnamed tribal chairman, which is not an unacceptable practice in Native America.

According to Snipp (1989), since blood quantum designations are becoming discredited and are disappearing from administrative use, the federal government has established several different approaches to establishing Indian identity. One of those is through the principle of "community recognition": "By this standard the testimony of one's neighbors is sufficient to establish membership in the Indian population. In practice, this often means that if tribal authorities are willing to extend tribal membership to an individual, this is sufficient to establish membership in the Indian population—regardless of genealogy" (1989, p. 35). Clearly, objective measures of authentic Indianness are challenged by such subjective designations. Yet tribes still rely on the federal rolls for membership. Brayboy concurs that his "policing" of Indian authenticity also stems from his feelings about his own authentic Indianness: "My sense of not feeling 'Indian enough' in certain contexts, however, led me to my being critical of others who might be labeled 'wanna-bes'" (2000, p. 423).

Members of the state recognized tribe are aware of the threat they pose to the existing tribal structure. Many describe the numerous state recognized tribes as rather antagonistic toward one another, explaining, "Well, they [all] want their federal recognition . . . because they didn't split up the money . . . . if they split up their recognition. . . . Now the pie gets smaller." He explains further, "So, uh, now you have all these groups. Our, we were pretty much one solid group . . . and now they've split into about twenty different groups who are all trying to get recognition. They've all got their own chief."

CONCLUSION

Reclaimers are constantly engaged in authenticity challenges and battles for legitimacy that need to be understood within a larger socio-political and historical context. Why are there such challenges to knowledge claims concerning such things as cultural practices? After all, we cannot all know everything there is to know about our culture. I think the situation is unique for Native reclaimers due to the fact we are dealing with groups who have experienced cultural genocide. There is no getting lost knowledge back; therefore challenging existing knowledge is perceived as threatening.

Almost every reclaimer questions others' approach to reclaiming. This leads me to believe that there is some insecurity in their newly reclaimed Native identity. Many reclaimers have limited exposure to Native culture and there is a lot they do not know and/or do not have access to. I think that makes them cling more tightly to the knowledge they do have. Only two people take the perspective that they have no right to judge others. One states, "The Creator put us all on this earth to follow particular paths," and this individual refrains from criticizing others. The other says, " . . . and the other thing that's very Cherokee as far as the old ones are concerned is [being] nonjudgmental. Whatever works for you . . . I don't have to live your life and you don't have to live mine and that's okay."

According to my Osage informant, no one can completely walk away from their Indianness; that a link, a connectedness, is always be there. She elaborates, "I believe, and this isn't just me, we've all sat around talking about this, that the drum calls people back. The drum is the center of life and it has a spirit . . . beating it activates it." Yet, there does not always appear to be much acceptance among reclaimers or non-reclaiming Indians of those who return. Is this evidence of internal oppression, where subordinate groups internalize their oppressor's standpoint and learn to view the members of their group in derogatory ways?

Brayboy (2000) critically interrogates himself over this very issue:

> My own tendencies to perform "authenticity tests" highlight my struggles with the notion of identifying "Indianness" according to the behavior and interpretations of those behaviors. In retrospect, I would have rather been more critical of the consequences of colonization on the ways I thought about this topic.

Ralph Wiley, an African American scholar, makes a similar argument about black people's tolerance for everybody but themselves. He views this "inhouse" racism as a direct result of the "outhouse" racism directed at them for centuries (Wiley 1991, p. 52).

Are questions of authenticity the result of the dominant groups' constant derogation of the colonized culture? To what extent do authenticity challenges contribute to sustaining cultures and to what extent do they strangle them? Sandoval-Sanchez argues,

> The danger of authenticity is that it anchors culture in ahistorical and apolitical domains, opening the door to stereotypes, perpetuating the notion of cultural

purity, and discarding the ongoing historical process and negotiations of cultural creativity and social change. In order to undo the mythification of authenticity, we must see authenticity as a social and cultural construction in the modern Western world. (2002, p. 155)

He continues his critique of battles surrounding authenticity in this way: "They are about incorporation, representation, and appropriation of the culture of the subaltern in a global economy from a dominant point of view." (2002, p. 158)

Similar legitimacy battles are unintentionally evident in the researcher/researched relationship. During a campus organization meeting that I observed in 1996, as final preparations for the first campus pow-wow are being made, I am part of an interesting interaction. Some of the group members were talking about rules of etiquette and such, and it was mentioned that photographs were prohibited if a dancer dropped a feather. I asked why, although I usually refrained from asking questions at these meetings in order to remain as unobtrusive as possible. The young man who mentions this became visibly uncomfortable with the question and mumbled something like, "Well, 'cause that's a ritual, not a dance, so no pictures." I felt embarrassed for putting him on the spot and irritated that he didn't just say he didn't know. It was clear he had no idea. Another student jumps in with the explanation: "It's because when a feather is dropped it symbolizes a spirit has escaped. And you don't photograph spirits." Clearly someone who is reclaiming their culture is not going to have full knowledge of all rituals and their meanings, yet my question appears to delegitimize this reclaimer, in his own eyes, possibly in the group's eyes, and maybe even in my eyes.

That incident generates considerable thought on my part concerning the availability of cultural knowledge between colonized groups and the study of such. First, since there is not a Native American culture per se, an individual who is reclaiming must learn his or her particular tribal culture. This is often difficult since so much of it has been lost or is not accessible. As the mood of the country has changed toward more tolerance, at a time when Indian identity no longer has to be underground, it is becoming clear that the colonizer's efforts to wipe out the indigenous peoples of this continent, from genocide to forced acculturation at BIA schools, has achieved a certain amount of success. Much indigenous knowledge has been irretrievably lost, yet the dilemma goes beyond this loss of knowledge, it becomes a question of how does one legitimize or affirm this cultural tradition in the face of constant challenges from the dominant culture?

At the same time, these authenticity battles are not simply evidence of the success of the colonizer; they are also evidence of the resiliency of Native American cultures. There are questions about right and wrong, debates over traditional versus modern interpretations of rituals, meanings, and beliefs, all of which expose the viability of Native cultures. These debates are resolved through *living* the culture, which is what reclaimers are engaged in. As Hall and Neitz point out, "It is worth remembering that 'culture' comes from the Latin for 'cultivating' or tilling the soil. Culture, in this sense, amounts to the ways of taking care of things" (1993, p. 5). Indigenous peoples, and re-claimers among them, are actively tilling the soil. In the process, cultures are bound to change, adapt, and be transformed, and be challenged for such changes, adaptations, and transformations. Yet, ultimately this is a sign of the survival of indigenous cultures.

NOTE

1. The debate over the additional "multiracial" category on the 2000 census was rather heated. The result was a compromise—while a multiracial category was not added to the census, individuals were allowed to check more than one box to indicate multiracial heritage.

Conclusion

Contextualizing Non-White Racial/Ethnic Identity Reclamation

A sociological analysis of Native American reclamation elicits a number of significant insights. First, it highlights the structure/agency tension at work in the lives of reclaimers. The sociological imagination is a useful tool for thinking about Native reclamation because it encourages an analysis of how individual reclaimers' lives intersect with history and social structure, exposing constraining and enabling aspects of structure and the role of individual agency. Cornell and Hartman also emphasize the influence of structure and agency for racial and ethnic identity construction: "Ethnic and racial identities and the groups that carry them change over time as the forces that impinge on them change, and as the claims made by both group members and others change as well" (1998, p. 72). According to the reclaimers that I speak to, there is recognition that there would be serious consequences to claiming one's Native heritage for their parent's and/or grandparent's generation. For some, this understanding of the threats their ancestors lived under is part of their family lore, while for others it is evidence in the silence. These reclaimers then piece together their understanding through persistent inquiries and investigations into their family history.

Second, a sociological analysis of racial/ethnic reclamation challenges us to broaden our understanding of ethnicity and race. It forces us, for instance, to recognize that a fundamental difference between white ethnic identity and the reclamation of a racial/ethnic identity is that the symbolic ethnicity that so many sociologists spoke of (e.g., Gans 1979; Alba 1990; Waters 1990) does not challenge the white, racial hegemonic structure the way racial/ethnic reclamation does. In chapter two, I analyze the various ways Native reclaimers challenge the racial hierarchy, through challenges to Native invisibility, stereotypical portrayals, and Native representation in educational

institutions to their challenges to mainstream American values of consumerism, materialism, and individualism, and the use of Native images as
team mascots. Essentially, reclaimers join non-reclaiming, lifetime Indians
in the deconstruction of the historical and ongoing white construction of Native peoples. It is necessary to recognize that while the battles reclaimers
choose to fight are generally not different than the battles non-reclaiming,
lifetime Natives are engaged in, what is unique is the socio-historical locatedness of reclaimers. They are individuals who voluntarily reject whiteness
and its accompanying race privilege. While their rejection of white privilege
is difficult to assess due to the fact that many do not assert phenotypical Native features, and therefore, they can effectively pass in day to day life, their
commitment to a racial/ethnic identity and conscious rejection of whiteness
is of significance. They, therefore, embrace what has been defined by the
dominant group as a subordinate racial status. This clearly challenges the
racial hierarchy as well as the dominant groups' power to define race. Instead of feeling pressure to assimilate and equating assimilation with "suc-
ceeding" in mainstream society, they reject an *already successful assimilation project* in order to embrace a racial/ethnic identity that does not come
with a package of unearned advantages otherwise known as white privilege.

Despite this powerful challenge to white racial hegemony, reclaimers' embrace of their Nativeness has some troubling aspects as well. For instance,
through their struggles to learn their indigenous heritage, they often reinforce
stereotypes concerning Nativeness and falsely portray Native cultures as
static rather than fluid. Their concerns with "tradition" and challenges to others' cultural practices occur in the name of preserving cultures, yet result in
cultural stagnation. Sociologists emphasize social change, which refers to "al-
terations over time in social structure, culture, and behavior patterns . . . [it]
is continual and universal" (Lindsey and Beach 2002, p. 643). According to
Hall and Neitz, "Changes in practices are an ongoing kind of cultural activity" (1993, p. 238). Nagel also emphasizes this point: "Individuals and col-
lectivities adapt, adopt, discard, and change continually, according to the
needs and vagaries of history and of the world around them" (1996, p. 63).

While sociologists emphasize the inevitabilty of cultural change, it remains
problematic for Native reclaimers primarily because they lack the cultural
capital associated with their Native heritage. In other words, they are not
raised within their tribes and therefore exposed to tribal practices in the *context* of ongoing cultural change and adaptation. The additional dilemma for
many reclaimers is that they often do not live in geographic proximity to Native communities and, therefore, do not have ongoing, daily exposure to the
lived culture. This presents reclaimers with a unique tension. They live in the
mainstream, non-Native world, yet seek to embrace their Nativeness and *be*

Native. Their distance and lack of cultural capital and their daily immersion in the mainstream culture all contribute to their zealous approach to cultural knowledge. Ultimately, their Nativeness is threatened by cultural ambiguities in ways that it is not for non-reclaiming Natives. Additionally, it is easy to understand why all indigenous peoples would resist cultural change and cling to "tradition" because so much cultural change has been the result of cultural imperialism, forced on them through colonization, rather than the arguably more neutral process of cultural diffusion and adaptation.

Gans (1979) describes symbolic ethnicity as "the feeling of being Jewish," Italian, Irish, or any European heritage. Cornell and Hartmann also emphasize this in their discussion of third- and fourth-generation Italian Americans when they state "they have gone from being to feeling Italian" (1998, p. 76). A dilemma reclaimers I meet seem to face is that they are struggling to go the other way—from simply *feeling* Native American, or generally a member of a specific Native American tribe, to *being* that. There is an ambiguousness regarding where "being" ends and "feeling" begins, although Cornell and Hartmann (1998) speak of it for Italian Americans, and white European ethnics in general, in terms of a distancing from ethnic communities, a distancing from European languages, intermarriage, and simply daily existence in the mainstream social, economic, and political arenas. Therefore, for Native reclaimers, the process of moving from being and feeling white to simply feeling Native, to being Native is relatively contested. Reclaimers remain part of the social, economic, and political mainstream (at least at the time of our meeting they were; and very few spoke of relocating to their respective reservations to live). They primarily speak English despite their intentions and efforts to learn Native languages. Even in the event of mastering their indigenous language, there is a question concerning its effect on their sense of being Native due to the limited opportunities to practice the language. Therefore, as chapter three exemplifies, there is some tension surrounding their cultural practices and ideologies. In many cases, the reclaimers I speak to are indistinguishable from mainstream Americans in terms of their practices and their Native reclamation is currently ideological, influencing their thinking and feeling rather than informing their being through cultural practices.

Physical appearance also plays an important role in Native reclaimers' construction of their racial/ethnic identity. Reclaimer narratives are replete with references to identity struggles they face between external racial ascriptions and their internal identification with Nativeness. Such struggles exemplify symbolic interactionists' perspective on the development of self—the extent to which it is the result of subjective definition and the extent to which it is objectively defined. Reclaimers engage in impression management, particularly through clothes and hairstyles, which attempt to influence external ascriptions and make them more congruent with their subjectively defined selves. Their reliance on physical appearance as an identity marker is evidence of two contradictory trends: that their embrace of a racialized discourse is a reification of the European social construction of race and, simultaneously, a deconstruction of white racial privilege. On the one hand, they still embrace the notion of race as real and objective, yet they reject the Euro-American racial hierarchy.

Finally, reclaimers face ongoing authenticity and legitimacy battles that need to be understood within their larger social, political, and historical contexts. Reclaimers lack the cultural capital (in terms of lived experience) and often the physical appearance that claiming Native membership requires, socially speaking. Reclaimers appear to be particularly insecure about their cultural knowledge, and this leads them to cling tightly to the knowledge they do have and feel threatened by challenges to or deviations from what they know. However, getting absorbed in authenticity battles presents a distorted view of culture in that it presents cultures as static, ahistorical, and apolitical. At the same time as authenticity and legitimacy battles can distort our perspectives of culture in this way, they are also evidence of cultural resiliency. Such debates over what is authentic, traditional, and meaningful are ultimately evidence of the viability of Native cultures because it is only through living the culture that these questions get answered.

I see reclaimers as ultimately challenging white racial hegemony and the racial hierarchy. Cornell and Harmann (1998) state, "Groups organized around ethnicity and race are reshaping societies, upsetting old assumptions, and challenging established systems of power. In essence, they are remaking significant parts of the modern world" (p. 12). Social scientists recognize race as a social and political construction, and Native reclaimers can effectively challenge the racial hierarchy simply through rejecting their white privilege and embracing a racial/ethnic identity that carries less status and privilege in our racialized society. These very actions challenge the assimilationist trends of the nineteenth and twentieth centuries.

I began this research wondering if reclaimers would see their newly reclaimed racial/ethnic identity in modernist, specifically symbolic interactionist, or postmodern terms. Kellner describes the postmodernist position on identity in this way: "In a postmodern image culture, the images, scenes, stories, and cultural texts of so-called popular culture offer a wealth of subject positions which in turn help structure individual identity" (1992, p. 173). If reclaimers take a postmodernist approach to their newly reclaimed identity, they would generate their sense of ethnic identity from images in the popular culture. One would expect the current era to provide fertile ground for such an understanding of Nativeness since we are currently in an era where portrayals of Native Americans are steering away from stereotypical images of the noble warrior and such, where instead movies like *Smoke Signals* receive widespread attention. I perceive it as an era where Native Americans are portrayed as living cultures rather than historical examples alone and where Native American literature classes are a standard part of an academic curriculum. My initial assumption is that such images create a context conducive to reclaiming a Native American heritage. The question remains, however—do reclaimers recognize the influence of such cultural forces on their identity choices?

What I find is that reclaimers rarely mention the influence of popular culture, and are more likely to critique Native images in popular culture, as chapter two exemplifies. When reclaimers did mention cultural imagery, such as the movie *Dances with Wolves* or books by the author William Least Heat Moon, they are highly critical because they see these as fabrications and ways for wanna-bes to illegitimately embrace Indianness. They also appear troubled by postmodernist notions of the fluidity of identity. This is possibly because as reclaimers, their identity is relatively ambiguous, and they therefore seek more concrete identity categories.

I do see the postmodern image culture as having an influence on their reclamation, however. Despite the fact that they do not speak of it as an influence, I think it is part of why the current structure enables reclaiming instead of constraining it as it had been for their ancestors. The increased presence of Native American authors in literature classes, films, music, and even the proliferation of Native American ideas within New Age circles is significant. The cultural presence of such increases the likelihood of individuals reclaiming an indigenous heritage. Author Alan Pomerance argues in *Repeal of the Blues: How Black Entertainers Influenced Civil Rights* (1991) that the increased black presence in the entertainment world from the 1920s to the 1940s paves the way for the passage of civil rights legislation. In essence, his argument is that as whites see more and more talented blacks, it gets harder to write them all off as "exceptions" to the race. In the minds of many whites, although certainly not all, extending civil rights to blacks became no longer inconceivable. I think the increased Native American presence in popular culture has had the same effect, only on people of Native descent rather than on white people.

Reclaimer narratives tend to emphasize the role of others in the development of their racial/ethnic identity, thus supporting a symbolic interactionist understanding of identity. They repeatedly discuss identity challenges they face from others, or identity validation for their newly reclaimed racial/ethnic identity. They do not see identity as completely fixed in the modernist sense, because clearly they are actively seeking to alter their sense of self through reclaiming. However, they appear uncomfortable with total fluidity of identity. Yet, embracing a Native American identity is clearly difficult for many reclaimers since they look white, they were not raised within their tribal cultures, and since they are, despite their reclamation, members of mainstream, white, dominant society. We need to find new ways to understand identity; we need to to recognize multiple identities rather than the fluidity of identity.

In chapter one, identity is problematized by Butler (1995): "The notion of identity carries several burdens: the meaning of culture . . . the problem of historical transformation and contextualization; the possibility of agency, social transformation, representability, and recognizability in both linguistic and political terms" (p. 440). This summarizes the experiences of those engaged in a racial/ethnic reclamation project. Reclaimers question not just the meaning of culture but also who gets to define culture. They do this through their challenges to the mainstream culture, as evidenced by their deconstruction of historical metanarratives in educational institutions and popular culture. And they also engage in this through challenging knowledge and authenticity claims made by other Natives and reclaiming Natives.

To the extent that reclaimers deal with the burden of identity in terms of historical transformation and contextualization, one can look to the overwhelming emphasis placed on physical appearance for evidence of the influence of history and context on their racial/ethnic identity claims. By reclaiming a Native American heritage, these individuals are positioned to respond to social, political, and historical constructions of Nativeness and race. For instance, the fact that Native Americans are deemed to be a minority race in this country affects a reclaimer's sense of self as he or she attempts to embrace this new identity. Their attention to and emphasis on physical appearance is a result of the Euroamerican social and political constructions of whiteness and Nativeness. Again, though, reclaimers are not simply replicating the dominant group's structural hierarchy with their embrace of Native Americans as a distinct race. Instead, they are transforming the racial hierarchy through this embrace.

Agency, for Butler, is another burden of identity, and reclaimers are no exception. Reclaimers act as agents to the extent that they actively pursue their Native tribal heritage and embrace this new racial/ethnic identity. However, their agency is limited by structural factors such as tribal enrollment criteria and often contrasting BIA criteria, the reliance on historical documentation as genetic proof of their Native descent, the unreliability of historical records, and the reification of race and its corresponding emphasis on physical appearance as criterion for membership.

Finally, Butler identifies representability and recognizability in both linguistic and political terms as a burden of identity that is also well exemplified in reclaimer narratives. They seek not only representation in educational materials and popular imagery but also recognizability for those reclaimers who do not hold stereotypical Native features. Therefore, reclaimer battles surrounding representability and recognizability happen within the mainstream, white culture as well as within Native communities. Within a nearly invisible minority, reclaimers are the invisible of the invisible. Lifetime membership in the mainstream Anglo-culture as well as often a lack of a congruent physical appearance presents them with ongoing challenges to their claim to Nativeness. They, therefore, find themselves immersed in battles of legitimacy and authenticity that non-reclaiming, lifetime members of Native communities do not have to engage in.

It is important to challenge Butler's language as well. While reclaimers' experiences fit the identity challenges she outlines, in most cases they do not seem to perceive their Native identity as a burden. It is an identity they eagerly embrace and in most cases, they view their ancestors' forced assimilation as more of a burden than the identity challenges they face as reclaimers. At the same time, describing identity as a burden implies something deterministic about one's racial/ethnic identity, which is congruent with how reclaimers view this aspect of themselves.

When one addresses the social, historical, and political context within which Native reclaiming occurs, one is left with the understanding that this process is more than the symbolic ethnicity that Gans speaks of. Gans describes white ethnic reclamation in terms of symbolic ethnicity, because, in his view, people are trying to find "easy and intermittent ways of expressing their identity, for ways that do not conflict with other ways of life" (Gans 1979, p. 203). In other words, this new ethnic identity does not affect an individual's status; therefore, the costs of being ethnic are slight. Reconnecting with one's white ethnicity does not challenge the racial hierarchy the way racial/ethnic reclamation, among Native Americans or any other racially identified group, does.

There is some evidence that racial/ethnic reclamation is a global phenomenon. For instance, Buruma (1997) describes the Jewish revival in Poland. As he explains, "It seems strange to me that these young people are trying to revive a way of life from which my grandparents had escaped" (p. 38). Due to their location and the historical persecution of Jews in Poland (beyond and including the Holocaust), these New Jews, as they are called, "have to start from scratch" in terms of reviving their heritage. He argues, importantly, that this revival of Polish Judaism can be problematic in that it "might seem to fit in with a climate of residual anti-Semitism. It makes the Jews visible again, and comfortably alien" (1997, p. 41). O'Toole (1997) also focuses on global indigenous reclamation, specifically in terms of the Griqua of South Africa and the Metis of North America. Additionally, indigenous peoples are organizing globally into an indigenous peoples movement, challenging exploitation and standing up for their own empowerment and for resistance to transnational corporations, environmental degradation, and human rights violations. Ultimately, reclaimers are evidence of the ongoing significance of race and ethnicity. As Cornell and Hartmann explain, "Construction refers not to a one-time event but to an ongoing project. Ethnic identities are constructed, but they are never finished" (1998, p. 80).

Bibliography

Adler, Patricia A., Peter Adler, and John Johnson. "*Street Corner Society* Revisited: New Questions about Old Issues." *Journal of Contemporary Ethnography* 21 (1992): 3–10.

Alba, Richard D. *Ethnic Identity: The Transformation of White America.* London and New Haven, CT: Yale University Press, 1990.

Babbie, Earl. *The Practice of Social Research.* Belmont, CA: Wadsworth, 2004.

Bahr, Kathleen S. "The Strengths of Apache Grandmothers: Observations On Commitment, Culture, and Caretaking." Pp. 500–16 in *Shifting the Center: Understanding Conteporary Families*, second edition, edited by Susan J. Ferguson. London: Mayfield Publishing, 2001.

Banks, James A. "Multicultural Education: Approaches, Developments, and Dimensionsions." Pp. 83–94 in *Cultural Diversity and the Schools, Vol. I*, edited by J. Lynch, C. Modgil, and S. Modgil. London: The Falmer Press, 1992.

Barrett, Michele. *Imagination in Theory: Culture, Writing Words, and Things.* Washington Square, NY: New York University Press, 1999.

Bernstein, Richard. *Dictatorship of Virtue: Multiculturalism and the Battle for America's Future.* New York: Alfred A. Knopf, 1994.

Best, Steven. *The Politics of Historical Vision: Marx, Foucault, Habermas.* New York and London: The Guilford Press, 1995.

Bloom, Allan. *The Closing of the American Mind.* New York: Simon and Schuster, 1987.

Boelen, W. A. Marianne. "*Street Corner Society*: Cornerville Revisited." *Journal of Contemporary Ethnography* 21 (1992): 11–51.

Bonvillain, Nancy. *Native Nations: Cultures and Histories of Native North America.* Upper Saddle River, NJ: Prentice Hall, 2001.

Bourdieu, Pierre. *Outline of a Theory of Practice.* Cambridge: Cambridge University Press, 1977.

Bourdieu, Pierre, and Jean-Claude Passeron. *Reproduction in Education, Society, and Culture.* Second edition. London: Sage Publications, 1990.

Bowles, Dorcas D. "Bi-racial Identity: Children Born to African-American and White Couples." *Clinical Social Work Journal* 21 (1993): 417–28.

Bowles, Samuel, and Herbert Gintis. *Schooling in Capitalist America: Educational Reform and the Contradictions of Economic Life.* New York: Basic Books, 1976.

Brayboy, Bryan McKinley. "The Indian and the Researcher: Tales from the Field." *International Journal of Qualitative Studies in Education* 13 (2000): 415–28.

Brayboy, Mary, and Mary Morgan. "Voices of Indianness: The Lived World of Native American Women." *Women's Studies International Forum* 21 (1998): 341–54.

Bruchac, Joseph. *The Native American Sweat Lodge: History and Legends.* Freedom, CA: The Crossing Press, 1993.

Bruner, Edward M. "Ethnography as Narrative." Pp. 264–80 in *Memory, Identity, Community: The Idea of Narrative in the Human Sciences*, edited by Lewis P. Hinchman and Sandra K. Hinchman. Albany, NY: State University of New York Press, 1997.

Buruma, Ian. "Poland's New Jewish Question." Pp. 34–55 in *The New York Times Magazine.* New York: The New York Times, 1997.

Butler, Judith. "Collected and Fractured: Response to *Identities.*" Pp. 439–48 in *Identities*, edited by Kwame Anthony Appiah and Henry Louis Gates Jr. Chicago and London: University of Chicago Press, 1995.

Callinicos, Alex. *Making History: Agency, Structure and Change in Social Theory.* Ithaca, NY: Cornell University Press, 1988.

Castells, Manuel. *The Power of Identity.* Oxford: Blackwell Publishers, 1997.

Charon, Joel. *Symbolic Interactionism: An Introduction, An Interpretation, An Integration.* Upper Saddle River, NJ: Prentice Hall, 2001.

Clifford, James, and George E. Marcus. *Writing Culture: The Poetics and Politics of Ethnography.* Berkeley, Los Angeles, and London: University of California Press, 1986.

Cornell, Stephen. *Return of the Native: American Indian Political Resurgence.* New York and Oxford: Oxford University Press, 1998.

Cornell, Stephen, and Douglas Hartmann. *Ethnicity and Race: Making Identities In a Changing World.* London: Pine Forge Press, 1988.

Creswell, J. *Qualitative Inquiry and Research Design: Choosing Among Five Traditions.* Thousand Oaks, CA: Sage Press, 1998.

Crow Dog, Mary. *Lakota Woman.* New York: Harperperennial, 1990.

Dalmage, Heather M. *Tripping on the Color Line: Black-White Multiracial Families in a Racially Divided World.* New Brunswick, NJ: Rutgers University Press, 2000.

Dandaneau, Steven P. *Taking It Big: Developing Sociological Consciousness in Postmodern Times.* London, New Delhi: Pine Forge Press, 2001.

D'Antonio, William V. "Confessions of a Third-generation Italian American." In *Ethnic America*, edited by Marjorie P. K. Weiser. New York: H. W. Wilson Co., 1978.

Davis, F. James. *Who Is Black? One Nation's Definition.* University Park: Pennsylvania State University Press, 1991.

Dean, Mitchell. *Critical and Effective Histories: Foucault's Methods and Historical Sociology.* London, New York: Routledge, 1994.

Dei, George J. Sefa, and Irma Marcia James. "'Becoming Black': African-Canadian Youth and the Politics of Negotiating Racial and Racialised Identities." *Race, Ethnicity, and Education* 1 (1998): 91–108.

Delgado, Richard, and Jean Stefancic. *Critical Race Theory: An Introduction.* New York and London: New York University Press, 2001.

Deloria, Vine, Jr. *Custer Died For Your Sins.* Norman, OK: University of Oklahoma Press, 1988.

Denzin, Norman. "Whose Cornerville Is It Anyway?" *Journal of Contemporary Ethnography* 21 (1992): 120–32.

DeVault, Marjorie L. *Liberating Method: Feminism and Social Research.* Philadelphia: Temple University Press, 1999.

D'Souza, Dinesh. *Illiberal Education: The Politics of Race and Sex on Campus.* New York: Vintage, 1991.

DuBois, W. E. B. *The Souls of Black Folk.* London: Penguin Books, 1989 [1903].

Edwards, Rosalind. "Connecting Method and Epistemology: A White Woman Interviewing Black Women." *Women's Studies International Forum* 13 (1990): 477–90.

Escobar, Arturo. *Encountering Development: The Making and Unmaking of the Third World.* Princeton, NJ: Princeton University Press, 1995.

Eshbach, Karl. "Changing Identification Among American Indians and Alaska Natives." *Demography* 30 (1993): 635–52.

Farley, John E. *Majority-Minority Relations.* Third edition; fourth edition. Englewood Cliffs, NJ: Prentice Hall, 1995; 2005.

Feagin, Joe R., and Karyn D. McKinney. *The Many Costs of Racism.* New York: Rowman & Littlefield, 2003.

Feagin, Joe R., Hernan Vera, and Nikitah Imani. *The Agony of Education: Black Students at White Colleges and Universities.* New York: Routledge, 1996.

Fitzgerald, Kathleen. "Reclaiming Ethnic Identity: The Native American Experience." Presentation given at Indigenous Peoples: An International Symposium. April 8–9, 1997. University of Nebraska–Lincoln.

Fitzgerald, Kathleen J., and M. Angie Jones. "White Like Me: Reproducing the Racial Hierarchy in a Teacher Education Program." Presentation at the Midwest Sociological Society annual meetings. April 2001. St. Louis, MO.

Foucault, Michel. *Power/Knowledge: Selected Interviews and Other Writings, 1972–1977.* Edited by Colin Gordon. New York: Pantheon Books, 1980.

Frankenberg, Ruth. *White Women, Race Matters: The Social Construction of Whiteness.* Minneapolis: University of Minnesota Press, 1993.

Fuchs Ebaugh, Helen Rose. "Creating the Ex-Role." Pp. 330–45 in *The Production of Reality*, 3rd edition, edited by Jodi O'Brien and Peter Kollock. Boston and London: Pine Forge Press, 2001.

Gans, Herbert J., et. al. *On The Making of Americans: Essays in Honor of David Reismann.* Philadelphia: University of Pennsylvania Press, 1979.

Germov, John, and Lauren Williams. *A Sociology of Food and Nutrition: The Social Appetite.* Oxford: Oxford University Press, 1999.

Giddens, Anthony. *The Constitution of Society.* Berkeley and Los Angeles: University of California Press, 1984.

Giroux, Henry A. "Rewriting the Discourse of Racial Identity: Toward a Pedagogy and Politics of Whiteness." Pp. 224–52 in *Becoming and Unbecoming White: Owning and Disowning a Racial Identity*, edited by Christine Clark and James O'Donnell. Westport, CT: Bergin and Garvey, 1999.

Glazer, Nathan, and Daniel Patrick Moynihan. *Beyond the Melting Pot.* Cambridge, MA: MIT Press 1970 [1963].

Greeley, Andrew. "The Ethnic Miracle." In *Ethnic American*, edited by Marjorie P. K.Weiser. New York: H. W. Wilson Co., 1978.

Grim, John A. "Cultural Identity, Authenticity, and Community Survival." *American Indian Quarterly* 20 (1996): 353–77.

Grossman, Kandice L. "Mother Mystics: Understanding Mystical Experienes During Pregnancy and Childbirth." Unpublished honors distinction paper, Columbia College, 1999.

Gunn Allen, Paula. *Off The Reservation: Reflections on Boundary-Busting, Border Crossing, and Loose Canons.* Boston: Beacon Press, 1998.

Hall, John, and Mary Jo Neitz. *Culture: Sociological Perspectives.* Englewood Cliffs, NJ: Prentice Hall, 1993.

Hamer, Jennifer. *What It Means to Be Daddy: Fatherhood for Black Men Living Away From their Children.* New York: Columbia University Press, 2001.

Haney-Lopez, Ian. *White By Law: The Legal Construction of Race.* New York: New York University Press, 1996.

Hansen, Marcus Lee."The Problem of the Third-generation Immigrant." Pp. 202–215 in *Theories of Ethnicity: A Classical Reader*, edited by Werner Sollors. London: Macmillan Press, 1996 [1938].

Harner, Michael. *The Way of the Shaman.* San Francisco: Harper Collins, 1980.

Hinchman, Lewis P., and Sandra K. Hinchman, eds. *Memory, Identity, Community: The Idea of Narrative in the Human Sciences.* Albany: State University of New York Press, 1997.

Holst, Wayne A. "Native American Religious Identity: Unforgotten God." *International Bulletin of Missionary Research* 23 (1999): 90.

hooks, bell. *Black Looks: Race and Representation.* Boston: South End Press, 1992.

Ignatiev, Noel. *How the Irish Became White.* New York: Routledge, 1995.

James, William. *The Varieties of Religious Experience.* New York: Macmillan, 1961 [1902].

John, Robert. "The Uninvited Researcher in Indian Country: Problems and Process and Conducting Research among Native Americans." *Mid-American Review of Sociology* 1–3 (1990): 113–33.

Joseph, Sarah. *Interrogating Culture: Critical Perspectives on Contemporary Theory.* London: Sage Publications, 1998.

Kellner, Douglas. "Popular Culture and the Construction of Postmodern Identities." Pp. 141–77 in *Modernity and Identity*, edited by Scott Lash and Jonathan Friedman. Oxford: Blackwell Publishers, 1992.

Kibria, Nazli. "Race, Ethnic Options, and Ethnic Binds: Identity Negotiations of Second-generation Chinese and Korean Immigrants." *Sociological Perspectives* 43 (2000): 77–95.

Korgen, Kathleen Odell. *From Black to Biracial: Transforming Racial Identity among Americans.* Westport, CT: Praeger, 1998.

Ladson-Billings, Gloria. "Preparing Teachers for Diverse Student Population: A Critical Race Theory Perspective." Pp. 211–48 in *Review of Research in Education* 24, edited by Asghar Iran-Nejad and P. David Pearson. Washington, DC: American Educational Research Association, 1999.

Ladson-Billings, Gloria, and William F. Tate. "Toward a Critical Race Theory of Education." *Teachers College Record* 97 (1995): 47–69.

LaDuke, Winona. *Last Standing Woman.* Stillwater, MN: Voyageur Press, 1997.

Leary, Kimberlyn. "Passing, Posing, and 'Keeping it Real.'" *Constellations* 6 (1999): 85–96.

Lewin, Ellen, and William J. Leap. *Out In The Field: Reflections of Lesbian and Gay Anthropologists.* Champaign: University of Illinois Press, 1996.

Lindsey, Linda L., and Stephen Beach. *Sociology.* Second edition; third edition. Upper Saddle River, NJ: Prentice Hall, 2002.

Lipset, Seymour Martin. *The Continental Divide.* London: Routledge, 1990.

Lookingbill, Brad D. *Dust Bowl USA: Depression America and the Ecological Imagination 1929–1941.* Athens, OH: Ohio University Press, 2001.

Lorde, Audre. "The Master's Tools Will Never Dismantle the Master's House." Pp. 22–23 in *Feminist Frontiers*, fifth edition, edited by Laurel Richardson, Verta Taylor, and Nancy Whittier. Boston: McGraw Hill, 2001.

Matson, Madeline. *Food in Missouri: A Cultural Stew.* Columbia: University of Missouri Press, 1994.

Maynard, Eileen. "The Growing Negative Image of the Anthropologist among American Indians." *Human Organization* 33 (1974): 400–404.

McIntosh, Peggy. "White Privilege and Male Privilege." Pp. 29–36 in *Feminist Frontiers*, fifth edition, edited by Laurel Richardson, Verta Taylor, and Nancy Whittier. Boston: McGraw Hill, 2001.

McIntyre, Alice. *Making Meaning of Whiteness: Exploring Racial Identity with White Teachers.* Albany: State University of New York Press, 1997.

McLemore, S. Dale, and Harriett D. Romo. *Racial and Ethnic Relations in America*, seventh edition. New York: Pearson, 2005.

Mercer, Kobena. "Black Hair/Style Politics." Pp. 420–35 in *The Subcultures Reader,* edited by Ken Gelder and Sarah Thornton. New York: Routledge, 1997.

Meyerhoff, Barbara. *Number Our Days.* New York: Simon and Schuster, 1978.

Michener, H. Andrew, and John D. DeLamater. *Social Psychology*, fourth edition. Fort Worth, TX: Harcourt Publishers, 1999.

Mihesuah, Devon A. "American Indian Identities: Issues of Individual Choices and Development." *American Indian Culture and Research Journal* 22 (1998): 193–226.

Mohawk, John. "In Search of Humanistic Anthropology." *Dialectical Anthropology* (1985): 165–69.

Moore, Robert B. "Racism in the English Language." Pp. 171–78 in *The Production of Reality*, third edition, edited by Jodi O'Brien and Peter Kollock. Boston: Pine Forge Press, 2001.

Nagel, Joane. *American Indian Ethnic Renewal: Red Power and the Resugence of Identity and Culture.* Oxford: Oxford University Press, 1996.

Nahirny, Vladimir C., and Joshua A. Fishman. "American Immigrant Group Ethnic Identification and the Problem of Generations." Pp. 266–81 in *Theories of Ethnicity: A Classical Reader*, edited by Werner Sollers. London: Macmillan, 1966.

Nakano Glenn, Evelyn. "From Servitude to Service Work: Historical Continuities in the Racial Division of Paid Reproductive Labor." Pp. 57–73 in *Feminist Frontiers*, fifth edition, edited by Laurel Richardson, Verta Taylor, and Nancy Whittier. Boston: McGraw Hill, 2001.

Naples, Nancy A. *Grassroots Warriors: Activist Mothering, Community Work and the War on Poverty.* New York: Routledge, 1998.

Native American Rights Fund: Twenty-Five Years of Justice, anniversary edition. 1995.

Neufeldt, Victoria, ed. *Webster's New World Dictionary*, third college edition. New York: Prentice Hall, 1994.

Neumann, W. Lawrence. *Social Research Methods: Qualitative and Quantitativ Approaches*, third edition. Boston and London: Allyn and Bacon, 1997.

Novak, Michael. *The Rise of the Unmeltable Ethnics.* London: Macmillan, 1971.

Nussbaum, Emily. "Return of the Natives." *Lingua Franca* (February 1998): 53–56.

O'Brien, Jodi, and Peter Kollock. *The Production of Reality*, third edition. Boston: Pine Forge Press, 2001.

Ogbu, John. *The Next Generation: An Ethnography of Education in an Urban Neighborhood.* New York: Academic Press, 1974.

Oliver, Melvin L., and Thomas M. Shapiro. *Black Wealth/White Wealth: A New Perspective on Racial Inequality.* New York: Routledge, 1995.

Omi, Michael, and Howard Winant. *Racial Formation in the United States: From the 1960s to the 1990s.* Second edition. New York: Routledge, 1994.

Orlandella, Angelo Ralph. "Boelen May Know Holland, Boelen May Know Barzini, but Boelen 'Doesn't Know Diddle about the North End!'" *Journal of Contemporary Ethnography* 21 (1992): 69–79.

Ortiz, Leonard David. "'And the Stones Shall Cry Out': Native American Identity in the Lawrence Indian United Methodist Church." *Journal of Ecumenical Studies* (Summer/Fall 1999): 363–76.

O'Toole, Thomas. "Who Is Really Indigenous? Comparative Ethnic Construction: The Griqua of South Africa and the Metis of North America." Paper presented at Indigenous Peoples: An International Symposium. April 8–9, 1997. University of Nebraska–Lincoln.

Outhwaite, William, and Tom Bottomore, editors. *The Blackwell Dictionary of Twentieth-Century Social Thought.* Oxford: Blackwell, 1994.

Persons, Stow. *Ethnic Studies at Chicago: 1905–1945.* Champaign: University of Illinois Press, 1987.

Pomerance, Alan. *Repeal of the Blues.* New York: Citadel Press, [1988] 1991.

Powdermaker, Hortense. *Stranger and Friend: The Way of an Anthropologist.* New York: W. W. Norton & Company, Inc, 1966.

Press, Andrea L. *Women Watching Television.* Philadelphia: University of Pennsylvania Press, 1991.

Prothrow-Stith, Deborah. *Deadly Consequences.* New York: Harper Collins, 1991.

Quadagno, Jill. *The Color of Welfare.* New York, Oxford: Oxford University Press, 1994.

Reissman, Catherine Kohler. "When Gender is Not Enough: Women Interviewing Women." *Gender and Society* 1 (1987): 172–207.

——. Paper presented at the Couch-Stone Symposium. Jan. 26–31, 2000. St. Petersberg, FL.

Rhea, Joseph Tilda. *Race Pride and the American Identity.* Cambridge, MA: Harvard University Press, 1997.

Richardson, Laurel. "Trash on the Corner: Ethics and Technography." *Journal of Contemporary Ethnography* 21 (1992): 103–19.

Roberts, Charles. "A Rising Cry: 'Ethnic Power.'" Pp. 158–62 in *Ethnic America*, edited by Marjorie P. K. Weiser. New York: Wilson, 1978.

Robinson, Randall. *The Debt: What America Owes to Blacks.* New York: Dutton, 2000.

Rockquemore, Kerry Ann, and David L. Brunsma. *Beyond Black: Biracial Identity in America.* Thousand Oaks, CA: Sage Publications, 2002.

Roediger, David. *The Wages of Whiteness: Race and the Making of the American Working Class.* New York: Verso, 1991.

Rosaldo, Renato. *Culture and Truth: The Remaking of Social Analysis.* Boston: Beacon Press, 1989.

Rothenberg, Paula S., ed. 2004. *White Privilege: Essential Readings on the Other Side of Racism.* Worth Publishers: New York.

Rubin, H. J., and I. S. Rubin. *Qualitative Interviewing: The Art of Hearing Data.* Thousand Oaks, CA: Sage, 1995.

Rubin, Lillian. *Families on the Fault Line.* New York: HarperPerennial, 1994.

Rumbaut, Ruben G. "The Crucible Within: Ethnic Identity, Self-Esteem, and Segmented Assimilation among Children." Pp. 119–70 in *The New Second Generation*, edited by Alejando Portes. New York: Russell Sage Foundation, 1996.

Sandoval-Sanchez, Alberto. "Paul Simon's *The Capeman:* The Staging of Puerto Rican National Identity as Spectacle and Commodity on Broadway." Pp. 147–61 in *Latino/a Popular Culture*, edited by Michelle Habell-Pallen and Mary Romero. New York and London: New York University Press, 2002.

Sandstrom, Kent L., Daniel D. Martin, and Gary Alan Fine. *Symbols, Selves, and Social Reality.* Los Angeles: Roxbury Publishing, 2003.

Schlesinger, Arthur. *The Dismantling of America: Reflections on a Multicultural Society.* New York: Norton, 1991.

Schumer, Howard, ed., et al. *Racial Attitudes in America: Trends and Interpretations.* Cambridge, MA: Harvard University Press, 1997.

Seidman, Steven. *Contested Knowledge: Social Theory in the Postmodern Era*, second edition. Oxford: Blackwell, 1998.

Smedley, Audrey. "'Race' and the Construction of Human Identity." *American Anthropologist* 100 (1999): 690–702.

Smith, Dorothy. *The Everyday World As Problematic: A Feminist Sociology.* Boston: Northeastern University Press, 1987.

———. *The Conceptual Practices of Power: A Feminist Sociology of Knowledge.* Boston: Northeastern University Press, 1990.

Snipp, C. Matthew. *American Indians: The First of This Land.* New York: Russell Sage, 1989.

Sollors, Werner. *Theories of Ethnicity: A Classical Reader.* London: Macmillan Press, 1996.

Stein, Arlene. *Sex and Sensibility: Stories of a Lesbian Generation.* Berkeley: University of California Press, 1997.

Stein, Howard, and Robert F. Hill. *The Ethnic Imperative: Examining the New White Ethnic Movement.* University Park: Pennsylvania State University Press, 1977.

Strauss, Anselm. 1993. *Continual Permutations of Action.* Aldine De Gruyter: New York.

———. *Mirrors and Masks: The Search for Identity.* New Brunswick, NJ: Transaction Publishers, 1997.

Sturm, Circe. *Blood Politics: Race, Culture, and Identity in the Cherokee Nation of Oklahoma.* Berkeley: University of California, 2002.

Taylor, Ronald L. *Minority Families in the United States*, third ed. Upper Saddle River, NJ: Prentice Hall, 2002.

Treuer, David. *Little.* New York: Picador, 1995.

Trimble, Joseph. "The Sojourner in the American Indian Community: Methodological Issues and Concers." *Journal of Social Issues* 33 (1977): 159–74.

Turner, Victor. *Dramas, Fields, and Metaphors: Symbolic Action in Human Society.* Ithaca, NY: Cornell University Press, 1974.

———. *Process, Performance and Pilgrimage: A Study in Comparative Symbology.* New Delhi: Concept Publishing Company, 1979.

Underhill, Evelyn. *Mysticism.* New York: Dutton, 1961.

van den Berghe, Pierre L. "Race and Ethnicity: A Sociobiological Perspective." Pp. 54–61 in *Majority and Minority: The Dynamics of Race and Ethnicity in American Life*, edited by N. Yetman. Newton, MA: Allyn & Bacon, 1985.

Vidich, Arthur. "Boston's North End: An American Epic." *Journal of Contemporary Ethnography* 21 (1992): 80–102.

Wahrhaftig, Albert L., and Robert K. Thomas. "Renaissance and Repression: The Oklahoma Cherokee." Pp. 80–88 in *Native Americans Today: Sociological Perspectives*, edited by Howard M. Bahr, Bruce A. Chadwick, and Robert C. Day. New York: Harper and Row Publishers, 1972.

Waters, Mary C. *Ethnic Options: Choosing Identities in America.* Berkeley: University of California Press, 1990.

Wax, Murray. "The Ethics of Research in American Indian Communities." *American Indian Quarterly* 15 (1991): 457–69.

Wax, Murray L., and Rosalie H. Wax. "The Enemies of the People." Pp. 177–92 in *Native Americans Today Sociological Perspectives*, edited by Howard M. Bahr, Bruce A. Chadwick, and Robert C. Day. New York: Harper and Row Publishers, 1972.

Wax, Rosalie. *Doing Fieldwork: Warnings and Advise.* Chicago and London: University of Chicago Press, 1971.

———. "The Warrior Dropouts." Pp. 146–54 in *Native Americans Today: Sociological Perspectives*, edited by Howard M. Bahr, Bruce A. Chadwick, and Robert C. Day. New York, San Francisco, London: Harper and Row Publishers, 1972.

Wax, Rosalie, and Robert K. Thomas. "American Indians and White People." *Phylon* XXII, no. 4 (1961): 305–17.

Weatherford, Jack. *Native Roots.* New York: Fawcett Columbine Books, 1991.

Webster's New World Dictionary. Third college edition. Prentice Hall: New York, 1994.

West, Cornel. *Race Matters.* New York: Vintage Books, 1993.

Whyte, William Foote. *Street Corner Society.* Chicago: University of Chicago Press, 1943.

———. "In Defense of *Street Corner Society*." *Journal of Contemporary Ethnography* 21 (1992): 52–68.

Wiley, Ralph. *Why Black People Tend To Shout.* New York: Birch Lane Press, 1991.

Willis, Paul. *Learning To Labor: How Working Class Kids Get Working Class Jobs.* Aldershot: Gower Publishing, 1977.

Wojcik, Daniel. *Punk and Neo-Tribal Body Art.* Jackson: University of Mississippi Press, 1995.

Index

About the Author

Kathleen J. Fitzgerald is Assistant Professor of Sociology at Columbia College. Her research and teaching focuses on inequalities along the lines of race, ethnicity, class, gender, and sexuality. She also works and publishes in the area of social movements and social policy.